306.874 MacI
McInnis, Dion.
Daddin' : the verb of being a dad /

34028085475417
FM $22.99 ocn694151668
05/23/14

Daddin'

Presented to

Clear Lake City - County Freeman Branch Library

By

Friends of the Freeman Library

Harris County
Public Library
your pathway to knowledge

Daddin'

The Verb of Being A Dad

Dion McInnis

Copyright © 2010 by Dion McInnis.

Cover photograph by Kim McInnis.

Library of Congress Control Number   2010913977
ISBN: Hardcover   978-1-4535-6441-7
              Softcover   978-1-4535-6440-0

All rights reserved. No part of this book may be reproduced or transmitted in any form or by any means, electronic or mechanical, including photocopying, recording, or by any information storage and retrieval system, without permission in writing from the copyright owner.

This book was printed in the United States of America.

To order additional copies of this book, contact:
Xlibris Corporation
1-888-795-4274
www.Xlibris.com
Orders@Xlibris.com
30248

Contents

Introduction	9
Havin'	13
Learnin'	41
Listenin'	70
Lovin'	79
Playin'	109
Fishin'	132
Growin'	175
Leavin'	252
Livin'	272

Additional Writings

Essays	279
Father and Son, revisited 2002	279
Father and Son	282
Young Love	284
Father's Day Writings	286
Father's Day 1999	288
Happy Father's Day 2002	290
Father's Day 2003	291
June 20, 2004 Listen to Life newsletter	293
June 19, 2005 Listen to Life newsletter	294
June 18, 2006 Listen to Life newsletter	296
Father's Day 2007	298
Father's Day 2008	299
Father's Day Memories 2010	301
Kid Art	303
Various pieces of art from the boys over the years	
Poetry	306
Family	306
Son's Room	306
Voices	307

Stories 308
    College Calls 308
    Daddy, Draw My Hand 310
    Family Vacations..313
    The Fork in the Path 315
    Justin the Shark Slayer...317
    Moms and Dads 321
    Napkin Art...324
    "Please Come Back: A Love Story" 326
    Raccoon Feet..333

Dedication

I dedicate this book, with love, respect and appreciation beyond measure to:

Dion Christopher, Justin Anthony and Cameron Matthew: The three greatest sons a man could have and the reasons for writing this book.

Dorothy Ann Sobieski McInnis and James Russell McInnis: My parents who I will forever love and miss, and who led me to believe that loving parenthood can be a wonderful thing.

Kimberly Carroll Barfield McInnis: My wife, and wonderful step-mother to the boys, who believes in what I do and why. Thank you.

Acknowledgements

Thank you to the many who have supported the concept and my ramblings about this book for years; thank you for your ears, shoulders and patience.

Thank you to Andrea Dunn, Charity Ellis, Theresa Presswood, and Cheryl Rohde for taking the time to review the entire book to provide me editorial input and thoughtful insights.

INTRODUCTION

I have started this book a thousand times and compiled idea nuggets and complete stories for years, all in hopes of conveying the verb of fatherhood. We don't have a word like that in the English language, so I made up one: daddin'.

If you were to say to someone that you saw a woman mothering her child at the park, your listener would likely conjure up tender images of a woman caring for, nurturing, touching, and interacting with her child. Mothers mother. However, if you were to say that you saw a man fathering a child, the listener would likely envision a man having sex. In our society, the most common connotations of the verb "to father" are "to beget" or "to sire." There is so much more.

This book is about the verb of being a father, from the perspectives of being a father to three boys, and as a son. You will learn more about my sons and father within these stories. Dad said to me "You can have as many kids as you want, but you'll never be a father until you've had a daughter." I didn't take that as an insult to me or my brother, nor did it place my sisters on a special pedestal. By the time that I came along as the family's caboose, Mom and Dad had already lost one daughter to leukemia and had one son in the military and another daughter. I was a surprise. But Dad saw in daughters, I believe, the chance to see inside another world. That did not diminish his love for his sons. My father passed away when my oldest son was one, so he never got to know them, though my sons know him through my stories. And that is a gift to them, providing a sense of perspective and insight into their own father and themselves. Perhaps through the stories in this book, you will learn about my family, and about your own in the process.

Part of the motivation for the book comes from memories. I treasure memories of time with my father, and I wonder about his life before my arrival. By blending stories, poetry and musings, I explore my past as part of the fatherhood story, for perspective and to share with my sons a bit about me. Hopefully, all of which they can share with their own children, to answer yet-to-be-asked questions.

In 2006, after I pondered again the framed newspaper clippings I have about my dad, I wrote:

Yellowed paper—clippings—behind glass
Reveal in snippets and sport speak
My father's time as boxer, scrappy
Professional pugilist.
Evidence of his life a quarter century before my arrival
Only my imagination can create the images
As he punched, deflected and danced
As he shed blood, drew blood and impressed the blondes and redheads—
I've heard the stories but know no one who witnessed him.
I must interpolate his rope-jumping demonstration at 60
To his workouts at 20
When he polished his skills as he drew headlines and praise
In small town San Antonio a decade before World War II.
My father who would not dance with my dancer mom
Out of embarrassment
Danced around competitors while pounding them proudly.
Yellowed newsprint and a vivid imagination
Beats back last memories of my dying dad
Paralyzed by modern medicine.
The ink tells stories of a man
Whose image fades year by year.

You don't have to be a son or a father to appreciate what this book reveals about time, relationships and the verbs of living as a child or parent. A woman who I have photographed a few times listened to a story and began to cry. It was a father-son story, but it struck a chord. Being blessed to have a father who understands the verb and not just the noun is a good fortune that this book celebrates, whether for sons or daughters. Perhaps that is also why every woman at a recent chamber luncheon asked to be notified when the book was finished: The verbs of fatherhood mattered to them as daughters and as mothers.

This hasn't come easy. Each time I have read this manuscript and its previous iterations, I have emotional moments that take me away from recording the beautiful, colorful kaleidoscope of fatherhood—the image changes each time you change the view a bit. So, how to begin? How to organize? In 2000, I jotted in my journal:

My book idea—daddin'—is so rich with material that I know not where to begin. Start again? I work and re-organize what I have in hopes of finding the pieces to the puzzle. Perhaps I need to try the other side of the pieces. My poetry—some of it anyway—is publishable. I would love to see under my name—writer, photographer, poet, dad, husband, friend . . . the richness of the options spoils me.

But this was a project that I could not not do. Just a week after writing the above, I jotted:

To call out to you, to many, to all
The joy of being
Father, dad, pop
To these three.

I've never really had a choice but to create this book.

I have no more control over this
Than over my heart beating or
My lungs taking in breath.
My boy comes into my view
And I smile
And swell with pride and love.

In developing the stories and the book concept over the years, I struggled with how to organize it all. And it came to me—by verb. To be a father is to live out verbs in moments. This is a book of moments.

Welcome to the world of daddin'.

HAVIN'

Havin' children is pretty easy. Make a baby and eventually it comes out if all goes well. Then the fun and the work begins. I guess that I always looked forward to the days of being a father. Of all the jobs that I have had, or expect to have, none compare to that of fatherhood. Perhaps, more accurately, fatherhood is an avocation, one done for love alone, which bears no financial remuneration. It helps us dads maintain our amateur standing when the Olympics begin to accept fatherhood as a competitive sport. On second thought, maybe many dads already believe it is: competition to be the coolest dad, the youth sports coach with the most victories, or the toughest. The real score is measured by joy, I believe. Maybe I looked forward to fatherhood because my dad handled the role with such poise, or so it seemed to me. He got flustered, frustrated and was human, but he handled the role with me quite comfortably, it seemed. Naturally. Genuinely. And perhaps that is because he had transformed and relaxed over the years by the time I arrived as the caboose.

Dad wasn't the super-attentive type that media now uses as the role model active father. But, he was present, loving and loyal to his family to an appropriate and healthy degree. Within that rich environment, I drew my own conclusions about being a father. At the age of barely 17, I wrote this poem.

Close your eyes, dear one
Let down your sails
And anchor for awhile
Dream on my love
Of our busy day
Tomorrow

Your dog'll be here
So don't worry 'bout that
Tomorrow
Joe, Brian, Charlie
Are sleeping now
They too will play
Tomorrow
Kiss your finger? OK
Scraped slidin' into third
You've stolen home so rest
Rest for your big game
Tomorrow
When I was young?
OK son, if you'll sleep
Tonight
Stories of youth
Make me so dearly want
Yesterday
Your eyes are sinking
Let them drown
They will rise again
No, no more stories
Yes, know 'bout the bike
And your finger, too
Your sails are in
The tide is at ebb
And the anchor is out
So rest for now
Your sails will hold
And catch the wind
Tomorrow

And, it pretty much worked out that way for me and my three sons. Pretty much. I learned over time that hasty go-to-sleep time robbed us both—father and son—of enjoyable end-of-the-day talk time. My father didn't provide those experiences to me, but my mother did. Lessons learned from both parents made me the father that I am. Thirty years after the poem above, I wrote:

I won't tell you to go to sleep
In fact, I hoped that you wouldn't
We've so much to say, to talk about
You can't go to sleep, you shouldn't

Tell me all about your school day
And I'll share the same of mine
Tell me about the games and fun you had
Tell me all—we now have the time

I'd love to hear all about your friends
While I rub your back and head
But don't get too relaxed right now
No sleeping for you in this bed!

What's the story of that scratch on your knee?
And why were you laughing at recess?
What did you see while playing hide-and-seek?
Did you say that in kick ball you're the best?

Your breathing is deeper, but awaken
There's so much more I want to hear
Your stories, I love to hear you tell
I know you have more, that is clear

Your head fits on the pillow so well
The quilt covers you up quite snugly
Perfect for you to keep sharing your day
Please, please tell it all to me

I laugh at your jokes and tall tales
Listen to your questions and your wonders
You're so busy and so full of fun
Of successes and some blunders

Don't close your eyes, we've just begun
Too soon your stories will end
Too soon you'll be my grown little one
And I won't be able to put you to bed

Sleep well, sleep well my wonderful child
Dream the dreams of what's yet to do
I'll watch you for just a little while more
Sleep well my child, I love you

Little did I realize the changes that were to occur after June 26, 1981 when Dion was born. On August 3, 1981, I wrote this essay for our Lamaze class' follow up assignment. The handout read, "On the following pages or page, please write for me the story of your labor and delivery. Tell how it began, how things evolved and any significant changes you noticed. Please include both of your feelings during the various stages and what class material you found to be most helpful. Just tell it like it was!!!" Page or pages? There are few single-page assignments for McInnis writers.

Miracle. Nothing more, nothing less.

To describe our feelings about the delivery experience is no simple chore, especially since the actual birthing is inseparable from the entire term. However, inner joy and pride are two words that would seem typical of the entire time span.

One notable fact is the impact of childbirth classes. The most important part of these classes was the information detailing the "real experience": to know the changes the body is going through and the functions of these changes. This insight led to a high level of confidence in our ability to deliver naturally. This confidence was shaken only one time, this being in the labor room. It seemed to us that total concentration was a requisite—this was impossible with the last shift of training nurses chatting, cracking jokes and being somewhat oblivious to the matter at hand: contractions and preparations for the birth of a baby. We genuinely feel this disruption rather than assistance caused the loss of control over the contractions. Coach cannot keep in front of the lady's face to control breathing while watching a fetal monitor that is incorrectly put on and not reading contractions. When the contractions were lost, we had no other assistance. The presence of a student nurse with less confidence than us did little to bring things back to normal.

We understand that experience is the best teacher, but by the same token there should have been someone to help in contraction monitoring, etc. as there was early on in the labor room.

Other than the latter period in the labor room, the entire process was wonderful. Everyone in the delivery room was understanding. What struck Mom and coach was the difference between witnessed deliveries and the one that was the result of an act of love nine months previous, 280 days of growth and concern and ultimately three pushes from an exhausted mother; the façade of education collapses into smiles and ecstasy. Films in childbirth and sexuality classes do not come close in preparing parents for the inner feelings resulting from the first cry—funny how emotions change concerning the same boisterous cry as time passes.

As an open comment to all parents-to-be, we would like to express views on "natural childbirth." First, it is a mistake for natural to be misconstrued to mean "medicine free." We had hoped that anesthesia would not be necessary but after eleven hours and the labor room problems, some assistance was needed. What is the benefit of modern medicine if it is ignored for some silly notion that epidural is Latin for "cowardly?" Second, for the couples who enjoy the team concept of pregnancy—and it is truly doubly rewarding—there is no experience like natural childbirth. It took both partners to become pregnant and both should experience the delivery. The sharing of the entire process, pleasure and pain make it more rewarding and more endurable; happiness shared is doubled, pain shared is halved.

(August 12, 1981)

This is an addendum to the first part—facts after emotion, as it were.

Nine months of changes, mostly not visible and none really "experienced" by the father, is hard to put into a nutshell. Suffice it to say that the awesome practicality of Mother Nature in preparing for childbirth is amazing. Even if she is a little off schedule.

Our newcomer was due June 22 (one day after Father's Day) and with Mom's activity level and the doctor's comments (two weeks prior—"any day now") we expected an early baby. So much for speculation. June 19 was a scheduled OB appointment and he offered an induction, for convenience sake, on Monday.

Total surprise. We balked, preferring the old fashioned method of getting up in the middle of the night if need be. It need be.

One minute into June 26, slight contractions started. Mom remained awake to monitor while Dad snoozed in one-hour increments until 3:00 a.m. Contractions every four to six minutes for 50 minutes. A quick call gave approval to go to the hospital. The real thing. We were calm outwardly but probably harboring all types of anticipations, questions (am I ready now?), etc. After a stop to drop the pet dog, we arrived at the hospital at 3:45 a.m. Check in smooth. All is ok. Breathing was under control. So far so good.

Then minutes in the labor room introduced two very nice, understanding nurses and a punch to our confidence. The blow was a woman's uncontrolled shrieking as she gave birth while being transported to the labor room. Things continued on well for approximately seven hours (until 10:30 a.m.); breathing and the fitness of exercise helped Mom ease through her exhausting activity. We also had the aid of our childbirth class instructor until this time; the calm and assistance in reading contractions offered by her were invaluable. This is something every couple should have, either from their instructor (if they are lucky) or the nurses on call. About this time new nurses chatting, distracting and not assisting, in conjunction with water breaking and an increased dosage of Pitocin yielded a greater work load and less help. At 11:00 a.m. a request, a plea, for an epidural became necessary. First attempt did not take but the second was successful. Labor and delivery heaven is a functioning epidural.

Once the rolling stone moves, there is no such thing as brakes. Contractions became longer, harder and more effective. At lunch time, the nurses were preparing Mom to push in the labor room; this was delayed to ask the doctor's permission. Thank goodness for common sense. After a brief check, the doc grinned and said, "Let's have a baby." Oh my God—it is real.

Mom was wheeled into the delivery room, leaving Dad, dressed in less than fashionable sterile wear, in the labor room with camera draped and ready for a tremendously important assignment. Finally, Dad was permitted in (Mom's prep was finished) and escorted to the best seat in the house. The doctor explained forceps (used for two seconds) and quietly gave instructions to the delivery room nurses. At 12:30 p.m., and in the middle of the third push, Dion Christopher McInnis came screaming into the world, mouth open and big feet flailing. While

Mom was being repaired (episiotomy stitches) Dad was able to touch the loud one as he was given APGAR scores and put on his warming bed.

Nurses quickly shuffled Dad out of the delivery room and to awaiting visitors to spread the news. First-time grandparents and sixth-time grandparents. First-time uncles and fourth-time aunts. Tickled neighbors. Happy friends. From the role of crier to consoler, Dad went to the recovery area to help a shivering Mom warm up and hold her new son. Photos here, too.

The next step was the hospital room. From these confines, the attachment typical of feeding would develop. The nocturnal visits of an eight-pound, 13-ounce boy rooting for mama's nourishment will forever be remembered. As it all will.

From these early recollections of a first son's birth by a young man with plenty of growing to do as a father, husband and writer, came decades of surprises and experiences. That pretty well defines fatherhood: birth, growth and plenty of surprises and experiences. So much more has happened between the poem written in high school and the one written in midlife.

For as much of fatherhood turned out as I envisioned or hoped, one can never expect things to turn out one way or another with children. In 2000, I wrote a note to my sons in my journal:

Dear Sons:

I remember your births. You asked how I felt about you being born—the answer then is the answer now: exceedingly proud, concerned about providing, hopeful for our futures, and connected to the future. While we awaited your arrival, I was anxious about the future; as we await your multiple milestones of growing up, I continue to be anxious. Not scared anxious, but like the anxiousness of bobber fishing, when we sit there and the bobber begins to move across the water and then pauses to bob and we know that something great is about to happen. We don't know how long it will last, how big the fish will be, whether the line will hold or not—we know nothing really of what is about to occur, so we are anxious, but we also know that is what we are here for. And so it is with having children.

Two months short of eight years after I wrote the poem in high school, I became a father. A year after becoming a dad, my dad died. Fortunately, I was well on my way to enjoying the verbs of fatherhood. About a decade after Dad died, my then-wife was pregnant again and while at work I received the post-doctor's visit update call. I usually went to the obstetrician with her, but this day I did not and the updates were important to me because we had already experienced the trauma of miscarriage. Work demands did not allow me to join her, so she called in her report: "Great news, everything is going well, it seems. And . . . well . . . we're going to have twins."

My spring day immediately became even fuller of life than spring days naturally are. I was excited by the news. After rattling on about all the people I had to tell, she said, "Wait, wait. Uh, April Fools. I thought it would freak you out. I was trying to surprise you." Being a father has been full of surprises, freak outs and unexpected occurrences. And it is still exciting.

When my first-born, Dion, arrived, I worked as a freelance writer and photographer. Among the jobs was being the beat reporter of the Fort Bend Independent School District for a weekly newspaper on the west side of Houston. The district was beginning its expansion, but it still had a country feel of familiarity and genuineness. I felt to be among good people when I attended their school board meetings and wrote about their work or editorialized against some of their actions. So it was great fun to bring cigars to the first board meeting after Dion was born. When the members of the board came from executive session to begin the evening's public deliberations, each found at their place a (cheap) cigar declaring "It's a Boy!" "Who has the good news?" a few of the members asked. Sitting on the front row reserved for the media, I proudly raised my hand. They laughed and offered their congratulations, and then most passed their cigars down to the superintendent, Lawrence Elkins. Whenever I hear of Elkins High School in the news, I think of the man who got the cigars that constituted my first public declaration of fatherhood.

Justin arrived at a curious time, as the Houston economy was in bad condition and my photography business struggled. I served on the board of the Alief/Southwest Houston Chamber of Commerce, and some of those compatriots shared the excitement, but the church family at Notre Dame was the most invested. We had had one miscarriage after Dion's birth, so fellow parishioners provided support, though we were not as entrenched in the parish as when Cameron was born. Justin came at a time of limbo—in terms of our finances, my career future and our social networks, but we had a strong family and extended family. He was still nursing when I opened the storefront studio, with Barbara having to lock the doors for short feeding breaks. Not that many people were coming to the door; I made a stupid decision and we ended up having to file for bankruptcy to get out of the lease we had in the shopping center.

By the time that our third son came along, Dion was old enough to go through Lamaze training so he could be in the delivery room, which he was until the "critical time" when he was escorted out. A lot happened between the time Dion was born and the time he was in the labor room to witness Cameron's birth.

By the time Cameron arrived, we had had two more miscarriages. He was to be our last attempt and we had much support from our friends and church family members. People would rub Mom's pregnant tummy in hopes of providing good fortune or blessings. At about month six, when it appeared that all would work out well, we attended a baptism at our church. At the offertory part of the Mass, the family brought the baby to the altar as the other gifts were brought forward, too: Wine, water, hosts, the collection's harvest, and a baby. Fr. Kealy blessed the gifts, and then took the baby, held him aloft and said a prayer. I said, "If he does that with ours, I will come unglued." Losing babies is hard.

Not all the celebrations equaled Dion's for fun. I worked at the University of Houston Cullen College of Engineering when Cameron arrived. Most of my staff of 12 attended school and worked part time and only a couple worked full time. We had had a challenging period of low work load (we provided support services to faculty, among other things) and low performance by several members of the team. The time had come for me to trim the ranks, which I did. One day before my surprise baby shower. I'll never forget the looks on the faces of the employees as I walked into the conference room for what I thought was a meeting. A couple of people smiled, like the young woman who organized the party and my boss' secretary. The others seemed less celebratory. Within 30 minutes, the party concluded with the two women and me laughing about the timing. "You picked a funny day to let people go," Lori said. There is no controlling timing or circumstances when you're a dad.

Time and timing is simply something that you have to work with as a dad. Going with the flow gets you through.

A hairstylist asked me, "Are you a father?" "Yes," I replied. "At what times do you feel most like a dad? My girlfriend is pregnant and I've been asking around. My friend said that he first felt like a dad when he paid the hospital bill and another said something about bills and responsibilities, too. When do you most feel like a dad?"

That was an easy question to answer. I told the young man that I always felt most like a father when I had one of the boys on my shoulders. I loved walking around with one of them up there, pulling my hair, resting on my head, drooling on my scalp, or bouncing along and laughing. I figure they enjoyed it, too. Even when Cameron was 10, he wanted to ride there, granted he only did that in the pool where I enjoyed the added benefit of the water's buoyancy to help.

As they got older and became more stable riders, each would straddle my back as I provided horseback rides all over the house. Perhaps it assured one way to make sure that we could always go places together.

As time went on, I created bedtime stories (remember the poem?) based on my son's life and his perpetual friend, Charlie the caterpillar. The stories would begin, "Once upon a time, there was a little boy named . . ." and he'd fill in the name. (On hindsight, which is not 20/20 as you get older, these stories may have only come around for Cameron.) I would then conjure up a story in which the main character boy would seek some time alone to think about something that I knew was on their minds. It never failed that as the boy was walking or riding around, he would come upon Charlie who would then come out of his cocoon to render friendship, advice and support to the boy. About six years before the family split by divorce, I wrote this story as a family Christmas present.

Once upon a time, there was a family, a rather large family actually: a mom, a dad, three boys and two dogs. And a caterpillar. This was the McInnis family and their multi-legged friend was Charlie.

Not many families were like this, and I don't mean the caterpillar friendship . . . although that, too! Not many families had the complete package of love, play, support, curiosity and fun that the McInnises did. In fact, it was on one of their play activities that they found Charlie.

Mom McInnis, Dad McInnis and Cameron (being carried alternately by his mom and dad) were hiking in a park while the two older boys, Dion and Justin, rode their bikes in extravagantly long loops to cover the same amount of territory. It was on this walk, at the rest stop in the fork of the path that it all happened.

"I'm pooped," Dad said amid mumbles about his creeping age and tired muscles. Everyone joined in the teasing because it was so easy to do. The other McInnis adventurers welcomed the opportunity for the break and joined Mom, Dad and Cameron on the log. And what a perfect log it was; well-worn from other hikers pausing for rest at the fork in the path.

The biking boys skidded to a stop alongside the log, laughing as they almost collided. Mom and Dad were too busy unpacking Cameron, stretching and enjoying the company to worry about it.

The conversations paused for just a moment as mom distributed fruit to the crew. And in that pause came a sound. A voice. "Hi, guys. I've been waiting for this for quite some time."

The family silence continued. No one knew where the voice came from. Or who it was.

"I'm Charlie, the caterpillar. Well, I'm a caterpillar now, but will be a butterfly soon. Hang on for a few minutes and we can meet."

Charlie? Caterpillar? Butterfly? Meet? Meet!?!

Everyone began looking for Charlie, although they had to be careful. They knew that if they stepped or sat in the wrong place, Charlie and his cocoon would be history. They looked under leaves, on trees, everywhere. No Charlie.

Then they heard a soft, gentle tap. And another. Blue eyes and brown eyes looked to where the sound came from: a small brown cocoon on the side of the log they were sitting on!

The tapping was coming from the cocoon on the log. Ten unblinking eyes watched closely as the little hatch door began to open. Justin crawled on Dion's back for a better view; Dion didn't even notice. Mom and Dad whispered.

First, two slightly damp black antennae poked through the opening. The sound of bug groans came from Charlie's tiny house as he pushed against his door. The McInnises didn't even breathe. But they could hear Charlie panting as he worked so hard to come out. They could hear his many feet moving . . . and then . . . slowly, he stumbled out.

"There's Charlie," Justin screamed, like he was seeing a long-lost relative.

The noise scared Charlie. He was so concerned with getting out that he didn't notice that he was surrounded. Surrounded by noses and eyes as faces, cheek to cheek, watched him make his not-so-grand entrance. He looked up. He smiled.

Charlie tried to stretch his wings. Dion said they looked like rainbows. Justin said they looked like bicycle reflectors. Mom said how lucky we were. Dad was quiet, for a change. And Cameron, well, he reached out to grab Charlie for a snack.

"I'm your forever friend," Charlie said. "Not many people have me, or the other special caterpillars like me as friends. I can visit with you whenever you like—sometimes as a butterfly and sometimes as a caterpillar—but I usually will find you when you need me. That's what friends are for. That's what family is for. Right?"

Everyone smiled and nodded.

Charlie dried his wings by taking a few erratic laps around the log. Cameron laughed. Dion and Justin chased him around. It was great fun. Then he came back to rest on the log and everyone knelt down next to the log.

"You are a lucky family to have each other. And I'm lucky that we can be friends. In fact, I'm the luckiest caterpillar or butterfly I know." Mom and Dad weren't sure, but they both believed they saw butterfly tears when he said it.

Charlie offered to lead the family on a tour of the woods and everyone gladly accepted. Charlie floated through the woods with Dion and Justin intently following along, listening to his stories of the woods. Cameron looked around

Dad's shoulders to watch his new friend. Mom and Dad walked, holding hands, watching their kids, knowing there was a little Charlie in each of them.

That's how the stories went, always involving the boys in life and interactions with their ever-available friend, Charlie.

What I didn't fully appreciate, of course, at the age of 17 when I wrote the poem is the continuum that is fatherhood. The verbs may be the same, but the context and depth change with time and age. A lot of the issues are consistent. I'm a word guy, and I've used several songs to help myself understand the process of having children and all that it entails, and the responsibilities thereof.

At each moment of living, there is the inevitable change process to what will be. Many songs remind me of the parenting transitions, and I have shared these with my sons, sometimes subtly in conversation, and sometimes specifically in asking them to listen. As I gained experience as a dad, and heard more songs, and life had its changes, I developed a list of songs to match the phases:

Having kids: Living Years by Mike and the Mechanics (birth); Arms Wide Open by Creed (birth);
Raising kids: Cat's in the Cradle by Harry Chapin; Younger Generation by Lovin' Spoonful;
Leaving home: Child's Song by Tom Rush; Father and Son by Cat Stevens.

"The Living Years" touched me for its message, and for its timing. I found the song around the time that my father passed away, making my firstborn son only one year old at the time. The song assures me that my father would pass through me and into my sons. Yes, I know there are myriad other relatives in them, too, but the song spoke to me about a father to son to son bond that meant much as I recalled my dad's death while holding a young namesake son. It was more than 20 years later that the song by Creed came along and became part of my father song collection.

"Arms Wide Open" found me during the time that I had moved out of the house and dealing with life decisions influenced by my desire to show my sons various truths about life, living, relationships and loving. I wanted them to understand that living—as the song described, with one's arms wide open—was not easy, nor something I had abided by all my life, but can be embraced throughout one's life. That the lyrics expressed the author's desire to teach his newborn son to live in such a manner touched me. We are constantly in phases of newly born chances and opportunities to learn how to live better. More fully. More completely.

As much as the first two songs speak to newborns and the possible futures for them, the second two songs provided me a way to express in other than dad-speak what my feelings and beliefs were about being a father. "Cat's in the Cradle" is familiar to probably everyone of my generation. The first time I heard it, as a mid-teenager, I knew in my heart that I would never want to be the dad in the position of the singer. Fortunately, it has worked out that way.

Written by Harry Chapin's wife, the song charts well the many, easy distractions that keep fathers and their children apart, and how this becomes a learned behavior. One would think that if you grew up without access to your parent, you'd learn to *not* be that way, but unfortunately many of the negative experiences that we have become affirmations for doing the same instead of illustrations of what not to do. But, there's an entire chapter about learnin', so we'll get to that later.

I heard "Younger Generation" the first time from Woodstock. Not at it, but from the movie about Woodstock. I don't want to falsely claim attendance at the original grand event, but I did appreciate the music and some of the dynamics that made such an event a possibility. While watching the movie, I heard a very stoned John Sebastian trying to sing, and then eventually making it through the song "Younger Generation." The words struck me because they spoke of the parent-child relationship in ways that revealed that parents aren't perfect, and we all have dreams.

I was about 14 when I first heard Cat Stevens' "Father and Son." It was the middle of the night and I roused from sleep. Playing on my Sony cube clock radio was a tune whose lyrics captured me immediately. Even in my dozing daze, I could recognize the beauty of the conversation between father and son regarding growing up. My mother would often quote someone (was it a pastor, perhaps?) with, "I once was what you are now," referring to the position of parent or elder to child or youth. Parents *were* once what our youth are now. Neither side should forget, for the children will be what we are now, with all that comes with aging. Powerful and wonderful lessons can be found in those sharing moments of conversation.

The song, and the experiences from that time on, illustrate the true nature of parenthood. The parenthood business is catch and release. You let your kids go, they do their thing, and you hope for the best. But you also know you'll reconnect another day, and when you do, it will be wonderful. Each visit, each call, each connection and re-connection reminds you of the joys and love of parenting.

I have to believe that my boys understand the depth of the song and the value of open father-son conversation. In fact, I know they do.

When my namesake got married in 2009, he caught me by surprise at the reception. The crowd had thinned somewhat as the post-ceremony event had been going on for a couple of hours. I figured my role had been completed; save for watching with mixed emotions the evidence of time and growth. It felt surreal at times, though the laughter and conversations with family and friends "kept it real," as they say.

"Dad? Where's my dad? Dad, come on up here," Dion said. Like his old man, he never met a microphone that he didn't like and he seemed to be enjoying the moment. I had no idea what to expect, and headed to the front of the room. As I stood next to this young man who used to ride on my shoulders as a wee one not so long ago, he talked about how special and important it is to have time with your dad. He called out to "all the fathers, sons, grandfathers and fathers to be" to spend time together. (One of his groomsmen's wives was pregnant.) "Sometimes it is just great to share a beer with your dad. So, Dad, let's go to the bar and I'll buy you a beer." As we headed to the bar, the song began. The Song. I stopped, turned and pointed to the deejay; he sort of shrugged his shoulders as if to say, "Hey, what can I tell ya?" It was "Father and Son."

My pause caused me to get to the bar a few moments after Dion had arrived. The bar was at the edge of the seating area. He stood at the bar, two Samuel Adams beers in his hands. "Here you go, Dad." I took the beer, wrapped my arm around him and with our heads bowed and together, we laughed, cried and put an emotional bow on what has been a wonderful relationship gift. For the four minutes of the song, we shared love, appreciation and more.

The "more" is the affirmation of what we have had as together we head to what will be.

Leaving home for me came fairly easily because, I believe, I was stepping away from a solid foundation and a feeling of being loved. Not every child is that lucky, and, no matter the circumstances of leaving, there is the call to grow on and grow up. "Child's Song" tells the story well. We are all called to leave the nest and it is a time of mixed emotions, optimism and concern, looking forward and looking back. But the move must happen. And the move changes the lives of children, siblings and parents, while creating a rite of passage for all.

As of March 2009, I have added another song. My eldest, his fiancé and I chatted after I created their engagement images. She asked about dreams and how a couple can work to fulfill them after marriage. "I don't want Dion to have to sacrifice his dreams. Nor I, mine. How does that work after marriage?" I opened my arms for a long hug. After the embrace, I said, "I am so glad to hear that." With tears in my eyes, I continued, "Because that's my son who has much to offer and much to live out. As you do, too." We continued the conversation and the next day I sent them the song "Dreams Go By" by Harry Chapin. The song became more significant to me.

Chapin, a master storyteller, uses "Dreams Go By" to share a tale of a couple as they grow up, grow together and their talk of dreams becomes only lost memories. Thanks to his style, most anyone can feel a sense of their own lives described in the notes and syllables of his song.

The lyrics of those tunes help describe the normal processes and can be used to help me say to my boys that I "get it." The August 2008 issue of Better Homes and Garden magazine cited how I gave Justin, my middle son, a CD of songs as he was dealing with the complexities of moving out and moving on. I burned a few songs on the CD, including "Child's Song," "Father and Son," and "Arms Wide Open" with a sticky note attached. The note simply said that what he was going through was normal and that the songs might help him understand.

For some reason, the continuum of growing, growing up, growing older and growing away has always moved and inspired me. As a child, I listened to "Puff the Magic Dragon," and innocently thought it was only about a childhood friendship lost to growing up. That innocence was destroyed when my friend Brian drowned on the Mississippi River while working on a barge at the age of 19. I could not listen to the song again for almost 30 years. The book "Giving Tree" by Shel Silverstein still moves me to tears. It, too, speaks about loving over the years which age and change us, while also changing our relationships. It speaks of sacrifice (some would say near-martyrdom).

Indeed, having children is easy, and surprises always occur because it is a never-ending journey, and script-less play, an ultimately goal-less destination. It unfolds, with some guidance, some instructions, and some helplessness. Such is life.

Age isn't the only time-based bridge that holds the mirror for me and Dad. There are the kids, three sons who would have sparked his smiles, pats and infamous summary of "dumb ass" to ideas he deemed crazy but worthy simply because they came from his offspring.

My Loin Fruit

My loin fruit
Defies the archaic phrasing that assumes they are mine.
They are themselves,
In my custody for whatever time God has X'd out on his planner
For them in our house and lives.
Turn the pages slowly Lord,
For they are growing fast, creating lives not necessarily to which we'll be invited
And I love them desperately.
With desperation.
To get as much in before the next decades slip by
And leave me without them
Or them as orphans.
Diapers become senior prom tuxes,
Cereal-sticky hands become the artist's or musician's tools,
String rings become wedding bands
And I am unprepared
To lose them.
The product of my loins is muscle,
The product of my soul is my children.

August 8, 1998

Havin' children is the first verb, and it is a gift. And the best that one can hope for is that in the learning, listening, loving and living, there is hope built for the future.

In the voices and eyes of my young men
I see inside them, and me reflected
Like a magical looking glass that looks into the future
And the past, at the same time.
The burning of their souls' passions
Were mine;
The curiosity and confidence of discovery
Were mine;
The confidence and knowledge that love will follow them the rest of their days
Were mine.
And in my eyes I hope they see smiles for a lifetime
Will be theirs;
Determination and courage, sometimes repressed, never vanquished
Will be theirs;
The belief in what can be and the confidence to ask for help
Will be theirs;
The humility of vulnerability and humanity
Will be theirs.
I can only hope that we're both seeing when we look
Father to son.

And as time goes on, the children become men and bring from the past as well as what they make anew.

Father and son
Two men, the same—but individuals
The younger carrying
Genes, demons and dreams.
The elder breaking ground
Carrying burdens, demons and legends.
Younger to become elder
In an undetectable blur of years
That ford the meridian that
Separates
Child and parent

Younger and elder
Father and son.
Two men—the same, but individuals.

Over the years, I thought often of the songs about being father or being son. And I fancied that perhaps I could write one, too, that revealed the years of son-who-became-father. This was my attempt at that method of conveying the story. I wrote it in 2007: I was 51 and my boys were 26, 22 and 15.

Refrain

Father, father
Dad of mine
Tell me your stories
Share some time
Remind me you love me
With a hug and a smile.

I look up to you
I copy your walk
I've watched and listened
Since the time I could talk
I look at your hands
While you wind the clock
< R >
We talk about jobs
We talk about life
We talk while we're fishing
You sharpen your knife
The clock keeps on ticking
We're running out of time
< R >
I lean against the granite
That lies above your head
I continue to ask questions
Even though you are dead
The clock is now silent
It and you rest

< R >
See your son's sons
The way we all play
Listen to our chat
And the things that we say
Father loves his sons
I learned it that way
< R >

Early in 2006, I wrote in my journal:

The circle is closing. I am now the age of my father when my first real memories of him began and Dion is the age I was when he was born. Cameron is the age I was fully into my first "relationship" with a girl—fittingly, it was by correspondence—and Justin is about the age that I forsook employment for freelance photography and writing. My memories of those stages stand boldly for review and I wonder what memories the boys and I are creating for each other now.

Later that year, Dion called to remind me that I was now officially a life father. "More than half your life has been as a dad," he said. At that moment, a myriad of influences came together like in a chemistry experiment blending ingredients creates a reaction so magnificent that it cannot be ignored. And when lucky, it is alchemy.

Like in old science fiction movies when the chemist watches as his concoction boils and gurgles, until he pours the last dribble of the final ingredient to the mix, only to yield a powerful brew, my son's comment was the "final ingredient" to the mix for this book. I had pondered this book since 1998 and struggled to find the catalyst to complete this book. His observation played an important role.

I held several roles over the late-teen years into my adult years, including writer, photographer, publications coordinator, teacher, public speaker and university administrator, to name a few. The boys played roles in all of them, particularly the crossroads that called for a change. Just having kids changes life's parameters. At each job, however, I told the employees that there was no need for them to try to curry their boss' favor or to think that I would have a "golden child" at work. I have only three: my sons.

Dion was just getting into elementary school and Justin was a nursing baby when I began the job search that would take me from my beloved photography to the great unknown. 1986 would be the year that we became one of the statistics for Houston's troubled economy: we filed bankruptcy, if only to get out of a business space lease. A long job search began while I continued with my freelance writing and photography. I still have the log of more than 500 phone calls, letters and cold calls in search of a job, but I didn't find much of a market for photographers. A visit to my old parish's career assistance volunteers encouraged me to sell my skills more than my job titles. The search for sustainable income continued until I found a job at the University of Houston Cullen College of Engineering.

I was hired to be the college's coordinator of publications. The dean who hired me, Roger Eichhorn, loves to brag that he gave me my first real job. There may be some truth to that. While my intention was to remain in higher education for about three years before returning to my beloved work, I have grown and remained in the field since 1987.

Hey Dad,

This is great. The job of your life in the town of your dreams. Just imagine, a hard day at work then you can head out to fish & walk, enjoy yourself. Do your best, Good Luck!!!!

Luv Ya,
Dion

PS - If your ever down - read this & remember - FISH!

Dion created a congratulations card for me when I accepted a job at Sam Houston State University that also provided great access to fishing. Fishing matters to McInnises!

Cameron was born while I worked at UH. Three mouths to feed encouraged my leaving there in 1994; a confluence of personal and professional reasons prompted my departure from Sam Houston State University in 1997. I returned home to Texas from New Mexico in 2001, influenced by my desire to be closer to my roots as the boys grew older. Justin was in high school at the time I was trying to decide whether to accept an offer at the University of Houston-Clear Lake. I struggled with the decision to move the family from Albuquerque and accept a less-than-expected offer. Positive signs encouraged me despite an inauspicious beginning.

My first interview for the job was via video connection. I arranged an appointment at Kinko's in Albuquerque to have the two-way video interview at an appointed time. When I arrived, the television screen showed an empty room. A woman then entered, asked if I was Dion McInnis and then apologized that a fire alarm had just been triggered. "They take it quite seriously, so we'll be back in a bit. Just hang on!"

The interview happened 10 minutes later and things went well. An onsite interview followed months later and then the job offer came. Then came the time to decide. As with many of my decisions, I engaged the boys for their perspectives at the ages of 20, 16 and 9.

With Justin (almost 16), I related the decision to a biblical situation. "I sure wish there was a burning bush, telling me what to do," I said. He paused, smiled and said, "Well Dad, didn't the job interview begin with a fire drill?" I accepted the job offer shortly thereafter.

The family was never the same after I left for the UHCL position in 2001. More of that story is in the "leavin'" chapter, but the family did not reunite until late 2002 and I moved out in early 2003. Our separation lasted 18 months before filing for divorce. A lot of things weren't going as planned, and I looked for another job, but again the boys influenced any and all decisions.

I had to make enough money to pay for my own life's needs, the debts of separation and divorce, and I fulfilled my decades old commitment to help their mom get her bachelor's degree. I also pledged that I would not leave Cameron. We needed each other, and I knew it. The job search was limited, but a great opportunity that would connect me even more closely to art presented itself. The phone interview went well and the same day I received a call for a personal interview. That interview process revealed to me again how important parenting is to all people.

There were about eight people in the room and two on conference call as they tag-team interviewed me. At one point an interviewer asked "Clearly you are looking for an opportunity to spread your wings and fulfill your vision for an organization. Why have you stayed in your current situation and not moved on to something else?" The room went silent as I paused to collect my thoughts and emotions. Only one answer could come out of my mouth.

"One word," I said. "Cameron."

People blinked. They looked puzzled as I assembled words in my head. I continued.

"I'm divorced now," I said. "When I separated, I promised my youngest son that I would not leave the area. He would never be far away. My middle son lived with me for a while and has gone on to college in San Marcos. But I will not leave this area before Cameron graduates from high school. We enjoy our time together too much, and we need each other. I made that promise, so all my job searches have been limited to the Houston area. Yeah, one word: Cameron."

The room remained silent. Three interviewers were in tears. One of the teleconference participants told me later that she struggled to keep it together to continue the interview. The simplicity of a loving father-child bond must be a powerful thing for everyone.

When you were young
You rode on my shoulders
Or I carried you in my arms
Together we could make it
Anywhere.
Distance today
Keeps us apart
More than I ever believed could be

But we can still make it anywhere
'Cause I'll always be your dad

August 2003

Years later, a counselor shared a breathtaking insight with me. He said that "There is an overwhelming sense of a call to something of great importance for someone in this room. A call that is so great, that it dominates all other." As much as I feel that I am called to a ministry of change and joy through my words and images, I felt confident he would comment on that. But, no. "It is you. And it is fatherhood. Being a parent. It is what you were called to be and do." My head spun, but I suppose he is right. No matter what other roles I have, or changes that may come, being dad dominates my decisions.

I would like to think that I would never have made decisions that hurt my children in any way. Parents hurt their children enough unintentionally, so it makes difficult decisions that may cause pain even harder. I hope that the boys realize the reality of imperfect fatherhood, both as sons and when they become dads themselves. Despite the challenges of love and tough love, patience and impatience, joys and sorrows, they remain treasures.

I've caused you hurts
And made you laugh
And together we grew, you and me
Struggling together
Struggling apart
Like the life struggling in a seed
Living our lives
Living our dreams
Always believing in what's to be
I've always loved you
As only a father can
You'll always be a treasure to me

2003

Having kids requires shifting roles as circumstances changes. Fathers serve as disciplinarians, friends, coaches, mothers and more. But, the basis for all the roles is the identity and responsibility as dad. When I relocated back to Houston and Justin moved in mid-school year, it was like having kids anew. A new situation, new processes, new environment, that I used old wisdom and experiences to help me through.

Two a.m. laundry runs
Two men's clothes—father and son.
Son sleeps to awaken in three
Father, day off, washes, softens, dries and hangs
Using lessons from his mom—
My mother taught me two-fisted scrubs,
Wipe around the washer ledge to keep it clean,
Snap the shirts before hanging,
Keep the complaints to oneself.
Clean clothes, sweet clothes, fresh clothes—
"No kid of mine is going out dirty"
She said, I echo.
In three hours, the young poet goes to work early
His father, having just gone to bed.
This is the new family,
Built on new realities and old lessons.

I am clearly the father I am because of both my mom and dad. Many of my behaviors are clearly mom-influenced, and in those ways my boys see some of their grandmother, I hope, and through stories I share they learn more of their grandfather. All three knew my mom to some extent and none have recollections of my dad. Sharing stories and insights about my father is part of the fun, but it is also part of the responsibility of helping my sons understand from whence they came. I am who I am largely because of Mom and Dad; the boys need insights into them. While I have the memories, I must share them. It is part of the role of father in having children.

I look up to old man moon
With a cigar in my mouth
And beer in my hand
And really hope and wonder
If that old guy

Could be my old man.
We fished by that moon
And I wonder if
He howled at it a time or two.
I use it for writing and thought
As I sit under it
Thinking the world and life through.
Old man moon keep shining
Keep shining down on me
And if you're Dad, wink just once.
I'm looking at you closely
And thinking of dear old dad
With beer, cigar and remembrance.

August 2003

Over the years, I have shared stories that relate to being son-to-father and father-to-sons under the same title as this book. My first daddin' presentation was to a Kiwanis group in Bay Area Houston shortly after I arrived back home to work at University of Houston-Clear Lake in 2001. At the time, Justin lived with me prior to Cameron and his mom moving from Albuquerque to Friendswood, Texas. The opportunity came for me to speak and Justin was interested in joining me for the luncheon. "Why not?" I thought. I figured the worst I could do is mess up and it wouldn't be the first or last time that I would mess up in front of one of my boys.

About two dozen people attended the lunch meeting. Sixteen-years old and always hungry, Justin appreciated the benefits of attending a luncheon at an Italian buffet.

Shortly into my presentation, it appeared that I had lost the men in the audience. They weren't looking at me, they allowed distractions to preoccupy them and I figured that Justin was witnessing his dad bust. But I continued on, and concluded the presentation with an invitation to share their thoughts about being a father. Twenty minutes later, most of the women had left and the men remained talking.

One man described that he didn't learn how to say "I love you" to his children until he returned from war; another father shared why he volunteered with his wife in the local La Leche League to help mothers and their children bond; one dad spoke about not becoming an active parent until the last child was born, actions necessitated by his wife's health issues. The latter said, "I wished I had known how fun it could be with our first children. I missed out on so much."

There are many verbs to fatherhood. They are words of action. Sometimes there are simply no words to say though.

Don't let my silence confuse you
As I watch you play and grow
As you laugh and cry over life
As you wonder and question and discover
As you see the world through your own eyes.
Sometimes I don't know what to say.
All the time I'm in awe of
What a wonderful person you are.
Silently I watch
Lonely my spirit calls out
That is my child
How lucky and blessed am I.

2003

LEARNIN'

There are many lessons to learn, my sons
Restraint of your spirit is not one
Nor finding others to blame all the time
Nor quitting before you are done.

Great wisdom to learn from others, my boys
From their experiences if you just listen
Add to those stories your own tales
Your own truths should not be missing.

It's true that we have just one life
And we each own thousands of stories
We all bring to this world
We all deserve our own glories.

Learn, too, that to conform is to die
If we shape ourselves to fit in
There are leaders and followers, too
Giving our Selves away is a sin.

Don't lose the joy that comes in your heart
The instinct to celebrate the sublime
The miracles that come from expressing yourself
The gift to do, which is time.

Resist at all costs the motivation
Of money and power for its sake
Inspired be your soul because it can give
What "expectation" cannot take.

Be open to truth and goodness, my sons
No matter where you find it
Listen to many, but most of all
Always listen to your own spirit.

2003

From the moment the baby exits the womb and the doctor says, "You want to take a photo?" (Well, that's what he said to me!), the learning begins. And the teaching commences. Everything from how to behave responsibly to how to walk like a busy man is covered. Usually the teacher doesn't know the student is paying attention, whether the parent is the instructor or the instructed. Through observation, conversation and specific instruction, I have learned and taught more as a son and father than all the years of school combined. The same is true for you; you may just not know it yet.

Maybe it was his simple background, or the Southern heritage, or maybe Dad was just much wiser than we recognized: Dad could open the world with just a few simple words. Among his many expressions used for love, frustration, or smart-aleck banter, several have stood out over the years. One in particular has stayed with me as husband, father, friend and boss.

"Ya ain't gonna learn any younger," my dad would often encourage. Not one for bad grammar, his choice of words was disarming, while also empowering. They were words of truth, of love, of encouragement. But then, that was Dad.

Unsure, lacking in confidence for the first 16 years of my life, I did not fully own the simplicity of his permission to try and fail, to learn. As I got older, perhaps with those words ringing in my brain, I felt greater confidence for most things.

Scrawny, holding a baseball bat that probably weighed nearly as much as I did, I faced his pitches on an overgrown baseball field near Bendwood Elementary School, not far from our house. Gravity, not a fence, defined the outfield boundary; the ball could carry forever. First I would have to hit it. I feared the ball, feared the new activity, but Dad would encourage—sometimes positively, sometimes in frustration—that I wasn't going to learn any younger and that I should hang in there and keep swinging. I learned a little over time. He encouraged me on a new niche: pitching. We'd pitch for quite a while in the backyard, he with bursitis and me with an attitude. But, I learned. And did well. Despite wanting to procrastinate, I jumped in knowing that I wouldn't learn any sooner than today.

He did what no substitute toy or friend could do: he returned the ball and encouraged me. Sometimes, with my mad/bad-ass teenage attitude, the simple tenacity of staying out there was encouragement enough. And I realized it. And when he would give up in frustration with my (in)accuracy or my audacity, he would say a few words, take off the glove and walk in. The pain of that usually sufficed to straighten me up for a while.

That pain could never equal the other pain that stands out as part of the little leaguer experience. My pitching ability improved with practice, and Dad often acted as my practice catcher at home. The fastball hummed; my curve ball broke; and my . . . well, that's all I had. But, for eleven years old, they worked well. I found a place in baseball; and, more importantly, I earned a place in the hearts of my team buddies. That was important. Dad and I practiced in our backyard "sandlot," a moderate size yard, just wide enough for the mound-to-plate distance. The boundary markers included a tremendous oak tree that Mom swore Indians pow-wowed under a hundred years before. A couple of smallish pine trees sat around the corner, out of the game except for errant throws or hits when a game was in play. Towering semi-Siamese twins—two trees almost joined, but not of the same heritage: pine and oak—created another boundary, thus providing an alley for our pitch-and-toss. Except for this day. Today, we pitched on the narrow alley, defined by the far edge of the twins and the redwood fence that delineated the further-most confines of my world. Oak branches draped down, creating shade and distraction. I share all this set-up for a simple pitch: my fastball sped and danced toward Dad, touched a low-hanging leaf, distracted Dad and, almost totally unimpeded, hit Dad square-on in the groin. Sons don't deal dads blows like that and expect to live to talk about it.

I had no idea what to do as he crawled into the house, this one-time professional boxer, brought to his knees by a low-blow from his son, through the intermediary of a white ball with red seams. I remember him lying in bed, an ice bag on the wounded area, moaning. If my life wasn't going to be over, surely my practice routine would be. Hours later, he said, "C'mon, let's toss some more around. You were pitching pretty well, but you need to keep working on it." I stammered a balk. "You ain't gonna learn any younger, so c'mon," he said.

During a crazy phase in high school—it was sophomore year, I believe—I thought that I might try the fight sessions. Guys would don boxing gloves and protective head gear and duke it out during lunch breaks as part of the entertainment. Since Dad was a boxer, I thought that perhaps some of that genetic tendency to scrappiness and built-in coach would serve me well. The fact that I had never been in a fist fight in my life, and that I weighed 110 pounds dripping wet, did not diminish my interest. Dad's laughter took care of that.

My older (by 18 years) brother boxed a bit early in college, as I recall. Certainly, I too could pick up the sweet science, if only for a semester in high school. Dad and I went into the garage for some basic fighting tips. I have to imagine that Dad had mixed emotions: one, perhaps his son would tackle his sport, and two, perhaps his sport would maim his son.

He guided me on foot position, and where and how to hold my fists. We worked on a few simple moves when he started laughing in a patient, loving, "I can't believe we're doing this" sort of way. "What?!" I barked, a bit incredulous that we hadn't even started the real work and he already found humor in my effort.

"We used to love guys like you in the ring," Dad said. "That long neck just reaches out over your hands and that nose and chin present such a great target." He took a light jab at my jaw, and smiled broadly. "We sure loved guys like you." I realized that nothing sounded fun about getting into a ring and punching wildly and embarrassingly out of control with another guy. I stopped the pursuit, and have never yet been in a fist fight. My sons have carried the McInnis scrapping gene sufficiently to make up for my DNA deficiency.

I learned about fishing early on; likewise, I taught the boys when they were young. All three of my boys came to love fishing—Cameron being the most enamored with it and being a student of it—and we've come to identify the times of "daddy fishing." This style of fishing involves the child fishing and the dad teaching, tying knots, retrieving lures from trees, wading to release hooks from stumps and such. Daddy fishing means Daddy doesn't fish. My boys picked up on the term and now use that themselves if they have taken a girlfriend fishing or found a stranger on the pier who needed help. They are willing to forsake their own fishing to teach others. They, too, have their daddy fishing moments. There is, in fact, an entire chapter on fishin'.

Dion had been away from serious fishing for about a decade, but returned to it as schedules and life began to align to allow the luxury of rediscovering his love of the sport. On one recent experience with some youngsters, he spent most of the day un-snagging lines, answering unanswerable questions about fish ("What kind of fish would make my bobber do that? How big do you think it is?") and watching his new fishing rod get broken by carelessness. "I finally understand a bit about all that goes into daddy fishing," he said. The learning will continue.

The learnin' verb is two way, and all three of the boys are good teachers, even when they don't know it. They have each shared a teaching goal at different times in their lives: teach dad to swim. Each got the bug to "be the one" at about the age of nine. All three are strong swimmers, swimming competitively since early childhood: Justin competed at all-state level in high school and in a triathlon, Dion swam competitively until high school, and Cameron made the varsity swim team freshman year as well as the water polo team. My dad swam like a fish and learned by being thrown by his father in the water at Brackenridge Park in San Antonio. I inherited my mom's fear (we preferred to call it a strong appreciation of and respect for . . .) regarding water.

Each son's attempt to teach me began the same way they learned: putting my face in the water. They encouraged and coached, and I could not not accept their assistance, despite their instructions being embarrassing as everyone nearby could hear them trying to bring me through the first steps, and strokes, of swimming. But, how could I not try?

The last year we lived in Albuquerque, we took a family jaunt to a lake where Justin and his mom would be certified in scuba diving. Dion was already in college at Texas A&M, so the four of us headed to Santa Rosa for a weekend of outdoors and certification. We arrived at the hotel, and to get to our room we walked through the indoor pool area. No one was there.

In the back of my mind was Dad's voice saying, "You ain't gonna learn any younger." I knew I had to at least try.

When I arrived in the room with everyone's suitcases, Justin and Cameron had already parked themselves on the bed waiting for what was to come next. I put down the bags and said, "OK, guys. Today's the day." Somehow, they knew exactly what I meant and they jumped up off the beds as if they had springs in their bottoms, grabbed towels and headed out the door. Class was about to be in session. I prayed for an empty pool. Prayer answered.

We entered the water. With a boy on each side giving instructions, passing encouragement and noting useful corrections in my style, we put class into full gear. Once I began to make progress, their mother took over and the boys stepped out. Shortly thereafter, others arrived and it became disquieting to be stroking in the pool with instructions being called from the side, so I got out. But, I had picked up the basics.

Shortly thereafter, I accepted a job that returned me home to Houston and for the first few months, Cameron would ask when I called him if I was still swimming. Cameron gave up on asking about two months after I moved. After I separated from the family, Cameron would visit and we would swim in the pool. "You remember how, right Dad?" That was a far cry from his query five years before.

He was about five, as I recall, when he quizzed me about not being able to swim. After all, he was already swimming on a team, as did his brothers. "Dad, how come you didn't learn how to swim when you were young, too? Didn't they have swimming pools back then?"

You gotta love your teachers.

Cameron went on to teach his friend John how to keep his face in the water, too. The boys teach others in the pool or pool table, on piers or workbenches. Teaching and learning are inseparable and they occur at various venues.

Baseball fields have been one of the great fields of learnin' for the McInnis boys. Dad taught me things there and in the practice field that was our backyard, and I've tried to teach my three there. They've gone on to teach each other and teams, too.

In the high, dry summer of Albuquerque came a splendid opportunity. Dion had not yet left for college, Justin was full of pee and vinegar, and Cameron played little league ball. It was a perfect storm of conditions, ripe for some thunder and noise.

Dion coached the team, bringing a new level of knowledge to the kids. He believed the kids were smart enough to learn the game and respect it; he also believed that passion rules the day. Some parents disagreed, particularly those from opposing teams. At one game, a parent from the other team admonished Dion from behind the fence on the first base side. I prayed Dion would not respond. After the inning, I reminded him to not get into it. I coached third base and could watch how things transpired. Sure enough, after the game, the parent began to gnaw on Dion and I could see him roiling as only dads can see in the young men of their DNA. I walked over to see if the parent had a problem, and as with most bullies, his problems disappeared. Committed, passionate, enthusiastic, and charged, Dion served as the coach. He was the calm one of the older brother influences.

By this time, Justin had established himself as the cheerleader from Mars or beyond. His forms of cheering for his younger brother in baseball and soccer games had already become stuff of legend. He could run a soccer sideline, screaming encouragement and jumping chairs and coolers as if they didn't exist. While baseball provided no such sidelines, he could clearly make a difference with his cheers of encouragement.

And then there was Cameron, the quiet little guy just trying to make a splash on a team. Nothing dramatic came of this McInnis confluence during one season, except that Cameron enjoyed the season, kids learned from and admired Dion, Dion enjoyed coaching and tested theories he is still using today, Justin inspired and enthused as he still does, I had the pleasure and the memory of watching all my boys involved with something at the same time, each with their own gifts and interests at stake. And we all came away with stories. Which is mainly what I came away from when my dad coached my little league team for one year. That one year made a difference to me, and influenced my decision to coach, or assist, with each of the boys' sports interests, including baseball, basketball, soccer and track.

As I mentioned earlier, Dad put up with a lot from his smart-aleck caboose child. What my body could not deliver, my tongue always could. In baseball, my body could deliver as long as the need was pitching. My miserable hitting prevented me from any role other than outfield when any other person coached a team. Dad gave me a shot as pitcher, after I proved I deserved it. I was not the ace of the squad, but I was good. And I came away from that season with confidence, success, stories and influences that affected how I coached kids 15 years later. So, it made a difference. Likewise, the last Cameron season of baseball made a difference for all of us.

Learnin' how to drive makes for stories, too, and for differences in the lives of both the teacher and the students.

Following Dad's philosophy of "ain't gonna learn any younger," I learned some driving skills when my sister worked on preparing for her driver's test. That made me about 12 or 13. Some of my early attempts to master the machine prove why it is important to not be too harsh on people when they first begin to drive, or learn anything new for that matter: I drove into a neighbor's yard, laughing uncontrollably with my mom; I skimmed the back bumper of a car on my first day driving to school with a learner's permit; and, I got a ticket within the first week or so of having a license. But, I learned.

Dad took my sister Molly on back roads a half hour's drive from where we lived to practice driving. I got to join and have a few minutes at the wheel. The most fun was learning how to stop. "When I say stop, I mean STOP," Dad said. This gave us permission to cram on the brakes and learn the sensation of abrupt stops without fearing them. Doing this on dirt made a great crunching noise, and on asphalt provided the lovely screeeech that all young boys love.

When the time came for me to practice with my learner's permit, Dad and I returned to Patterson Road. I think Dad chose this area for more than its isolation; he loved the country. Considering his upbringing in Mississippi, it made sense, but I didn't fully grasp the meaning and the comfort it must have brought Dad. We'd drive up and down, up and down, giving me practice and him the sights, scents and sounds that made him comfortable. He'd note the scissortail birds, the bobcat tracks. One time we had to stop so he could try to catch the armadillo in the road. In his late 50s and still young enough to grab a 'dillo by the tail as it burrowed into the side of a ditch. Usually Dad asked us to stop for something different, but nothing compared to snake day.

I recall it as snake day because, among the many times Dad would have us stop so he could infuriate or harass a snake (he'd do this on family outings, too, when we would drive around to pick berries, look at critters and appreciate the countryside), this occurrence most confirmed for me his thing about snakes. Whatever that thing really was.

"Stop the car slowly," he said with a hint of excitement and anticipation. "Look over there, we just passed it. A rattler." Sure enough, a rattlesnake lay coiled on the dirt road in a nice, tight circle like rope on a pier. Dad walked past it to pick up a big chunk of scrap concrete he found in the weeds on the side of the road. He returned to the nervous, rattling snake and stood over it, straddled the coil and dropped the concrete chunk. Somehow, he missed the snake! Being a practical guy, he reached next to the snake, picked up the chunk and tried again. The snake disappeared under the concrete with a crunching sound. I never understood Dad's deep desire to kill poisonous snakes and harass non-poisonous ones.

Perhaps it is that background of country driving practice that led me to use similar techniques for the first two boys, though it is harder to find such spaces for the third who is learning at the time of my writing this. Either way, country drivin' is the way to be, to twist the old "Green Acres" theme tune a bit.

Dion had the benefit of learning to drive at a ranch. Not ours, of course, but a ranch, indeed. I worked at Sam Houston State University at the time of his learning, so we practiced on the mile-long road that ran from the front to the back of the property that belonged to the university and was only a short drive from campus. It was pretty safe and I had all manner of things to test him with: "Stop with your right tire on that pinecone," "Drive over, not on that cow patty," and such. Of course, his brothers wanted in on the act, and Cameron sat on my lap as he steered us up and down the road. As I finish this book, he has now started driving solo, a year behind his contemporaries, but now gaining the independence at last. We still talk about his earliest lessons.

I recall my father taking me to Memorial City Shopping Center's parking lot so I could learn to drive the standard transmission Mercury Capri that he bought because I totaled mom's Plymouth Fury. His patience and persistence—he wouldn't let me give up on learning the machinations of clutch-shift-accelerate, even when the smell of the hot clutch became obvious—served as a good background for me to teach Justin how to drive a standard truck and to provide Cameron with the early basics. I used the shifting experiences for Justin and the parking lot times with Cameron, in particular.

I had a 1987 Ford F-150, five-speed standard, while awaiting the rest of the family's relocation from Albuquerque to join me in Houston when the serious driver training began for Justin. He wanted to learn; he hated learning. Justin has never been one to accept his self-perceived failure or even imperfection with much grace. Learning the process of shifting required great self-acceptance.

We drove into then-developing new neighborhoods in Friendswood. We'd switch seats, putting him in the driver's position. One of our first such experiences tested him, and the clutch. It also revealed his persistence to never back down from a challenge.

In the first 20 minutes or so of the lesson, we travelled less than a block. The aroma of cooking clutch was strong, filling the air around us, and his impatience was equally hot. He did not direct his anger at the process or the truck, but on himself for being unable to master something that looked so easy. Justin got out of the truck swearing that he surrendered, and other types of swearing, too. I got out and leaned on the truck, saying "Then I guess we're walking home because either you're driving us from here or we'll leave the truck here." As I declared the law of the road, I flinched because of the heat of the fender metal. We had to laugh, diminishing his frustration and the strength of my edict. He returned to the cab and we kept at it until he could drive straight, downshift for a turn and start from a stop. And for the clutch to cool down. Then I drove us home, and he was on the path to driving independence.

He drives a standard today. And quite well.

Cameron got a bit of a late start on driving, and it began in area parking lots when he came for his weekly and bi-weekend visits. As with all driving lessons, they included times of frustration and laughter, for both of us. I could not afford to have my car dented at the time, so I tried to keep his lessons to places that minimized the chances of accidents, and had to hide the extent of my concerns whenever he got too close to a light pole or wall in the parking lots of nearby schools, shopping centers, storage facilities and business parks. You'd have to ask him whether I hid things well or not.

I couldn't hide my belief that he *needed* to drive more than his brothers. All teens do as rites of passage and to develop independence, but Cameron was in a different circumstance than his brothers: his mom and I had been divorced for several years by the time his opportunity came around for driving. For myriad reasons, Cameron needed to learn to drive, to use the independence to grow as a young man and pursue his dreams.

After about six months driving on his own, the opportunity arose for Cameron to take a mini coming-of-age trip: going to Austin for an extended weekend with Justin for bank fishing, hanging out and spear fishing.

He and I discussed the best routes for navigating across Houston and onto the least nerve-wracking of the possible roads out of town. That is like searching for the least painful of a pile of glowing charcoal briquettes to pick up bare handed. I provided directions and asked to affirm his understanding.

"I don't know the names of any of the roads, Dad."

I tried to find other ways to describe the roads by the landmarks or possibly by past forays onto freeways. Still no luck.

"How many times have you driven on the freeway alone?" I asked.

He smiled and held up two fingers. Unfortunately, it was his middle finger and thumb to form a zero. His smile remained slightly out of focus in the background of my view as I paid specific attention to the zero.

He came up with a few examples of short drives at freeway speeds, but none during busy traffic times or requiring following highway direction signs.

The evening before he was supposed to leave for Austin, Cameron and I took the drive through Houston to get to the last freeway stretch to Austin. We left near dusk and arrived at the juncture at night. He did well, but that didn't ease my fears about other drivers. He drove to the turnaround and I drove back, but felt confident enough in his abilities and judgment to let him take the trip. My willingness was based on 20% confidence and 80% prayer.

My mother used to say, "I begin praying for you kids the second you walk out the door and don't stop until you return." As the boys grow up, Mom's wisdom becomes more relevant every day.

He made the trip without incident and enjoyed the man-to-man time with his brother in and under water, and got to know Justin's girlfriend, Roxie, even better. After 500 miles, he drew a few steps closer to manhood, learning from family and strangers along the way.

Of course, fathers aren't their children's only teachers. Nor should they be.

Dion rejected his early teachers. He believed he knew more than they did, which is not uncommon for students in high school or maybe middle school. Dion was in Mother's Day Out when he first expressed that attitude.

He did not carry the same attitude when he tried out for the baseball team in high school in Huntsville, Texas. He loves baseball. He respects it. He admires its history. Among the many gifts that God has given him, baseball athleticism is not on the list, though baseball passion is. He tried out in hopes that his passion for the game would push him past any athletic deficiencies. He tried for love of the game. And in the trying, growing occurred.

I arrived at the practice field a bit early. The lit baseball field held scores of young men who ran, caught, batted and played in hopes of catching the attention of the coaches. I stayed in the car, observing from a distance so as to not cause any undue pressure on Dion. I watched him push himself, attempting to use brute force and enthusiasm to get him over the challenge. I listened to a coach yell to the players, "Get naked for the ball." In those moments, I realized that other male adults would enter my first-born's life and call to him to reach further, teach him things that I don't know, influence him for better or worse. He was entering yet another era of influences on him, and the best that I could do is honor that with a dad's watchful eye.

From a father's perspective, Dion's next major influence could not have been more antithetical to the country-town baseball coach: Mr. Zuber. Mr. Z, as the students called him at St. Pius X High School in Albuquerque, could have been the poster teacher for liberal education. Not radical, but liberal, as in he tried to liberate their thinking. And maybe liberal in other ways, too, but that could be a book in itself. Mr. Z allowed the students to take just about any position if they could defend it in his English classes, which reminded me in some ways of my high school English classes at Strake Jesuit in Houston: read, write, think, proclaim and defend. Do those things and you'll do well.

Mr. Z provided a catalyst to Dion's re-invention of himself, which he did a bit each time we moved. I believe it was during those years that Hemingway met Kerouac in Dion's personality.

A Scout leader in Albuquerque, New Mexico provided Justin with some of his most significant other-than-dad influences, I believe. It wasn't the Scout-ness that provided such strong influence, but the activities that Merle led, the manner in which he led them, and his love of the outdoors. His active lifestyle included ultra-distance running, hiking, trail running and teaching. He was quiet, stoic and knowledgeable. Justin's natural love of the outdoors that began to develop when we lived in Huntsville came to full bloom in the environs of New Mexico and Merle's approach made for a perfect match for Justin. So much so, six years after leaving the state, Justin worked for Student Conservation Association, which teaches high school kids about the environment in camps around the country. He took his love and passion for the outdoors as a compass guide in his education, and was already working for the United States Geological Survey (using his GIS certification, master diver certification, love of geography, and new knowledge) by the time he graduated from Texas State University. Would he have chosen that path without Merle's influence? I don't know, but the student was ready when that teacher appeared.

Sometimes a teacher appears even when the student isn't ready. The wise pupil remains open to the opportunity.

At Texas State, Justin took a technical writing course from a teacher who drove him crazy with her expectations, demands and teaching methods. They argued, disagreed and butted heads. I received phone calls from Justin when he vented about something she said or did, or appeared to say or do, particularly when it related to her commenting on his work. Typically, I could understand what behavior or skill she was trying to teach after he vented sufficiently and I could re-state what she probably meant and what he should do in a way that I believed he could understand. And usually, that worked.

Near the end of the semester, he had put aside his frustrations and his work was sufficient to get grades that satisfied him, though he felt he deserved better. In that calm, he shared that he could see how the writing skills he learned might help him professionally some day. It didn't take long. He wrote a letter and some e-mails to Student Conservation Association to get a summer job working in national parks to teach high school kids about the environment. His communiqués were excellent and helped him get an interview and the job. Even now, as a gainfully employed professional, he reacts with frustration to the mishandled writings of others in e-mails, memos and letters.

Justin is an experiential learner. I believe the education profession calls that "kinesthetic learning." So, his eyes, hands and movements provide him great learning methods. During a summer session class in botany, the class had to learn 50 or five million plants a week. I forget which; I remember being amazed at the number. The students had to learn the common and Latin names, the genus, species and phylum of each. And each week there was a test. I recall his angst about one test, in particular.

"I think I did well, dad," Justin said. "But I got one wrong. I thought I knew what the leaf was, but I got it wrong. It looks a lot like another plant, but they are very different if you touch the leaves and not just look at it. I should have touched it, dad. If I had only touched it, I would have gotten it right." Learning comes with all five senses.

The role of other men-as-teachers for Cameron was quite different. I moved away when he was 10. Weekly visits and alternate weekends provided us far different teaching moments than I had with his brothers. Of course, I was cautious and watchful over where he would get his clues and cues in my absence. He learned on the job. Literally.

Thanks to a passing comment that I shared at a church men's group about him and his dream to someday work as a boat salesman, he got a job cleaning boats. He learned much about boats, work, dealing with others and life. His teacher was Norman, a middle-aged man whose company cleans boats in the 30- to 40-foot range and who enjoys nonconformity in the work world despite his otherwise conservative views.

Though dads can't choose their children's other teachers, I have been lucky in whom my sons found or sought out.

No matter who the teacher is, there must be the courage to try, to grow, to test. Lessons can be learned in school or on the playground, in the workplace or while seeking employment, in dreams considered or those attempted.

When I decided that I wanted to follow a photography career path, Dad provided support in any way that he could, though he didn't understand it. He proudly had some of my early color images professionally framed and displayed in his office and reception area. He taught me how to write my first business letters, and guided me on a variety of business planning concepts. I recall a time when Mom told me that Dad said, "I think the young man is going to make a go of it." Things didn't work out as I had envisioned, but my love of photography never died and it remains an avocation and part vocation to this day.

At one point in my development as a photographer, I decided to create more nude work. The experience in a photography class at University of Houston inspired me and I wanted to try more of it. I fretted about whether that was the right direction and what others may think. It was all quite new and foreign to me. After sharing my concerns with Mom and Dad, he replied, "Don't be a coward, son. Do what you have to do." I didn't interpret his comments as pejorative, but quite affirming. Indeed, should we fear life and choices? In our doubts we must fear less, even if we cannot be fearless. Dad's words still remind me to fear less as I tackle new challenges or face old demons.

I see the living out of dad's guidance in my boys, in all phases and aspects of their lives. It will serve them well; it already has.

Watching the boys stand for their convictions, or their right to discover has been source of both entertainment and inspiration over the years. As with all things parental, it has also provided opportunity for worry.

We lived in the western suburbs of Houston that were part of the Alief area from 1979 to 1994. Our subdivision, known as the first master planned community in the area, took a great hit in the economic downturn of the 1980s. The financial institution behind the development went out of business and the "master plan" degenerated to general oversight. Still, it was a pretty good place to raise a family though as foreclosed properties became rental properties, the conditions changed. Several gangs were represented on our street. During these changing times, Dion took a stand because of an incident in the band practice hall. We learned of the situation when a school counselor called to say that we didn't have anything to worry about. We had no idea what she was talking about.

Between her information and Dion's story when he got home from school that day, we learned that a fellow band member had showed Dion a large-bladed knife at school and declared that he had brought the weapon to "Cut myself a n****. But don't you tell anyone or I'll cut you." Dion knew wrong when he saw it and told his teacher and counselor about the circumstance. The principal removed the student from school the same day. In watching the behaviors of our children, we realize what lessons they have learned. And sometimes you wonder where their levels of strength and courage come from, but admire it nonetheless.

That story crossed my mind about five years later while working in New Mexico. When the boys sold candy for various fundraisers, I maintained a box in my office for others to make purchases on the honor system. A little old black lady would occasionally come by my office to chat, and she would sometimes buy a dollar candy bar or two so she could have a snack for the bus trip home. She would usually need to purchase on the installment plan, which meant I also got to visit with her when she came by to make a payment. On one such payment visit, she and I chatted about the boys. She said, "Your boys are sweet. You haven't taught them prejudice have you?" I hope not. I hope they have learned about human dignity instead, and this is best taught in the moments and the stories.

Dad shared with me a story that forever shaped my thoughts on self-reliance and dignity. He was an accountant, and for reasons that I am not sure of, he would never charge widows to do their tax returns. I recall the story of him offering pro-bono services to a custodian of meager means after having seen the man's circumstances. "This was an easy return. No charge." "No, sir.

I want to pay my bill." "It's okay. I know how much you made, of course, and I'm happy to have done your return for you." "No, sir. I want to pay. Don't be taking my dignity."

Dad's best intentions were completely misunderstood; however, his offer and then his acceptance of the man's position revealed to me differently that my father had a generous spirit, an appreciation for the days of struggling with little, and respect for other's self-respect. His generosity was about helping others as they needed or wanted, not about glorifying his own image.

I learned a lot by watching or hearing about Dad's kindnesses to strangers. Hitchhikers benefitted from his generosity. Two experiences, in particular, gave me insights into his simple helpfulness.

"I helped a couple of hippies today," Dad said when he returned home from one of his regular roundtrips between Houston to San Antonio to work with clients.

Dad described the hippies' circumstance with their car broken down on the road in need of something simple. I don't recall the need, but I do remember him commenting on how nice they were, how short the young woman's skirt was, and how they smelled nice. He gave them money to cover the cost of the part or repair. The woman asked for Dad's address so she could repay the money. He had no expectation, but two weeks later a check arrived in full payment of the "loan" along with a thank you note. Dad gave without expectation of return.

On a fishing trip, we came across a black man hitchhiking on a farm-to-market road. It was the mid-1960s, I believe.

It didn't take long before Dad's attempt to draw our new passenger into conversation revealed that the man was a deaf mute. I remember being the conveyor of messages, writing Dad's questions on a note pad and passing them to the man in the back seat, and then reading his answers to Dad. We carried on this way for quite a drive. I remember feeling good that dad and I, together, helped the man. And I remember his scent—it reminded me of Johnson's baby cream that came in small white jars with pink screw tops (Mom always had a jar by her makeup mirror). I don't know what it was that he had on, but I sure know what it reminded me of.

All sorts of learning happens in school. Stories from the halls and classrooms reveal a lot about what children learn about subject matter, and also about people, relationships, trust, loyalty, leadership and life. And careers, too.

Cameron declared in first grade that he was a doctor and could take care of medical things in the house. I inquired as to which medical school he attended. Without pause, he confidently replied, "Preschool." Case closed.

I don't imagine that any of the boys will be doctors, and that is fine by me. Justin encouraged my submission of an article to an outdoors magazine and when I thanked him for his "gentle" reminders to do so, he replied, "No problem, Dad. I just want to help you get rich so you can buy me all that land. See, I'm going to ride your coat tails, Dad." I replied, "Son, I believe you've already made your own coat."

All three of the boys have boldly chosen their own paths in school, relationships, jobs and life. I am pleased to still be a source of information for them, but also realize that my input is merely that. After gathering information, they will make their own decisions. While Dion's and Justin's routes to college could hardly be more different, Cameron admitted to wanting to live with me and his step-mother while attending community college once he graduates from high school. Justin lived with me after he graduated from high school, and then took a five-year path through community college and Texas State University and the dean's list before taking a job in the field of his dreams, despite believing five years before that he was "too stupid to go to college." Cameron believed in Justin's model. I had to remind him that his approach would have to be his, possibly influenced by what he had seen in his brothers, but his path nonetheless. "With your swimming skills, you may find yourself getting a scholarship to a small college if you keep your grades up. You may find an altogether different path than either of your brothers, and that is perfectly fine. Find your path, buddy," I said, and he is on a new trail. Being the wise, insightful, curious thinker that he is, his paths will be well-considered courses of growth.

For his 18th birthday, I created a card for him. On the cover are two photos—him at three years of age looking upward into a flock of seagulls, and him at 17 diving into the pool at the start of a race. The caption states, "You've always looked ahead to see the good and beauty in life; you've never been afraid to dive in with all you've got." The message continues inside, "Which is why we're sure that as you leave childhood and enter manhood, your life of dreams, joys and successes will outweigh the mundane frustrations of the day. The life that awaits you is grand, bold and wonderful, because the man entering it is . . ." Where he goes with that in college and career is yet to be determined.

I'm confident that Cameron's path will be special. Years after his crack about medical school, he made another humorous comment that required me to remind him of his early medical training. He laughed and replied, "Yeah, ain't I a piece of work?" Indeed, he is . . . they are. Seeing how they apply the things they learn about life and themselves along the way keeps the "pieces of work" interesting and surprising.

The boys have exhibited various elements of their character in jobs and career steps.

After a variety of job steps, Dion established a web design business. While the other jobs he had along the way revealed things, the consulting business provided different views of him as a man and a manager. The business grew, as did his confidence and self-awareness. When he first tried to hire some part-time assistants on contract, he created an ad to convey what he wanted and expected. He called to read his verbiage to me.

He felt that anyone who called after reading the ad was worthy of an interview. I don't know if anyone had the courage to seek a job with someone so clear about his expectations and self-awareness regarding management and leadership style. But he clearly conveyed more than a job opening—he described a leader's vision . . . his.

Courage begets confidence, and the same can be seen when living out the verbs of fatherhood.

Little moments allow glimpses into how a child's confidence is coming along. The backyard baseball field, front yard gridiron and driveway basketball court each provide opportunity.

Playing basketball with the boys always provided learning and entertaining moments, and more spirited clashes as they got older, stronger and needier of expressing their ability to muscle around Dad on the court. In a surreally fast blur of time, they moved from sitting on my shoulders taking shots at the hoop to standing toe-to-toe with me and stuffing my best jump shot.

In between those stages, Justin showed a bit of the cocky confidence that continues to serve him well in life. He and Dion challenged me to a basketball game under the pines in McInnis arena (the driveway in Huntsville, Texas) in time between supper and sunset. As I prepared to bring the ball into play, Dion moved over to cover me. Justin gestured him away, and stood in front of me with arms spread out like an eagle. He swayed back and forth as he smiled and declared, "I got it covered." He was 10.

I have tried to remind the boys of many such stories so they can see their development. It is no accident that they are the strong, wise, caring, independent, unselfish, risk-taking individuals; they have been in development to be the men they are, and the men they are becoming as they continue to learn.

Perhaps there is no way to instruct one's children about relationships, but they certainly learn by watching. I'm pleased to see how deeply the two older boys have loved the important women in their lives, and how generously they give of their talents, energy and attention to the special woman in their lives. As of this writing, Cameron has a girl who has caught his interest. From what I have seen, he treats her kindly and with humor.

I know that their behaviors aren't affectations to simply attract a sweetie. They have been genuine with their feelings and respect since they were kids. I have no delusions about any of them being perfect with every girl or woman in their lives. Growing up guarantees flaws and mistakes are made.

Justin had a girl friend as a kid while growing up on the west side of Houston. His Jessica was the carrots to his peas. When we moved to Huntsville, she wrote in chalk on our driveway a heart with the words "Please come back" inside. While they did not remain in touch, I believe his early friendship with her charted a path of female friendships for him, not unlike my early friendship with Kathy Meyer. Though she and I never lived on the same street like Justin and Jessica, our correspondence relationship of sharing and occasional visits between the ages of 12 and 25 set the mold for me that men and women can be good friends. The boys heard stories about my girlfriends. Being open about living, loving and learning seemed like the best way to teach about relationships.

We don't always end up teaching as well as we think.

By the time Dion was in his early teens, there had been many open discussions about sex to help him understand sexuality and relationships. His mother and I tried to provide him age-appropriate information and be available to answer whatever questions he had while growing up. For all the straight talk, some perceptions came out a bit squiggly. It was at this stage, while on a family errand, Dion affirmed from the back seat of the van his understanding of dating. We had been talking about dating, which was to come in a few years, and about his friends. He asked for clarification. "So, let me get this straight," he said. "Couples double date so one couple can watch while the other has sex?" Our laughter could not be contained, despite valiant attempts to do so. We tried to re-explain, though I wonder why he never mentioned anything about double dates to us in all the years since.

Laughter becomes a great tool in teaching. Teaching and learning aren't always done under ideal conditions, but rarely is meanness called for.

Humor is an important tool for teaching. It also helps to have it when watching how the lessons have been learned. Teaching also requires toughness.

When Cameron was an early teen, he said that he understood that there were times when I had to be a mean dad. I didn't know what he was getting at, so he explained his understanding of how dads sometimes have to teach lessons about responsibility and that requires being mean if necessary "Because your kids need to learn to grow up." That may count as a benevolent definition of "tough love."

Each son learns in different ways, which requires some adaptability in teaching methods. A common thread among the three is a sense of independence that moves them to learning at their own pace and method. Experiential learning rates high. They come by it naturally.

I was a slow learner on many things, like riding a bicycle and jumping rope. As a little kid, I struggled with those things and showed minimum interest. When I became discouraged that I didn't know how to do what many of my friends did, my mom would say, "You know how you are Dion. You'll learn when you want to learn, and not a minute before. You'll know when and no one will stop you when you're ready. That's okay." It has proven to be true for 50-plus years. I recall her wisdom while watching all three of the boys.

Dion picked up on almost any subject matter quickly and easily. In Mother's Day Out programs, he had already decided that he was smarter than his teachers. He absorbed information like a sponge, and sought out new information with great curiosity. One Christmas while he was in his early 20s, I asked him for gift ideas by inquiring about what he really loved. Work and responsibilities had taken him from some of his old hobbies like fishing, so I inquired as to his interests and passions. He answered with needs. I pushed, "But what do you love to do, buddy?" He paused before stating, "I love to learn." I gave him a year's subscription to Encyclopedia Britannica that year.

A couple years later as we discussed different methods of leadership and sharing information with others, he said, "I love to learn; I just don't like to be taught." His mom and I were separated at the time, and on the mirror of my apartment I had written with dry erase marker, "Don't tell me what to say, think, feel or do." Times like those remind me how I often see the boys when looking in a mirror, or see me when looking at them.

Moments of life and living reveal a lot about what children have learned, as do moments of loving, joy and sorrow. Times of death and dying have also provided me great insight into the boys' character and strength. I could not be more proud.

Dion was in high school when his maternal grandmother, Heidi, suffered a heart attack. As she lay on her death bed, kept alive only by machinery, he completed a scheduled interview for a position with a Congressional program that would allow him to spend his junior year in Germany. His grandmother was born and raised in Germany, leaving only after her American Air Force husband was re-assigned to America. His mother was born in Wiesbaden, Germany. Dion nailed the interview and was offered a position; he declined it because of the new family situation and the need for all of us to help his grandfather after having lost his life partner. Twelve years later, Dion made it to Germany, for his honeymoon.

Dion's gift to his grandmother was his German fluency and the offer to go to Germany to study. Whether she heard the news on her death bed is a matter of debate, though in our hearts we all believed she knew in her own way.

We also feel sure that she heard Justin's gift to her, too. He was doing well with his piano instructions, proudly playing tunes for her whenever they visited. After she died, he shared that he wanted to do something special for her funeral. "Can I make a tape of me playing her favorite song? We can put the tape in her casket, okay?" At her memorial service, his tape played as his last performance for her.

The boys lost both of their grandmothers in a two-year period. The circumstances were different, with my Mom's death not being unexpected. She was older and of failing health. After my mother's death, their reactions were poised and supportive. As we left the cemetery, Cameron asked that we stop long enough to see the casket disappear as they lowered it so we would not be leaving her alone. Their understanding of loss was born in their understanding of the people involved. They had learned well.

More than a dozen years later, Heidi's widower passed away. The boys lost the only grandfather they had ever known and it was a test of all they knew about themselves, family dynamics, spirituality and courage. They shone as exemplars.

Henry, their grandfather, suffered with failing health for several years before the multitude of problems beat down this hard-headed man who came up the hard way in life. He had gone into the hospital many times and everyone expected him to leave it again, despite conditions that indicated otherwise. That was Henry's way.

As Henry battled, Justin prepared for his exams. Justin studied for his *final* final exams—his last couple of exams of his last semester of college, accomplishing what he at one time, had never thought possible. He has to work many times harder to read and study thanks to dyslexia and Attention Deficit Disorder, yet there he stayed in his grandfather's ICU room—studying while attending to his grandfather's every gasp and whispered breath. With one hand, he held his grandfather's hand, and with the other he turned pages on textbooks and notebooks. Henry died; Justin graduated. And everyone who witnessed the tireless love was touched. The photograph used for the back cover of this book was taken at Justin's graduation.

One of those inspired was Justin's older brother, Dion. When Dion gave a final presentation on leadership to a class during the summer before *his* graduation, he cited Justin as an example of perseverance, will and strength. Dion used in his presentation an image that Justin had taken of him holding his grandpa's hand; he told the Justin story at his wedding rehearsal dinner months later.

We see what our children have learned by how they react, and by what they give of their time and talents.

After grandpa died, Dion created a video celebration of Henry's life that was moving, inspirational and beautiful. Later, he made CDs for the family members, giving them a tribute that also serves as a poignant visual story of a man's life as he did the best he could do with what he had.

Cameron was about the same age at Henry's passing that Dion was at Heidi's. He had no interviews scheduled, no possibility of a return to the homeland, which was Kentucky in Henry's case. He had the courage to ask for some time by himself with grandpa; he was the only person in the room when Henry accepted death.

Why is all this death in the chapter about learning? I believe that the best test of what someone has learned about life, love, courage, conviction, giving and supporting is their responses in time of death, be it their own or of others close to them. As I have watched my sons, I have seen evidence of strength, generosity and depth that will serve them and those they love for years.

Death has a way of maturing one's thoughts, providing a learning environment for thoughts of mortality, spirituality and purpose. A few months after grandpa died, Cameron queried, "If you and Mom hadn't lost so many babies (three miscarriages), would I have even been born?"

I replied that had the miscarriages gone to term, there likely would not have been the sixth pregnancy, which was him because each pregnancy presented more difficult physical challenges for their mother. I opted for a vasectomy after Cameron's birth due to issues relating to dangerous blood pressure for their mother, becoming higher and riskier with each pregnancy.

"Then what would have happened to my soul? Would it be in some kid in Nairobi or something?" he asked.

The resulting hour-long conversation reminded me that the learning and inquiry never stops. As it should be.

Life and inquiry takes place below the high realm of spirituality and the perfection of soul. It lives in the stupid and memorable.

My friend Steve still recalls the story and memory of my dad and the "dead soldier." The incident happened about 1975. My sons will have their stories, too.

Dad fought the demon of alcohol through his entire adult life. By the time I came around, he had things pretty much under control and my observations of his drinking were typically of the funny, congenial drinker. He also loved Mom desperately and struggled without her around (it is a blessing that he died first). One summer, those two conditions came together: Mom was out of the country with my sister, but the bottle was in the cabinet.

My friend Steve and I drove into my driveway and saw Dad sitting on the front porch in one of the aluminum frame, webbed folding chairs that were popular in the 1970s. He had a strange smile on his face. When a few words broke the smile, it was clear he had been sitting there, enjoying a few highballs of rum and cola. His tongue was a bit thick, as was his charm.

We meandered into the kitchen so he could pour another drink, offering us a chance to join in his combined good feelings and loneliness.

"You emptied the bottle, Mr. McInnis," Steve said. "Have you ever killed off a dead soldier?"

"Whassat?" Dad inquired.

"You drop a lit match into the bottle and it burns off the remaining alcohol. That's a dead soldier."

"Let's give it a whirl."

Dad lit a safety match and held his hand precisely over the opening of the bottle. He dropped the match in full flame and the process worked to perfection. A lovely blue flame shot up the neck of the bottle and exited the opening with the brilliance of a Bunsen burner in chemistry lab. Dad had not yet moved his fingers.

"Dammmmn," Dad proclaimed, proving that you can still feel pain after rum and cola. "I burnt my finner."

To this day, Steve comments on my dad's burnt finner and I smile. Every time.

My sons may have a similar response if and when our time together before my second wedding day comes up in conversation. In lieu of a bachelor party, I took the boys, my step-father-in-law and uncle in-law for a guided bull red fishing trip. The day before the wedding, however, was to be time with only my sons and me. The four of us sat out on the backyard deck to have a drink and cigar—one of the traditions we have instituted in this phase of our lives. All the conditions were set for a memorable moment. We learn a lot in moments.

Leaving me on the deck, the boys went inside to return with my wedding present. They presented me with a .22 caliber, Ruger semi-automatic rifle with a banana clip for those I-need-to-shoot-a-lot days. This night I needed only one shot.

As I reviewed the gun and its features, they challenged me to take a shot. In the backyard. In the suburbs of League City. It made perfect sense in the moment.

I took my now-empty 7-Up can into the yard, and left it behind as a target for a long rifle shell only 20 feet from where I was sitting. It had served its job in blending with the other half of 7&7 drinks. I loaded my present, and fired off a shot. Time and drink changed my recollection of how loud a .22 actually is. The neighbor's lights came on. The smell of gunpowder hung in the humid November air. Imaginings of our very responsive police force had them arriving at the door before the sound waves finished moving down the street.

I hustled double time to put the rifle in its case (also a present) and run inside to slide it under the bed, only to return and pick up where I left off with the cigar that I had left behind. I remember the night fondly for a variety of reasons. The boys will remember it as another day that dad proved he was as stupid a human as anyone else.

The backyard has provided other interesting insights.

I love grapefruit, but I can't eat it because I also take Lipitor. Oh, I really love grapefruit. I don't believe there is a wrong way to eat it, and the best is to simply peel it open and devour like a big orange. One of the things that I noticed when I looked at the home I bought in 2005 was the large grapefruit tree in the yard behind the house and the overhanging branches full of fruit. I ate one during one of the home visits. I wasn't taking Lipitor yet so I could still enjoy the full, pink, juicy, tasty, plentiful fruit. I knew I'd like the backyard neighbor, or would have to learn to.

Since moving in, the medication change created the change in my eating habits when it comes to grapefruit. The pharmacist, not my doctor, told me about the possible problems and the worst-case-scenario with the Lipitor-grapefruit mix is being poisoned to death. No more grapefruit.

Cameron takes every opportunity to remind me how scrumptious the fruit that drop into the yard are. They make great snacks while working in the back yard—pull one off the branch, break it open (they are so juicy and full that they can be broken, not peeled) and enjoy.

When Justin and Cameron helped me build a fence after the ravages of Hurricane Ike (and we made out quite luckily), the tree provided them juicy rejuvenation. Cameron noticed the irony of my wanting the forbidden fruit that was within such easy access in my yard of trees, bushes, pond and plants.

He broke open a juicy fruit, devouring it out of the peeling while smiling broadly. Juice ran across his cheeks, down his chin, along his arms until dripping off his elbows. "Hey Dad, I guess this really is like your Garden of Eden now." Smart boy.

We learn from each other by positive messages, well-chosen behaviors and from mistakes. We also learn about imperfections, foibles and stupid behavior.

My eyes focused on the underside of the beige Ford Tempo, an affordable car if you don't count repairs. And repair, I did. Stymied by the lack of cooperation from the oil cover, I laid with my chest all of a foot from the oil pan of the car, this working margin supported by garage sale special jack stands. Hours and hours of trying to get the oil pan reattached had drained any enthusiasm for self-repair; I surrendered.

Several attempts to replace the cover succeeded; none of them eliminated the oil leak. Totally frustrated, and almost completely oil covered, I lay on my back, knees propped up just outside the confines of the bumper . . . and I stared. The automotive muse was going to speak to me at any moment, giving me creative inspiration and divine mechanical intervention. I felt a gentle touch, and a soft voice speak to me, "Whatcha doing, Dad?"

It was Justin, who was four. He rested his head on my propped-up knees, simply watching his old man in a moment of total defeat. I looked up at this overgrown cherub giving me the simple message: "I'm here, Dad; don't worry about the car." I had to grin and divert my attention to him instead of the leaking, provoking car. Blonde, curious and seemingly proud of his dad's efforts, he merely wanted to watch. Shortly thereafter, I was able to again reattach the pieces, only to have it leak again. The subsequent trip to the dealer informed me that the pan was warped and could never seal, no matter how many times I tried.

Of all the things that parenthood teaches, perhaps the most profound and recurrent theme is humility.

Cameron was about 13 when I had my first book published. Titled "Listen to Life: Wisdom in Life's Stories," the book uses simple stories from everyday life to remind us all that everything we need to know about everything we need to know about can be found in the stories and interactions with those around us. Much can be learned by listening. Cameron and I discussed what an appropriate cover photo would be.

"What photo will you use, Dad?" he asked.

"I'm not sure," I replied with what was likely a contemplative look on my face because he followed up with "Yeah, I mean which of your photos can convey what it means to learn about life?" He has always been a deep, thought-filled boy, and clearly this was another moment of deep and thoughtful conversation.

"The photo is really important," he continued, "because you need something that is eye catching. Something that will attract a buyer when the book is in a garage sale."

LISTENIN'

He (Justin) and I discussed fatherhood, too. He said he/"we" like having me as their dad. I said I enjoyed it, and largely because I know enough about them—their strengths, weaknesses, failures, rebounds and demons—to be proud of how they deal with their humanity as strong, self-identified men. No assumptions of any perfection. We look at each other as real, genuine people with great mutual respect. To see how they've dealt with their demons and learned from their experiences is a magnificent thing.

July 8, 2008

During the final push of writing this book I shared with Justin that I had three binders of notes, previously written documents and stories, and copies of journal pages that I used for creative fodder. "Wow, Dad. I'm glad that you think our lives have been so interesting."

Perhaps I believe their lives are interesting because we are not superficial with each other. We can tell dirty jokes or we can compare notes as we read Dante's Inferno. We can laugh until we snort or we can cry in pain. Justin was in his early 20s when he asked rhetorically, "How many kids can talk to their dads about life?" All three of the boys have asked similar comparisons on topics related to parent-child relations. And I never know the answer because I don't know their friends' parents, and I don't hang out with people and talk about parenting.

Observation reveals the wonderful dynamics of watching sons grow and listening opens the door to remain in their worlds. Of course, listening requires a lifelong commitment and free exchange between all participants, like when Dad's not listening properly.

Even with best intentions, sometimes listening does not work right, with the parent not hearing what the child is really trying to say. Cameron provided great clarification when he was a young boy: "You haven't been listening in the right kind of way. You're listening in a 44 way and I'm talking in a seven way."

Perhaps that is the great beauty of listening: it is about give and take, and clarifications along the way. There is much room for misunderstanding.

Understanding requires knowledge and some degrees of patience.

Cameron and I had time to kill while visiting Navasota, Texas for him to receive a photography award for a competition he entered. As we explored the river and railroad tracks, I paused often to take photographs of buildings, stairs and other aged structures that caught my attention. Distractions (inspirations) sometime came in close proximity to each other.

During one pause, I photographed an old, metal external stairway that was built against weathered red bricks. Cameron was not yet a teen and didn't see or appreciate what caught my eye.

"If I didn't know that you loved photography so much, I'd be irritated right now," he said. His honesty led to laughter and an awareness of how my actions were perceived, as well as how wise he was.

Listening provides a window and a door, allowing me to see their lives and thoughts, and to enter at times. In combination, I am honored with access to their ideas, thoughts and growth.

The boys are good listeners—to life, to themselves and to others. It will serve them well, if not also drive their friends and significant others a bit crazy.

There is a stocker at the local Kroger store. A guy named Charles. He's a great guy, someone we always seek out to say hello to, and who prompted a chapter in my first book. We always like to check on him, his mom and life. I met him in late-night shopping trips when I lived alone during the separation period, and have since introduced him to the boys, and to my girlfriend. Of course, he now knows her as my wife. We have been talking for that many years.

On one night's trek to the store with Cameron, the three of us got into a variety of topics during a short conversation with Charles: his mother's 60th birthday party, her regular chores for him, his dad's passing ten years previous, times fishing with his father, Father's Day visits to the veterans cemetery where his dad is buried. We covered a lot, and Cameron clearly paid attention because when we left the conversation and moved onto the next aisle, he said, "I think we learned more about Charles in that five-minute conversation . . ." "Yes! Wasn't it great? Isn't open, candid, genuine conversation great?" I was proud that he realized how much can be learned by listening to others, thus helping connect us to people around us. He finished his interrupted sentence: "Yeah. Charles likes to fish!" I nodded and smiled, reminded that one's listening is affected by one's own perspectives, and the world is measured in fishing terms for Cameron. But, he listened.

Of course, it could be said that I perhaps listen too intently, always looking for opportunities to grow, learn or engage in gnarly conversation. It is possible.

Dion made the first toast at the wedding reception for Kim and me. He made his comments with his brothers at his side because I had no groomsmen. I had three best men: my sons. And there they stood, Dion confidently toasting, Justin smiling and Cameron shyly observing. Dion said, "Most of you know my dad well enough to know how he is. You can come to him to borrow a stapler and the next thing you know you'll be talking about the meaning of life. And then you may find that conversation ends up in his newsletter." Guilty as charged, but the apple doesn't fall far from the tree. Thankfully so, I might add.

On one of Justin's solo hiking trips in the San Juan Mountains of southern Colorado, he took Emerson with him and hiked to the top of the continental divide. He said later, "I sat there on the gray granite, looking over the world. There was nothing but gray, blue skies and patches of white (snow). I read Emerson. I felt like God was sitting next to me." I know he was listening in the moment, like he often does in his beloved outdoors. He listens to his heart, soul and creation. He hears the stirrings of his curiosity and spirituality. He hears his life. It is this sort of awareness that prompted him to drop into a church after Houston's Christmas snow of 2004. Not a church goer, he went in "to tell God thank you for snow."

I am blessed to be able to hear insights from all three of the boys, though each shares quite differently than the other. I recall a 24-hour period when both Justin and Dion called to say they had to share their recent realization. They wanted to be motivational and inspirational with their lives. It was less of a want and more of a need. Those calls came in 2006. Both have graduated from college since and ensconced themselves in jobs, and it is clear in how they live their lives, both personally and professionally, that they *do* inspire others, motivate others, and live examined lives to the betterment of those around them.

Listening provides insights into the boys that sometime prove disquieting, though the increased understanding of their great complexities provides me a treasure. Some of Dion's college years were difficult in myriad ways, exacerbated by the situation with his mother and me. I heard stories, but only some of them. Much of what I heard felt alien to me, his college life being so different than mine. Then I watched Good Will Hunting and realized I was watching a story of the collision of rage and genius. I understood Dion better though the roots of his rage bore little resemblance to the character in the movie. Likewise, as I listened to Garry Wills' audio book about the life of Saint Augustine, I realized that I better understood Dion by learning about the study of contradictions that was Augustine. Dion's no saint, but he has always had the scholar-philosopher mindset, and a rougher hewn side that appeared at times. Augustine was a blend of daytime scholar-philosopher and nighttime rowdy; Dion could easily be talking philosophy of leadership during the day, and in a bar fight at night during those more difficult years.

Listening provides insight because yin and yang are revealed; rage and compassion are demonstrated; query and exhortation present themselves; and, reality is exposed by an emotion-based exfoliation.

Listening involves tears, seen and shed. I've heard the stories, witnessed the tears and shed my own in the stark environment of sharing soulfully with the boys. I can't say that I had experiences like that with my father though. Such openness and interchange certainly came from the gentle acceptance of my mother as she earned the words that now appear on her tombstone: "A tender mother and a faithful friend."

The boys' lives have been good, but not without their pains and struggles. I can't comment on how hard some things have been because I am not in their shoes, nor do I know the extent of their circumstances, so I assume that in the stories that I have not heard are examples of wins and losses, joys and sorrows, love and pain. Welcome to the human race. Amidst their circumstances, each has shared an interest in seeking professional counseling to help them. While they have not accepted the offers to arrange and pay for the sessions, they were not afraid to admit the times when they believed their youthful omnipotence and power was finding their limits. It takes great strength to admit when you have none left.

Because of the mutuality of listening, we have all seen into each other's minds, thoughts and beliefs. Where we go with these concepts frequently includes collaborations or commonalities.

Dion was about 16 when we engaged in a life-path conversation while we drove around Albuquerque.

"Dad, you know that when I grow up, I want to be a history teacher and coach, right?"

"Yep."

"And you know that I want to be a professional fisherman with a column in a national fishing magazine and my own line of lures, right?"

"Yep."

"And you know that I want to be a vice president for music distribution like Uncle John, right?"

"Yep."

"Well, in between those things, I want to take a break and travel the south to fish the ponds, lakes and rivers. Just stopping where I want, seeing who I want to see, and fishing when I want. I'd write about it, too. I'd write a book about that journey."

"I didn't know that, bud. When I was 19, I had a young gal on my arm and was looking at pick-up trucks with camper tops thinking I wanted to travel the south of my dad's heritage while taking photographs, fishing and writing. Now, the young gal with me wasn't pleased that I wasn't talking about her coming with me. I didn't take the trip, but I gained three sons. That gal ended up being your mom. But, I had in mind that there would be a book about traveling the south for fishing and writing by Dion McInnis. Maybe I had the wrong Dion McInnis."

In my peripheral vision I could see his head turn towards me at the end of my statement. He smiled broadly. "Yeah, maybe so," he said. The next day while at church, I doodled out a drawing of a book cover titled "Stories of Fishing the South by Dions McInnis." I passed him the note. He nodded and smiled.

That was not the last project idea born through shared ideas. In 2004 I crafted a title for a book that came from Justin's desire for him, Dion and I to have a tape recorder capture some of our conversations about topics about humanity and existence. He was on a rant after some encounters with people at work, and he wondered why other people did not respect each other. Keep in mind that he worked retail at the time, and it was near crunch time during the holiday shopping period when he witnessed enough to rile him. He had witnessed enough to believe that he wanted to be a roaming philosopher, of sorts. We discussed some of the great roamers in history: Jesus, Whitman, Emerson, Thoreau, and Gandhi. We discussed Dion's heroes, including Ben Franklin, and how each of us has strong ideas. Cameron was too young at the time to participate in the project that we created a working title for: "Three Idealists, Different Ideals." Amidst the chat, he asked whether he believed my life would be different if I had taken the trip photographing and fishing the south. That, of course, led to another conversation.

Each conversation, no matter the boy's age or circumstance, provides me a chance to have an effect and to be affected. I choose to hold up their potential instead of holding down their spirit. It has been a lifelong commitment, and I believe it has made a difference.

One day I was hanging up clothes from the dryer. Cameron called out a question from the next room, "Dad, do you have a plan for your life?"

"Well, yes, actually I do."

"Oh, okay."

That ended the conversation so the next day I asked him what prompted him to ask a question like that.

"I just wondered if you did," he said. "It seems like you probably do."

"You're right. Do you know how many people actually have plans?"

"Nope."

"I read that it is less than 20 percent."

"That's actually a lot, Dad."

"Yeah, but there are four times that many who don't. My point is that it is pretty amazing that a 12-year-old would even be thinking about it at all."

Of course, I've also shared with the boys that "plans" come in all shapes and forms and levels of details. I would be remiss, too, if I didn't remind them about "best laid plans of mice and men."

I'm a fixer; it's in the chromosomes, I'm told. I have to intentionally listen and not step in to help at times, but it isn't easy. Dion was in his mid-20s and called to vent about some financial challenges and the challenges of cash flow in his business of e-commerce web site design. At what I felt was the appropriate time, I said that I was unable to help in any way that I knew of. There was a long silence before a sigh of exasperation on the other end of the phone. "I'm not asking you to fix it Dad; I just want you to listen." I should have realized that; there are times I simply want my sons to listen to their crazy dad with no expectation of them fixing anything, and it only makes sense that it should work both ways.

This mutuality creates a wonderful ebb and flow. Justin called to apologize for not having returned my call from a day or two before.

"That's okay, buddy. You have a life to live. If it was an emergency, I would have called again. And again. I understand you can't be around for every call."

"Yeah, but it's not fair. All of us expect you to answer the phone whenever we call. And you usually do, even when at work and such. We want you to always be there and you are. I'm sorry."

There will come a day when I won't be around to answer their calls, so taking them now is easy.

There were no cell phones, text messages and e-mails when my dad died. It was 1982 and I had just turned 26. At the time of this writing, Dion is 28, Justin is 24 and Cameron is 17 and between them, all manner of communications is used. I still had access to dad, including that which was not available to his clients on work days. He worked long, hard hours and almost always took a one-hour nap during the day. If I was out and about conducting my photography business and was in his area, I would drop by. If his office door was closed, it meant that it was his rest and recover time. His secretary had instructions to not allow anyone in, unless it was one of his kids. I appreciated that unique and special access, though I sometimes thought it better to let him rest when I came by. But knowing I had access to my father was a special gift to have, and now one that I gladly give to my three.

When Justin and I lived together after the divorce, I began a form of communication that worked for our lifestyles of mismatched work schedules. If there was something important to share—whether some sort of information or encouragement—I would jot a note on a piece of paper and leave it at the door of his room. He usually kept the door closed—he was either sleeping or the room was enough of a mess that he closed it when he wasn't home. At any rate, I would leave a note at the door, not dissimilar to how I used to leave notes and drawings in his lunchbox by writing on napkins. The note-at-the-door approach ensured that we shared despite life's demands.

The process works both ways. I woke up the morning that I was to deliver a presentation to a regional women's conference. As I left the bedroom, I saw the note on the floor. He basically wished me well, said I was going to do a great job, and hoped that I sold a lot of books. I changed the opening of my presentation that day to read the audience my note.

Cameron and I have the same routine, too, when he stays over. "Listening" of all types—be it on the phone, in person, or with notes—is critical. It is the essential ingredient to all the verbs of relationship.

DaD have a nice party
"You are the Gratiste Dab aver.

LOVIN'

To my mother, to my father
As I sit beside your stones
There is so much I want to ask you
There are times I'm so alone

I have to remember that our times
Were not perfect and that's fine
And remember that with all the demons
It was love that kept us alive

I don't strive for perfection
Though I strive for your strengths
I strive for your grace and charm
While owning what it is that I think

You gave much though we had little
You gave me a sense of self
I fight to reclaim that inheritance
That matters, but little else

I know there's a lot I do not know
About who you really were
But I do know that I can say
"I love you" to my mother and father

I wrote that poem while struggling with life and decisions after divorce, and hoping to tap into all that I could from my past. By the time it was written in 2005, Dad had been dead for 23 years and Mom for a decade. Living loved by parents provides great strength and a critical anchor long after the parents have passed. My boys know they are loved, and we say, share and give it in many ways.

Thirty one years before the conversation at the cemetery, I wrote this during freshman English class in college. My sister rewrote it in calligraphy onto paper that we secured to boards with decoupage—one each for Mom and Dad—that we gave as Christmas gifts in 1974. I used it in my Mom's eulogy in 1995.

There are two stones
Simple rocks of granite
Which have held me up
And kept me at it.

Rocks so soft
On which to lay
Tablets of wisdom
And words to say.

Shiny and smooth,
But weathered on edges
Nonetheless strong,
Steady and rigid.

Slabs to lean on
When exhausted and old.
Foundation for a home
When winds get cold.

These enduring stones
Are part of my life.
Forever Mom and Dad,
Husband and wife.

Why is it that I felt the way I did in high school, and also the desire to seek Mom and Dad long after they were gone in order to find comfort, counsel and direction? Love. I loved them; they loved me.

Lovin' kids is something that becomes reality by words, actions, gifts, empathy, sympathy, strength, stepping in, easing away . . . what demonstrates love is the fullness of emotion and action. Your children will learn along the way. Learning to love in their own, personal, genuine way takes a lifetime of experience to master. Okay, no mere mortal ever masters it. Our ability to love and show is always a work in progress. Watching the work can be fascinating.

I've shared with the boys my mom's warning to me about my driving and other growing-up activities. She would say, "If you let anything happen to you, I'll pee on your grave every day."

I knew, based on her comment and our other conversations that the death of her child would pain her. She and Dad had already lost their first daughter at the age of five to leukemia, and I grew up knowing that parents are not supposed to bury their children. And once was more than enough.

So it was that when Cameron prepared for his road trip to visit his brother in Austin, Justin cautioned him to make the trip only if ready, and "if something happens to you, you'll be taking years off of Dad's life."

The boys realize the gifts that they are to me.

When asked to say the family prayer at major events during my first marriage, I would often end the prayer with ". . . and thank you God for our many gifts, including the greatest which is love." "Love" and "gift" often go together.

In the mid- to late-1960s a new shopping center was built in Houston near the corner of Memorial Drive and West Belt. West Belt was a dead end road to the south at Buffalo Bayou at the time, so the new center was, in some ways, near one of the city's natural boundaries. The center remains, still called Town and Country Village, but it was very different in its formation with only a grocery store, a department store and a sporting goods store. My friends and I would ride our bikes to Minimax for donut snacks, to Sakowitz to toss in or remove pennies from the indoor fountain, and to Oshman's for all else male: fishing gear, sports equipment, stuffed trophies and conversation with patient salesmen. There were a few other shops, but none mattered as much as those three in my pre—and early-teen years.

Oshman's had a salesman—I believe his name was Ken—who was quite patient with my friends and me as we looked often and spent occasionally. Fishing gear was the greatest temptation, and I still have the Heddon spinning rod and Mitchell spinning reel that I bought there with his help in the mid-1960s. He was also instrumental in another purchase that was a gift for my father on Father's Day. It must have been 1968. I could not have been more proud of my idea and purchase, and I almost messed it up.

In April 1968, Dad was able to buy a boat for the first time in his life. I was a month short of 12 and he turned 55 that month. His dream come true had taken a back seat to the other financial demands of life for decades. Thanks to a special arrangement with one of his clients, he was able to get a 16-foot Hollywood boat with a 65-horsepower Evinrude motor and trailer for $1800. Brand new. It was a source of joy for him until the day he died, and the venue for many wonderful times for him, for us and for others.

The boat was not outfitted like the boats of today. Fish-finder equipment was largely unheard of. Two seats and a bucket for a live well was about as good as it got. So, in 1968, I came upon the perfect gift for Dad: white rod holders: basically white plastic tubes in aluminum straps that secured to the boat. They would make the perfect addition to the boat, and the price was just right for a kid too young to have a job-based income. Enter Ken.

A friend and I shopped together. I was proud of the selection and Ken affirmed that I was picking a good present that Dad would really like. I was confident of being on the right path. To celebrate, my friend and I went to Prince's hamburger joint for a cheap burger. Once we got home, I realized that I had left the perfect present at Prince's. A maniacally fast bicycle ride to the shop was not fast enough to forestall my active imagination's surety that the "best gift ever" was now gone, as was all my money. The present and burger pretty much emptied my resources.

Thankfully, the Oshman's bag still sat in the booth where we ate. Tragedy averted. We pedaled home. In my bedroom, I examined the greatest gift a fishing son could give his fishing father who just bought a lifelong desired boat. There, on the price tag, it listed the price. Per pair. Another panic. I was elated to see that we would each have a rod holder in the boat, but how would I convince the grownup people at the store that this kid had only taken one of the rod holders and wasn't just trying to pull a fast one? Luckily, Ken remembered my purchase and allowed me to take another holder when we returned to the store after another speedy bicycle ride.

Why all the trouble as a kid, and why does the story stick in my mind so clearly some 40 years later? That gift and the effort evidenced my love for Dad and for the enjoyment we shared for something in common. Many gifts have those qualities.

Justin was probably less than five when he made a paper note for my office. It was folded like a table tent and it said in childish scrawl, "I love you Dad." Of the many things that I have kept from the many presents my sons have given me, I do not have that one. It was stolen.

I had a century-old wash table in my office at University of Houston at the time, which made for a great place to put memorabilia items. A few days after I put the note there, I realized it was missing. The custodial crew was very good about not throwing things away, and if something fell off my cluttered desk, it was always placed on my desk. But this item was gone. I wasn't happy and shared what had happened with Justin; he made another for me to place in the appointed place on the table. I did. It, too, disappeared. I was livid.

After the second one was stolen, I placed a few irate phone calls to make sure that no one ever entered my office again. I told the powers that be that I would sweep, mop and clean my own office; I wanted no one inside my office, and only the custodians and a few administrators had a key that would open my office. Justin took it hard when I told him the news, and he tried to understand why anyone would do such a thing. "Don't they realize that you are my daddy and I love you?"

I have few normal ties. Most of my ties are a bit goofy, and usually sport some sort of theme. And rarely do I buy a tie; people give them to me as gifts, and they are always ties that I want to wear, contrary to the popular norm. In the mid-1990s, Cameron made a tie for me for Father's Day. It was paper. It was colorful. And it was broad. Think 1970s wide, and then add some. But it was also the work of a little lad who made a gift in preschool for his dad.

When I came out of the bedroom, ready for church that Father's Day Sunday, Cameron beamed. I had his tie pinned perfectly in place. The blend of many colors went well with my shirt.

"Are you going to wear that to church?" Cameron asked.

"Of course. It's a tie, and it's a tie that my boy gave to me. How could I not wear it?" I replied with a smile that could not possibly match his.

His smile returned as we walked down the aisle at church. We were pretty well known in the parish anyway, so when others turned to say hello, they burst into smiles and nods when they saw the very obvious tie. Both he and I were proud of the tie and the attention it brought, but he not so much as to be able to stay awake during Mass. He was still young enough to enjoy being held, and as I held him on Father's Day, his movements tore the tie off the pins securing them. He looked up, smiled sleepily, and said "That's okay, Dad. Thanks for wearing it." "Thanks for giving it to me," I whispered.

The fun of gift giving starts young and lasts a lifetime. While ultimate choices are influenced by one's financial position at the time, the sentiment and reason never changes for giving. Christmas has a way of bringing out the best for such things.

One such thing for Dion is procrastination, but he comes by it rightfully.

He was probably 16 or 17 when he tackled a renovation project as a gift for me with just barely enough time to complete it, particularly since he had never tackled something like it.

He spent many hours, up to the "last minute," to clean, sand, and repair a Buddy L toy dump truck that I received when I was about ten. (Have I mentioned that McInnis men tend to hold onto things that are meaningful to them?) He found paints that almost exactly matched the original pale blue and white colors. The truck now sits atop a book shelf in the living room.

Christmas 2005 marked a time of change for me that had me re-invigorated, and my sons seemed to be, too. They needed the energy that year, in particular, as they convened in Houston for a few days of hither, yither and then yon to make all the houses of family and friends. Blended families make for pureed schedules, particularly during the holidays.

The two older boys had in mind that they would build something for me amidst the hustle and bustle. That sort of idea always intrigues me, particularly because all four of us fully possess the procrastination gene. I knew their intentions, and figured with the time constraints, they may be looking at another set of bookends a la their Cub Scout days. Truth be told, I knew it was something involved. They live fully, and they give fully. All I really knew was that it was happening in my garage between their other scheduled activities.

The pressure of the holidays had gotten to Justin, and he and I ended up in the emergency room thanks to a bizarre fainting spell. We spent the midnight between Christmas Eve and Christmas at the hospital, with him shivering under layers of white blankets while they drew blood time and again, trying to find the cause of this most recent event. Christmas day, Justin and Dion had their rounds to make, while I attended other activities. It was my first year in a house since I separated from the boys' mom nearly three years before.

They returned from their day's activities. I was already asleep. Sounds of laughter and noise in the garage disappeared as my sleep became deeper. The bed began bouncing to the rhythm of Justin bouncing his butt up and down on the corner of the bed while Dion was calling out like a six-year old, "It's Christmassssss! Time to get up. Get up! Santa came, Santa came, Santa came. Come on!"

Even without my glasses, I could see that, indeed, the time was 3:30 in the morning. Christmas festivities were just wrapping up . . . in Alaska. I don't remember what was covering the present when I walked into the living room, but the item was of consequential size, and I could smell wood.

The boys had designed and built a fish-cleaning table. It had a kitchen counter, bar sink and faucet, and attachments so I could connect the garden hose to it for running water. I have a vision of that table being under a cover near a stock pond where their children can clean the fish they catch at grandpa's.

When Kim and I married in November 2007, I chose to have no groomsmen. This came as a surprise to those who know about the relationship between my boys and me. I had no groomsmen, though I did have three best men. They had a special job to do and needed special gifts.

Their assignment was not to throw a crazy bachelor party for the groom. Instead, I took them, two of my in-laws-to-be and me on a guided bull red fishing trip. So, they had no party to throw.

Their assignment was not to calm the groom's nerves, arrange for transportation from the wedding site to the reception venue, or assure that the groom got to the church. Their role was to bring Kim to me and into the family.

Kim and her father processed toward the altar, as usual, but they stopped a bit short of the first pew. There, she kissed him—"No one gives me away," she told him weeks before. "I am going where I have chosen."—and then the boys approached her together and brought the bride to the groom. They were the first to officially express that she was entering the McInnis family, which included all four of us.

The boys had an important role, and I needed to select a special gift for them, and each gift had to be the same while allowing personal sentiment. After much thought, the choice was made, then purchased and prepared for presentation at the rehearsal dinner. They have yet to use their gifts. They likely never will, and each of us is fine with that decision.

They opened their presents simultaneously and each had a similar reaction. The wrapping paper, put on in the male-style of their father, covered a pine box less than a foot long and about four inches wide. A small gold-ish clasp had to be moved to allow them in. Inside was an engraved knife: "To a dad's best men/Dion, Justin and Cameron/November 3, 2007." The box was given as a thank you for the many memories and they have chosen to place memories inside. Cameron later placed his boutonniere and cigar stub in it.

I've enjoyed watching the gifts that the boys give others, too, as expressions of their love for the other person. Dion has stayed up more than 24 hours to hand carve the top of a small table he made for a girlfriend. Justin recruited me and his brother to rent a metal detector to comb over a soccer field and parking lot in search of his grandmother's ring that his mother lost. He wanted to return the ring to his mother as a Christmas present in 2000.

Almost a decade later, Justin, the adventurer, decided to surprise his girlfriend with a fancy kitchen knife set. She loves to cook; he loves to explore. It only made sense that he decided to have her find the present one knife at a time via a scavenger hunt. When he shared the story of his birthday game, I smiled to myself at how genuinely the activity portrayed both of them. Love is about accepting the nature of your partner, I'd say.

Cameron has his first girlfriend. She's a cute young woman on the high school swim team, and he is learning the ropes of courtship. His naturally generous heart outstrips his unemployed capacity to do much in the way of gifts. Valentine's Day provided a test.

He planned to take her to Valentine's lunch at a reasonably nice place. It was his first Valentine's Day with a driver's license, vehicle and girlfriend. It was not his first without a school-year job. On the morning of the big day, he called to ask if it would be okay if he brought her by the house and cooked something for her for Valentine's. Normally, that would be a wonderful, romantic gesture. Unfortunately, there isn't much that Cameron cooks. He doesn't eat as much as he grazes in the pantry and refrigerator.

"Dad, can we just come by the house today so I can cook something for her. I can make sandwiches or something. I just don't have any money."

"Come on by the house, and tell her that you left your money in your desk here. I'll put some money in your room so you can take her out. Gentlemen don't make sandwiches for Valentine's."

He laughed. "Yeah, Dad. I guess you're right. Thanks. I really hate to do that, but thank you."

Thoughtful gifts stand as the norm, rather than the exception, for the boys.

It was about 2000 when the musical group Creed came out with their CD titled Human Clay. I loved the song "Arms Wide Open," and the boys knew it. One morning, as I prepared things for the boys' school day, Justin came into the kitchen with a cassette tape of the CD. He had used money he earned working in the neighborhood to buy the CD and then recorded it overnight. As I recall, he said he had to stay awake to be sure that a song was not split when moving from the first side of the cassette to the other.

Making things for the people they love seems to be another trait common among the boys. In high school, Justin schemed with me to create a portrait of his girlfriend so he could make a gift that included the image. He also gave much of his time to her and her family when her brother required much attention and time after coming home from the Iraq War with major head injuries. His current, very serious relationship has included projects of bookshelves, mirrors and various other labors as expressions of love and appreciation.

Dion has reconditioned old toys for me, built tables for girlfriends, and now builds for his wife a variety of things ranging from custom-designed, moving herb garden containers to a custom-designed table for gift wrapping.

My mom and dad remained married for more than 40 years before Dad died. I know there were great trials and tribulations, but I don't know how it must feel to have a remarriage to deal with as a child . . . how to accept the new step parent, how to evaluate the love the new person brings to parent, siblings and self.

Of the three boys, Cameron has had the most exposure and interaction with Kim. When he proudly announced the high grade he received for an assignment in speech class to deliver a toast, I figured he chose to present a toast to his recently married big brother. Instead, he opted to write an anniversary toast to Kim and me:

Hi, I'm Cameron, Dion's son and Kim's stepson. I just want to thank everyone for coming out. You all are so important and all close to my dad and Kim, and in being that close you know my dad and how big a dreamer he is. At the age of 50 he was still finding time to dream even with a stressful time-consuming job. But with a divorce added to it, his dreaming was put on hold. With all of the stress he became a small shadow of what he was until Kim came along. She brings out the best in him and not only allows him to dream but chase his dreams. They both glow when around each other and they get giddy like schoolgirls.

Personally, I find it creepy but I guess it's a good sign we will be coming to a lot more of these anniversaries. Cheers.

His words revealed his love, as well as his vision of what he sees in his father and his father's new life. A few months before that assignment, he created a Christmas 2009 card for Kim. He didn't have any money, and said, "Dad, I'd like to make a card for her to say thanks for the things she does. That would be okay, right? I mean, it isn't something to unwrap but she'll know I appreciate what she's doing being a stepmom and all."

"I can't think of a better gift, buddy." Little could I predict the outcome.

First, he took photographs of his bed, covered with the new comforter set that Kim bought for him, and then he created images of a container with candy in it, the couch with a sheet on it, and a "still life" of various products for cleansing hair and skin. He printed wallet size photos. On a speckled sheet of paper, he placed four purple rectangles of construction paper, each a bit larger than the size of the photograph; he placed one photo on each. On the back of the sheet of paper, he wrote:

This Christmas I had a hard time deciding what to get you. With everyone's gift I try to send somewhat of a message. The message I decided I wanted to be incorporated with your gift was my appreciation for everything you do and how you are the best stepmom I could ask for. My predicament arose when no kitchen appliance or hand sanitizer (there is an inside joke on this, folks) *seemed to send this message. So, I made you this card and on the front of the card I put a few things I appreciate you do and truly make you the best stepmom ever.*

1) *Noticing my blankets were bad and hooking me up with "sweet threads"*
2) *Not allowing my hair to go back to cotton. I never really admit it but I do appreciate it.*
3) *The non-peanut chocolate placed next to my sofa and always making sure food is peanut free for me* (he is VERY allergic to peanuts)
4) *Accommodating my nudist brother and his sleeping habits by putting sheets on your sofa so he can "be free."*

All these actions and efforts say "I love you."

The boys are not embarrassed or afraid to tell me or each other "I love you." I hear the stories of fathers and children who have to learn how, and I am thankful for having parents who were unafraid of expressing their love in their own ways. There is no one right way.

Love is often expressed by actions. Sometimes it is years later, if ever, when the receiver's appreciation for the action is discovered.

It was some years before high school, as I recall, that my dad did not arrive home on time from a day's work. Mom worried; she knew his history of years before that I was largely unaware of as a kid. Alcohol remained one of my dad's demons and a much-later-than-expected return home could mean many bad things. On this night, my grandmother was staying with us and by the time I went to bed, Dad had not yet returned home. Later, the phone rang and we then headed to pick up Dad from the city's "drunk tank."

I joined Mom for the trip downtown to get Dad. I remained in the car when Mom went inside to take care of things, but I wanted to ride with my father on the trip home. Along the way, he conveyed how he had been under a lot of stress, and the "drink or two" that he had after work did not sit well with him. He pulled over, as the story went, because the drink and his flaring ulcer made him sick to his stomach. I listened while also noticing the puke on the inside panel of the driver's side door, and on the carpet of the gold-ish brown carpet of the Chevrolet Impala. None of that mattered. I was going home with my dad because I loved him and believed in him. I also believed him.

Not until after his death did I hear from Mom how much it meant to Dad that I joined him in the car that night.

Of course, years passing gave me insights, conversations with my mom, and wisdom to realize that he had had too much to drink that night, was sick from the amount of alcohol, and that the stress and ulcer were likely made worse by his mom's stay at the house. He loved his mom, but she always created great stress in him. She had never really learned how to say convincingly that she loved him; it was always his late brother who was "the best son." I cannot imagine the pain of hearing that for decades.

Despite demons, Dad showed love by his time with me, and patience on myriad projects. By the time I arrived, he was 43 and more patient thanks to having had three other children, losing one when she was five to leukemia, and the ever-patient, constantly praying influence of my mom. I guess he had no choice but to mature and calm down with those influences at play.

Supportive efforts and actions can convey love more than any words could.

Justin was about 14 when he decided to write a note to Rosie O'Donnell to advise her of his dad's actions in creating a nonprofit to save women's stories and the images they inspire. At the time, he struggled mightily with writing, grammar, spelling and handwriting. He provided me the note so I could type it in an e-mail to her. With all its mechanical errors, it flawlessly explained how he was a good kid and Scout, and how proud he was of his father's efforts.

Dion has always been the creative combiner of words and images for any purpose, ranging from gift cards to editorials to blogs. Always creative and always honest, his messages always communicate.

I believe he was in his early teens when he developed a Father's Day booklet for me, comprised of colored sheets of paper stapled together, each page containing a drawing and message.

Page one: "For Father's Day I was going to make you a card. Didn't have the time."
 A picture of a clock face set to 1:30 in the afternoon on the June 18.
Page two: "I was going to buy you something. Didn't have the money." A picture of a five-dollar bill with wings on it.
Page three: "So I was going to make you something. Had to watch T.V." A picture of a kid in a baseball cap watching a television.
Page four: "Then Mom told me that if I couldn't find anything better to do I had to separate and turn the whites right side out." A picture of a kid with a sickened look on his face and a pile of smelly clothes in the background.
Page five: "I made you a card." A picture of a kid working at a desk with wadded up papers on the floor and in the garbage can and a shaking boom box radio.
Page six: "Happy Dad's Day."

The calendar says that once a year we are to honor each parent: one day for mothers and another for fathers. Of course, children naturally do things for their mothers with jewelry of macaroni and paint, or other gifts throughout the years. Random gifts from child to father tend to stop earlier than for mothers, I believe.

That said, the one-day celebration also provides an intense focus, revealing the feelings between parent and child over the year and years. I have had several poignant Father's Days.

The last such holiday of the 1990s was particularly poignant.

We trekked by van from Albuquerque to Corpus Christi for some time at the beach. The three boys, their mom and I were chattering when the idea surfaced for an impromptu visit to the cemetery in San Antonio where Mom and Dad are buried. Despite the intermittent rain, we adjusted our course slightly to go to the cemetery. Across the street from the entrance were vendors braving the weather so those paying respects to their deceased fathers would have something to place at the graveside.

We arrived at the site. We all stood at the grave. I quickly became lost in thought with my family around me. Sprinkles camouflaged my tears. I reviewed "tender mother and faithful friend," and "he left for us a most noble pattern" on the stones, along with the photo of the sister I never knew on hers. After a few moments, the sprinkles became a deluge and everyone returned to the van. I remained a bit longer to finish my thoughts with Mom and Dad.

Only the sound of the engine and blowing defroster filled the van. I sat in the passenger seat, shaking off my tears and shaking to the cold of the air conditioned van and my wet clothes. From the back of the van came the sweet sound of Cameron's voice, carrying a clear message from his almost-seven year old heart, "Dad, I'm sorry that your daddy died."

Not much could be said in response to such an honest show of love. After a long minute, I mustered a "Thank you, buddy" in reply.

My mom and dad met, courted, married and lived just under half of their married life in San Antonio before coming to Houston in 1956. McInnis

Lane, named for Dad's dad, stands as a small reminder of my largely untended roots in the Alamo City. But, I know I can always visit them there.

All sorts of actions remind our loved ones that they are so. Sometimes the action is one of effort, and sometimes an expression of ease. Either way, acting out speaks volumes.

During the difficult transition phase of separation-to-divorce, I invested much time in discernment, thought, and consideration, as well as actions of writing, speaking and creating photographs. In many ways, I felt I was thoughtfully blooming, or blooming thoughtfully. At any rate, I took to new levels my belief in a self-examined life without the process turning into navel gazing. The more I questioned and wondered, the more I learned and understood; the more I learned and understood, the more I created and expressed. Yet, there were always questions and self-doubts.

During a conversation in this phase, Dion, then about 23, said, "You were supposed to be a photographer." He has reiterated that message several times, and supported my callings in various ways, including setting up my first web pages. Having a web site to showcase my photography, presentations, writing and messages projected me into a different realm and sense of credibility. Years later, I then hired him to develop a new site. I believe in him, and he believes in me.

Loving can be learned early and shared youthfully. Even seeing the expressions of genuine friendship between youngsters provides some insight into how a child learns about loving and sharing.

As a child, Cameron heard often the story of the "Kissing Hand," a wonderful book by Audrey Penn that his mother found and she or I would read to him. The message of the story stuck.

From the Amazon.com review of the book: "Chester Raccoon doesn't want to go to school—he wants to stay home with his mother. She assures him that he'll love school—with its promise of new friends, new toys, and new books. Even better, she has a special secret that's been in the family for years—the Kissing Hand. This secret, she tells him, will make school seem as cozy as home. She takes her son's hand, spreads his tiny fingers into a fan and kisses his palm—smack dab in the middle: Chester felt his mother's kiss rush from his hand, up his arm, and into his heart. Whenever he feels lonely at school, all he has to do is press his hand to his cheek to feel the warmth of his mother's kiss. Chester is so pleased with his Kissing Hand that he—in a genuinely touching moment—gives his mom a Kissing Hand, too, to comfort her when he is away."

As a young boy, Cameron would perform the act of the Kissing Hand when he left the house for school or other activities. Even as an "older" child (not yet a teen), Cameron kept the intention of the Kissing Hand. As I dropped him off at his new middle school in Friendswood after the family relocated, he would hold his index and middle fingers together and kiss them, and say "kissing hand" as he got out of the car. As much as the boys have grown, and continued to grow, to be independent men, their "own men," we all enjoy spending time together and appreciate the love and fun of our time together.

Sometimes, best intentions to be generous with time together go awry. Usually, laughter ensues.

Cameron was about 14 when he decided to provide a surprise for me.

"Dad, what time did you say you would be home?" he asked in a phone call while I headed home from the other side of town one night.

I gave him my best guess of ETA.

"Ok, I'll have something good for you to drink."

When I arrived home, a frozen smoothie awaited me, a dark berry mix of frozen fruits combined in a cold tasty mix in the blender. I thanked him for the effort as I watched him prepare to pour the mix into a glass. I couldn't help but notice the evidence of smeared berry concoction on the kitchen counter, revealing a teen's attempt to clean up a mess.

"Have a little trouble with the blender there, buddy?" I asked.

"I guess so. And I think I messed up one of your spoons when I tried to . . . ."

He removed the white plastic stirring spoon from the blender as he spoke. The rounded end appeared squared off with a tooth on one corner, and seemed to be about one-fourth shorter. I couldn't help but chuckle.

"But I think it will still be good! I hope you like it, Dad."

"I'm sure I will, but maybe we should sort through it a bit so we are sure to not swallow a sharp shard. That might not feel good inside, or coming out."

"Oh, I didn't think about that. Sorry about the spoon, Dad."

I poured the drink-gift into a glass through a sieve to help remove the plastic pieces. Between that and picking out white chunks, I sorted out a drink and shared the mix with him.

"That's not real sweet is it?" he asked.

"Did you put in sugar or anything else?"

"Just the frozen fruit and ice."

After another sip or two, he decided he didn't want any and I drank what I felt was safe to ingest, considering the potential of sharp plastic.

"Thanks for making it, buddy. It's really pretty good."

"Well, at least it isn't pine tea, huh?" he replied.

Years before, he had come up with a recipe for tea made from pine needles, honey and who knows what else. I don't remember where he found the recipe—an outdoors television show, perhaps—but with great enthusiasm he concocted the mix and provided me a serving of the supposedly healthy, earthy brew. He made it; I drank it. We still laugh about that, though I'm not sure whether the reason is for the taste, the appearance of pine needles floating in yellow-tinged water, or his strong belief that it would taste really good. Either way, never turn down acts of love.

I was probably 18 and crushed by love. Sue and I had tussled enough for me to feel that it was over. My first-ever love, girlfriend style, was coming to a heart-crushing end. I lay on my bed, sad and tearful. I felt the bed move from the weight of company, and expected to hear my mom's voice or feel her gentle hand on my back. Instead, I felt the roughness of Dad's unshaven cheek on mine, a small kiss and a pat on the back. I don't recall if he said anything. It changed my perception of Dad. It also taught me that love's pain can, and should, be eased by both mother and father.

At the time of this writing, only the two oldest boys have experienced the ache of losing a "true love." Perhaps the only thing harder than losing to love, is watching your child pained by their own loss. I have been privileged to hear from them both the intense feelings, and the confusion. Joy and sorrow are both valid topics. For all the conversations we have, I also know that sometimes the best thing a father can do is literally or figuratively give their son a kiss on the cheek and a pat on the back. It reminds us that some types of love survive.

In love's survival comes the opportunity to do and share and give again and again.

Love hurts. It just does. There is no way around it, and being honest about the emotions of love experienced in life prepares one to help or understand another, even when that is between parents and children.

In early 2003, Dion was 21 and I was 46. He had just crossed one milestone and I was bearing down on another. We both battled with love issues; I recall the type that comes at 21 and I hope that he doesn't have to encounter the kind that I encountered at 46 through separation and divorce. We are also both, at our cores, sentimental fools in various ways. So it was that I wrote:

I can better understand my oldest son's pains of love at 21 now that I have fallen and been trampled by it at 46. Never has he felt the way he does; never have I. Yet, he is without, as am I. Where do a father and son turn for healing and clarification when wounded in love like never before? His options are greater than mine. We both want to escape the pain, and want the healing to come from our chosen ones. Apparently it is not to be.

A counselor once told me that whatever lessons the boys have learned from me and my actions in the realms of love and relationships would come to light when they had serious relationships. I can only hope that they learned good things.

Hey dad, American History X was a good movie huh. Well photography for me is getting better. I am kind of understanding it now. Well enjoy the goodies and stuff we gave you, please enjoy yourself with them. Don't forget to catch a 7 pound bass for me before I get down their. See you soon love Justin.

Dad you running. Love ya, Justin.

Yee haw

Gee wizz what a bate!

7 pound bass

you catching a 7 pound bass.

Oh on my time for the District race I put it on my number card thing. My number was 845

Justin drew this image for me shortly after I accepted a job at University of Houston-Clear Lake in order to keep me apprised of things. The image includes my Olympic Torch run, fishing and an update on his track activities.

In late 2001, I had the opportunity to carry the winter Olympic torch in Albuquerque as it made its way across the United States toward Salt Lake City for the events. The torch resides on a bookshelf in the living room and my official attire hangs in the closet. It is sort of like a special bridesmaid dress, worn only once and as part of the supporting cast to the real stars. But the youngsters at the end of my segment knew nothing about the "real stars" and asked for autographs and photos nonetheless.

That occurrence may have been a special moment for some of the people there. It was a memorable one for me, but not just because I was able to carry the torch for a quarter mile down a street lined with people watching. The most memorable element of the torch on the bookshelf is how I was chosen. I was chosen because of a son's pride and effort.

Justin was proud of the things I had done to create a nonprofit that saves women's stories and the images they inspire. He was proud of the work's purpose and my willingness to try and to share. And he wrote about it. He wrote an essay about his dad's work and submitted it as a nomination for me. I was chosen.

Putting pen to paper as an act of love provides many great memories, and moments. When Justin was in middle school in Albuquerque, there was a time when I would put drawings or notes on the napkins in his lunch. As I prepared his lunch, I considered what may be an appropriate message for the day. Not every day had a message, but one day in particular prompted a note that we both still recall.

Justin had left behind a good buddy in Huntsville. He and David had played in the forest, and goofed around as eight and nine year olds do. As a surprise, we arranged for David to visit us in Albuquerque. The plan was for Justin's mom to pick David up from the airport before picking Justin up from school. I knew that morning that I had to create a napkin that intrigued him but did not expose the surprise. A white napkin and red and blue ink pens can go a long way.

The napkin showed mountains and a road leading from the foreground into them, and a sunset (or was it a sunrise?) coming from behind the mountains' shape. I only drew lines and stayed away from complicated things like shading. I could say that the medium wasn't appropriate, but the truth is that I am a photographer for a reason: I can't draw. Anyway, in the front of the image was a pickup truck on the road. The sun and the truck were red—I had a red Ford F-150 at the time, that Dion has now, 12 years later—and the road and mountains were blue. Above the mountains I wrote something like, "Be open to surprises today." Considering the types of conversations that we had, it should have made perfect sense that I would be simply reminding him to have a good day with his eyes open to what the day may bring. That evening with the family and David together, he said, "Dad, the napkin was about David coming wasn't it?"

A couple of years later, he and I participated in a Boy Scout expedition into mountains that could have been those on the napkin. Being a winter campout, everyone had backpacks full of gear, including sleeping bags that had to be rated at zero degrees. The hike was—and I know you won't believe this—uphill both ways, except for the times that it was downhill at a 45 degree angle. The group hiked along long open areas until we reached a ravine named on the topographic map as "The Alamo." The New Mexican leaders who loved picking on anything Texas related, said to me as we stood on the ridge looking down, "A lot of Texans died at the Alamo, right?" I smiled while catching my breath, "Yes, and let's not add one more to the list."

Like mountain goats, we navigated narrow paths down the steep decline to then cross the dried river bed and worked our way up the other side. There wasn't a smooth or flat surface anywhere to be found.

Once we made it back up to another open expanse—uphill, I promise—we finally reached our destination. It was close to dusk and the temperature differential between the shade and the areas lit by the dwindling sunlight revealed it was going to be a cold night, indeed.

This particular troop, and the hike's guide in particular, prided itself on being able to take safe, well thought-out treks that presented challenges to all things Scout. Because of a fire ban, everyone set up their tents as quickly as possible since there could be no fires. Everyone was experienced; tents went up quickly, gear was unpacked and people settled into their areas.

Justin came to check on me.

"Pretty well, bud," I said, "Except that my sleeping bag is missing. It must have fallen off somewhere on the hike. Want to help me gather some leaves? I'll fill the tent with them to make a bottom and then I'll sleep with all the clothes I brought on. It's gonna be cold."

Justin has always been an intense young man, and a problem solver. He shared my situation with the scout leader who affirmed our plans. He also agreed that, despite scout rules prohibiting it, Justin could join me in my tent if temperatures dropped too low. They did and he did.

With a tent full of leaves and me bundled up to look like the Michelin man, Justin came into the tent with his sleeping bag and used it as a blanket to cover us both. We made it through the night, and found out later that the temperature in the area had dropped into single digits that night.

"I wasn't going to let you die, Dad," he said in all earnestness. Clearly no one would have allowed that to happen, but Justin placed himself in charge of his dad making it through the night.

As for the next day's hike back . . . did I mention that everything was uphill both ways?

On the hike back to our beginning, we ran into a hiker with an interesting question.

"Did someone is this group lose their sleeping bag? You're the only people that I've seen out here, so I figured it was one of you. I left it against the rocks at (something or another) spot."

Sleeping bag found; memories made.

I left the house in February 2003. I lived in a small apartment with a sleeping bag for a bed until Dion gave me the trundle bed that he had been given and didn't use. Despite putting boards between the mattress and springs, it never quite made it to "comfortable" status. There was little in the apartment except for my hopes—for mental clarity and direction of what to do. Justin graduated from high school in May 2004 and sought the same things. We became roomies. But first, a quick digression.

Soon after I left, when I came to the house where he and Cameron and their mother continued to live in order to spend some time in conversation with them, Justin and I had a memorable blow. All the confusion about the circumstances and the rage of being almost 18 came together in an explosive moment followed by an hour of aftershocks. It was necessary.

He and I were shooting pool. His tongue was much sharper than his game. And mine, for that matter because I jumped a shot off the table and he perceived it as a threat. I forgot what he said, but I recall saying something in return that basically said we could talk about it but we're not going to be taking verbal shots at each other. "If you want to talk, we can go outside." We went. The "conversation" and queries began and I realized there could be many moments when I would have to take the painful experience of my sons' pain and confusion expressed in vitriolic expressions, and merely listen. Listening before reacting served me well then, and many times since.

Justin felt pain, confusion and anger, and not just at me. A volcano erupted thanks to the circumstances. The magma flowed. As I stood, he paced around the backyard swinging an axe handle at branches and tree trunks. He needed the pressure release valves of both vocabulary and actions. Both were scary at times, but the pressure began to subside and we had a good conversation. I declined his mother's offer to step into the conversation. Our talk had to be man to man, father to son.

When he graduated from high school and had no clue of what to do nor where to go, except perhaps for a stint in the military, he clearly needed a place for mental clarity and a direction of what to do. I offered to him a chance to move in with me in a larger apartment. The apartment would not be great, but he'd have his own room. I was still living on credit card debt and borrowed funds, so our times would be meager, but together we would work on helping him find a path. A Justin path. He accepted the fringe-free offer.

He and I roomed together previously, too. I accepted a job in Houston and started in August 2001. Over the Christmas break in 2001, he moved to Houston to join me in a small two-bedroom apartment in Friendswood so he could begin high school there during his junior year. It was one of the few parts of the family transition master plan that worked out.

We lived in a modest environment, and I had to count on his good nature. January 1, 2002 I attempted a downscaled version of New Year's dinner with ham, mashed potatoes, black-eyed peas and such. Two bites into the ham, we both admitted that it was the saltiest, least edible meat we had ever tried. Reading the directions about placing the ham in a bit of water while cooking to help extract the salt would have made for a better meal, but would have prevented us from having a memorable story for an interesting start in Houston by living together.

In July 2002, I wrote:

I told J this morning how I'd always remember the six months we had together. How I knew he was a cool kid but how much more amazing he is that I know him better. I said how happy I was that we got to know each other so well and how I wished it hadn't taken this to know each other. He agreed. In 45 minutes he said about 10 times how special it was. He said, "there were good times and bad." "Buddy, I don't recall any bad ones," I replied. "Well, the ham," he said.

Good times and bad, indeed. Two months later his mother and brother moved to Houston to join us. Five months after that, I separated from the family.

In June 2004 he enrolled in a local community college to take a biology class after he graduated from high school. I knew the teacher and her love for teaching. We hoped that Justin would experience a classroom environment with an impassioned professor that could diminish his high school-based cynicism for school. He had been turned down by the three universities he had applied to—his grades weren't great and he applied to difficult-to-enter schools—and wondered aloud if he was "too stupid to make it in school." At the last minute, feeling some pressure because his girlfriend was accepted to one of the schools he applied to (because she did), he enrolled again at the community college to begin his post-secondary educational path.

About 18 months later, he began to contemplate his next steps. I was doing the same thing. In October 2005, I felt the urge to move out of the apartment and into a modest "starter" house. Starting anew at almost 50. Between relocations and related temporary quarters, this would be my sixth "home" in three years. I enlisted the input of him and a friend of mine in choosing a neighborhood that kept me close to work and to Cameron, and Justin close to his school.

"Thanks for involving me, Dad," he said, "but I probably won't be here for more than another few months. Don't buy a house for me."

"I'm buying a house for me," I replied, "and should you be able to spend some time with me, so much the better. And whenever you come to visit I want you to feel like this is home."

He nodded. We picked a house.

A few months after that, with solid grades under his belt, ongoing employment supporting his growth, and a desire to continue growing (with his girlfriend, too), he decided to continue his quest of discovery.

July 2006 marked his relocation from home to Texas State University in San Marcos, Texas. After an exhausting—physically and emotionally—move, it came time for us to part. Several hugs, well wishes and "I'll miss you" moments wrapped up our parting. Then, I said, "You're a wonderful roomy." As I drove home, sorting out emotions as well as pride for his growth, he sent a few text messages about me being the best roomy ever. Roommates part, but have the relationships to bring them back together. Catch and release.

After a couple years at college, he called to apologize. I was surprised by the unexpected apology for an unknown offense. He had been with high school students, working with Student Conservation Association that provides youth the chance to learn about the environment while undertaking useful work for parks and reserves. He said that the kids in his group had been sitting around at camp and talked about divorce. "I'm sorry. I feel bad for the things I said and did that were hurtful. I didn't appreciate that we (his mom, brother and him) were in a nice house and you were in a sleeping bag." The conversation continued and I reminded him that he had a right to the feelings he had when we had the blow up, and that he had great maturity and courage to make the call. As long as there is mutual respect and love, the doors remain open for conversation. A child's time is not a parent's, nor is a parent's the child's. We have no right or expectation for our children to do, say or act as we want in the moment, as they cannot expect the same of us. Some things just take time.

Each time a child grows away, it opens the parent's heart for joy and sorrow, fear and optimism.

Dion tried his first semester of college at University of New Mexico, where I was working when he graduated in 1999. The call home to Texas was strong for him and he had been infected by the Texas A&M bug thanks to a camp experience he had there between junior and senior year of high school. To enter TAMU mid-year, he had to come in as a member of the Corps of Cadets, which he aspired to anyway. It seemed that the delay in getting there forced his hand to do what he had hoped for all along.

The family was still together when we took him to College Station, Texas just a few months after the famous bonfire tragedy that killed several and put an end to the university's tradition of a student-built bonfire prior to the annual game pitting TAMU and their rival, University of Texas.

Once in town, we went through the local Walmart to gather all the necessities for a new Corps member, which were primarily socks, underwear, shoe polish and a trunk to put it in. Mission accomplished. We assembled in our green Ford Aerostar and headed back to Albuquerque while our first-born started his growing away adventure at the university of his dreams. A child's dream is sometimes a parent's nightmare.

A few weeks after leaving Dion in the hands of the Corps leaders, we received a call at 3:30 in the afternoon. It was a weekend. I answered the phone.

"Is Mr. McInnis there?"

"This is Dion. Can I help you?"

"This is Scott, first sergeant with the E-2 unit of the Texas A&M Corps of Cadets . . ."

My heart paused and my imagination began to play out possible scenarios. In three seconds, I had more than 300 possibilities to sort through. The young caller narrowed down my list quickly.

"Dion had a seizure. EMS is here to take care of him, but we wanted to let you know."

I interrupted him to pass the phone to his mom who I knew would retain the details with more clarity. We had known that he was under great stress and to this day we don't know what prompted the incident.

He remained a fan of the Corps and became an important leader in the Student Bonfire, which remains as a student-led, student-run, student-managed commitment to tradition at the university. He has shared much, yet there is much that I don't know, about his college times. There was much Ernest Hemingway-ness to it, and we were all quite proud when Dion, class of 2003, graduated in summer 2009. Don't ask; it's an Aggie thing.

While Dion was in college, we both went through much transition. We both grew, separately, but not disconnected.

Son Turns 22

I've had a lot of beer
Tonight
In my boy's name
No matter how much I drink
I can't impinge on his fame.
He's 22 as of today
And tonight he is getting juiced
Six guys one keg for the fun of it
Not exactly busting loose
I called him on his cell phone
This was a birthday present from me
Told him congratulations and
"I'm buying special beer to toast, you see?"
We laughed as we always do
Father, son, and our chosen brews
And then we finished our call as
We always do . . . "Love you . . . ."

June 2003

It was in college that he met the woman who would become his wife in 2009.

Where does lovin' your kids get you? The truth reveals itself on a daily basis, but I received a poignant glimpse of it at Dion's wedding reception. The full story is in a previous chapter. The truth I mentioned can be seen in the smiles and tears of joy in both Dion and I as we embraced. Loving means staying connected and being so by choice.

Dion sent a thank you card in appreciation for my attending his engagement party. It read, "Thanks for making the party Dad. We love you. Thanks for helping to make me someone she wants to spend forever with."

Times with the boys change over time. Father-son moments are influenced by age. The things we do together and the things we discuss are certainly different now than when they were single-digit ages and I was not yet 30. Or 40. Father-son moments are influenced by conditions. Divorced father and son moments reshape perceptions, as do remarried-father and son times. But they all remind me how much I look forward to the next time.

I told you goodbye
Again
After our 30 sunrises
30 tucks in bed
And my soul cried its tears
As I hugged you
And tousled your hair
As you stand, head at my shoulders.
I told you goodbye
Again
After our 30 sunrises
And my heart held you close
As it will for thousands of sunrises.
A decree can't dampen a father's love . . .
A decree can't dampen a father's love.

June 30, 2006

Those sentiments were no surprise, though more hopeful than the feelings a few months after the boys' mother and I separated.

*I miss
The feeling of my sons'
Arms
Hands
On my shoulders or back or head.*

*I miss
The feeling deep inside
Reserved only for them.*

June 8, 2003

There is always a loving place for the boys.

I Love Being Your Dad

*Of all the jobs I've had
Or will
The greatest ever is
Being your dad.
You've given me joy and a challenge or two
As you've grown on your journeys
Of learning and being and becoming
The great person that you are.
Your hand once fit in my palm
And your feet on top of mine
Your arms barely long enough to enwrap my neck
As we went places together.
The fit of all of us is different now
Except where you are in my heart
The only thing I love more than being your dad
Is you.*

August 10, 2003

At the end of the day, loving your kids doesn't require them to be like you, believe like you or even agree with you. They don't even have to make sense to you all the time. I'm lucky in that mine do to me *most* of the time.

I'm reminded of the movie "A River Runs Through It" for an important observation. The father figure—played by Tom Skerritt—is a preacher who presents a sermon shortly after his prodigal son is beaten and murdered for his gambling debts. The father's message during those times of pain and confusion work well at any time: "We can love completely without complete understanding."

PLAYIN'

Let's play!
Whatcha say?
Today?
Okay!
You and me
Your dad and thee
Let's see
What we see
Take a walk
Around the block
Never stop
Never stop enjoying you
Never stop being true
I love you
Yes, I do.

August 16, 2003

Something about playing football in the front yard, learning pass patterns amidst the solid defensemen named Ash, Pine and Oak becomes part of a boy's passage and a dad's play. Or is it the other way around? "Head straight to oak, then hook in front of pine where I'll catch you. Watch out for ash and go for the touchdown."

I learned that way. The china berry tree was just a tree until a branch clothes lined me after catching a pass from my dad, and then the tree became the Faust Lane version of Ray Nitchke, the feared linebacker of the Green Bay Packers. My youngest learned at 10 how to run pass patterns amidst the tall, green-headed, unmoving linemen of the front yard in Texas, his first chance to learn having been confined to the ping-pong table sized yards of Albuquerque for the previous five years.

After returning to the Houston area, he learned football in the lush St. Augustine of the home field advantage.

His quarterback was an aging never-could-be, never-really-wanted-to-be, a far cry from his friends whose fathers are former football athletes. My gridiron heroics were limited to sandlots and street "fields," preparing me perfectly for what started anew for him in 2002.

Because Cameron is the youngest, I remember some play and playfulness that exemplified things for all three of the boys. All were active, play-minded kids with great senses of fun and humor; video games and television watching never predominated their lives, though their energy levels and laughter did sometimes remind me of cartoons.

When we lived in Huntsville, Texas, Cameron developed a routine as "Speedy Gallez," as he called it from the Speedy Gonzalez cartoons. When I arrived home from work, he would run to my car to place a handful of grass on the hood. Running, laughing and completing his routine, he took care of his task and then dodged me until ready for his hello hug.

His play was the last of my child play—until grandkids come along—and comprised a variety of stories and fun. Cameron and I could make a tremendous "mess" in the bathroom at bath time, as I frothed up thick bubbles in bubble baths for him which then were called into duty for throwing at each other. Miniature clouds of bubbles stuck to the walls, carpet and nearby sink. Laughter filled the room.

For him, the characters of conversation included "Franker" the tiger (from his Winnie the Pooh books), and Pocahontas bandage strips to cover the boo-boos of the day. Each of the boys had their characters and stories that migrated from their books and movies into their lives and conversations. The times of early childhood—including the tub time fun, the motor boat sounds they made in the water, horsey rides on my back or knees—go through phases and changes. For each son, the rude awakening of their growth hit me like a cold shower when the fun times in the tub with baby shampoo hair washes, flotillas of toys ships staging war, and drowning dinosaurs complete with all sorts of sound effects were cut off with "I'm going to take my bath now. You can't see me naked." Their first steps away from the Garden of Eden of youth. Play provides a way to keep one foot there.

Play is not just a verb of certain types of actions. Play constitutes a spirit. And playin' with kids can last mere moments or hours or more. Play becomes part of life.

My dad and I didn't have a lot of play time, but I recall play and playfulness. In fact, it was playing with Dad that proved I had physical "issues."

As a tyke, I ran around the house with Dad in hot pursuit. He would chase me and before long I would be flat on my face or wheezing from asthma, or both. "After laughter, comes tears," my mother would say in Polish, harkening an expression from one of her immigrant relatives. Indeed, after the laughter of play (with mom, dad or sis), tears usually appeared soon thereafter. When it came to running around the house, the tears usually ended up being mine because my left foot crossed and I'd trip over my own feet, usually at high speed. Corrective shoes resolved the problem and kept me in very un-cool shoes until seventh or eighth grade when I was finally able to wear side-buckle slip-on shoes, but that's another story.

Diamonds are a girl's best friend
And for ball-playing little boys
A bat, a horsehide and a glove
Are better than the closet of toys

Dreams are made, lessons learned
On red sand and grass between chalk lines.
The smell of the first cut, the sound of the bat
Last them all their lives.

Both diamonds are indestructible
Able to cut through all life brings
Boys like their diamonds in the sun
Girls like them in their rings.

A woman remembers her first diamond
A man remembers his, too
Remembering his teammates and stories
And the dreams yet waiting to come true.

September 25, 2006

Not only did my left foot cross over, so too did my left eye. We discovered that by playing baseball. When I began to learn to play catch with my uncle's old baseball mitt, I missed everything, but usually by just a bit. The glove was old; the fingers were not even laced together. Dad wondered about the problem and Mom agreed that maybe I needed a glove from the current century, so I then became the owner of a Montgomery Ward leather glove. All leather. I loved the scent; all men and boys do.

Alas, even with the new glove, it and the ball usually never came to full union. Nor did my Sears Ted Williams-approved 28 bat and the ball. The problem was so persistent, and frustrating to Dad, that I ended up at Dr. Speer's office. Then I learned about "lazy eye." The glasses helped, but major league baseball would never be in my future, despite daydreams of taking the mound like my hero Sandy Koufax.

In fact, at 43 years of age, I still hoped to hit a homerun over the fence in a baseball game and feel the exhilaration of "touching them all" as described in the 1985 song "Centerfield" by John Fogerty. I added "hit a homerun" onto my list of things to accomplish before I die, as part of an exercise described in the book "The Aladdin Factor" by Jack Canfield and Mark Victor Hansen.

After turning down a couple of offers to play adult softball while living in Albuquerque, I agreed to play with the logic that "I can never get my homerun if I don't at least go to bat." I played with the team as their pitcher—ah, just like the "old days"—and batted and pitched with more confidence than my earlier forays into the sport. I played with them for three seasons.

The second season occurred in the summer, during Dion's first summer away from home. He had left University of New Mexico after one semester to return to Texas. As luck would have it, he spent some time with the family in Albuquerque on a break from his job and the team appreciated having a young man participate for a few games. Dion was happy to join; he loves baseball with every fiber of his being.

Well into the second season, I still awaited my desired homerun. Luckily, we had some pretty good hitters (and a great pitcher!) and fared reasonably well. We also did not have a bunch of guys with "I coulda been a contender" mentalities to ruin the fun for everyone as they pursued their missed fame and acclaim. Dion fit in well, with a great sense of humor to match his intensity for the game.

I recall one game in particular. Throughout the game, I could hear from over my shoulder, the voices of the players encouraging me pitch after pitch. The voice from third base or left field, depending on the inning, was Dion's. Hearing one's son calling out, "Way to go pitch!," "You got 'im. Great job pitcher," makes for a special surprise. During a troublesome phase, everyone did well to hold off our opponents in a challenging inning, keeping them from scoring despite opportunities. As our team ran off the field to the sound of our small fan group's cheers, Dion ran to my side and wrapped his arm around my shoulders. With his other hand, he pointed to me and said, "That's my dad!"

I don't need to hit a homerun anymore. By pursuing something that I thought I wanted, I received something I never even imagined, and much better.

Playing uncovers a lot more than crossing eyes and feet. It uncovers character, wit, humor, patience, courage, joy and laughter, among other things.

I've learned a lot about my sons' senses of fun, fairness and frivolity by playing with them. They have learned the same about me, as my dad and I did about each other.

The boys and I have never shied from playing where visible.

During our few years in Albuquerque, Cameron attended a small Catholic school for a while. It was close to my work and we believed it would provide some of the things we hoped for in a child's education. As luck would have it, the school's parking lot also provided more memories for Cameron and me.

Albuquerque can be cold. From September through March, there can either possibly be cold days or there will assuredly be cold days. Either way didn't matter, the children were still expected to stay outside in the asphalt gathering/play area on the other side of the fence from the parking lot. There they talked with each other or sat alone. Cameron was in second or third grade at the time, and I would usually take him to school on my way to work at University of New Mexico.

One day I noticed a hopscotch pattern on the lot. I asked Cameron if he wanted to play a bit before school. He agreed. A new tradition came to life.

A few times a week we would play. He in his uniform and I in mine—coat, tie, dress pants and cowboy boots. We both wore smiles.

We'd use my car keys, flat rocks or whatever else we could find for a marker. And we'd play as long we could until his job or mine beckoned. He was a kid and I was in boots, so it made for a pretty fair game. I noticed some parents watching as they dropped their kids; teachers noticed; playground overseers noticed. And then other kids began to act on what they saw.

Soon, kids—boys and girls—gathered and waited for an invitation to play. While it seemed that Cameron enjoyed having play time with his dad, he also seemed to enjoy being an agent for play for kids in the playground, including those older than him.

Kids are expert at hopscotch, of course . . . particularly, little girls. Even those who opted not to join us provided encouragement and tips on how to throw the marker just right, how to pause on our spot without falling, and other nuggets of expertise. Neither Cameron nor I would qualify for hopscotch Olympics, but we sure showed some people a thing or two about playing . . . playin'!

At least I stood a chance when playing hopscotch, or most anything when the boys were young and I was younger. Once I hit the half-century mark, game playing became a far greater challenge, and Cameron provided the tests.

Until the magic five-o, I could manage in a game of soccer with Cameron. Then puberty hit him and midlife hit me. In short-field soccer games where I could beat him, then tie him, there was only frustration now as he annihilated me, ten-zip, ten-one or maybe ten-two. No matter the score and the victor, laughter remained a component . . . even while gasping for air was added.

Although Dad did not have as much play time with me as I have had with the three boys, he did join me in a variety of activities that changed as I aged—baseball, football, basketball, fishing, volleyball, pool, badminton, and dominoes come to mind. He also helped construct things occasionally—like a wood go-kart for street races and a sword for a school play (complete with kid-approved red paint on the tip) that ended up being a home toy, too. He was no St. Joseph; carpentry was not one of his areas of craftsmanship, but he could cobble together things well enough to provide some additional fun for me and my friends. Likewise, he allowed us to experiment and play with boards, hammers and nails, to the demise of a couple of car tires, if I recall correctly.

Kids in those days (early to mid-'60s) built forts for themselves in their backyards. As luck would have it, there were many homes being built within reasonable driving distances of our home in Memorial Bend. At times, Mom would drive us to some of the sites and we'd ask the workers for some of the scraps for me to use. (Those were **definitely** different times.) I was too shy to ask, so she would do so for me. We'd come home with a few pieces of 2x4, 1x6 and other useful pieces which I collected in the garage. They became the makings for fun.

Those blocks and pieces of wood, along with a hammer and random nails allowed my friends and me to build boats (that looked more like the Merrimack than a boat) to float in the street gutters on days of heavy rain.

Dad grew up poor, and married Mom during the Great Depression. Needless to say, they never had a lot of money. Their backgrounds and the times included the practice of rarely throwing away nails. He showed me how to straighten a nail out sufficiently to make it useful again. His dad built things, including homes (one still stands in San Antonio some 60 years after grandpa built it) and there was little wastage under those conditions.

While nails were maintained separately according to the little brown bag they came home in from the nearby Wagner's hardware store or Sutherland's lumber yard, once used or taken out of their bags they ended up in a red coffee tin can—Folgers, I believe. The can held a hodgepodge of nails of various sizes and conditions. My friends and I could dump the inventory into a pile and sort through the mound to find the perfect nail for the project at hand. We had access to, and permission for, fun in the garage and with some, but not all, of Dad's stuff. Access and permission go a long way with a kid's imagination.

Somewhere between sixth and eighth grade our physical education coach taught us to high jump. The arrangement included two vertical poles with nails set for different heights. Across the nails we placed a bamboo cane pole. A sand pit comprised the landing area. Not high tech, but certainly high fun. Such were the conditions for the new Catholic school of St. Cecilia's serving the burgeoning west Houston area.

It seemed logical that I could make the same sort of play at home. So, with access and permission, we built the stands, measured to place the nails and used Mom's cane pole to create a high jump set for our backyard. The McInnis yards—front and back—were the most likely place to find many of the kids in the neighborhood as we used them for all manner of games, plays performed by neighborhood kids (including my sister) and much more.

Quick digression: the wear and tear on our yards was brutal, causing the ire of the homeowner's association. I remember that the association contacted dad about the condition of the front yard, including the well-worn base paths on the makeshift baseball/kickball diamond. The yard wasn't that big, but neither were we at the time. But we played hard and constantly, and the yard showed the worse for the wear. When the association contacted Dad about taking care of the yard, he basically told them to butt out. He said something like, "The kids won't be young forever, and this provides them a place where they can all play safely and supervised. Too bad if you don't like it." And that is the last I heard of that. When the next door neighbor complained about the condition of our yard as a possible negative reflection on his, Dad told him that whenever he wanted to find his daughter, he knew he could find her in our yard. All the kids played there and if he preferred that Mom and Dad shut it down so the kids would have to leave the street to find another playground where they couldn't be seen and supervised, just let Dad know and he'd do it. "After all, your daughter is one of the kids over here the most often." The neighbor quit complaining. Again, Mom and Dad provided access and permission to have fun.

Back to the backyard high jump venue. After we built the stands with old nails, old wood and young excitement, we set the arrangement for scissor-jumping madness. The Fosbury Flop had not yet become famous and certainly not for a yard of scarce grass and packed Houston gumbo dirt. Mom and Dad agreed that we could use an old mattress and then Mom made an oversize bag to hold rags. It was like a soft punching bag and we laid it on the ground to land on. Usually we just stepped on it. But we played, sometimes into the night under the light of the back porch. Playing, just playing. Because we could.

As I got older, my taste in games changed. In my early teen years, I picked up pool and Dad bought a pool table for us. We turned the garage into a makeshift game room that served us well. It took a while to get the pool table, and I was anxious. I had learned how to play on a slate table at the house of one of my friend's mom's boyfriends. It had leather pouches to catch the balls: very impressive to a kid. The table we sought had a honeycomb bed, not slate, and its arrival was contingent on a particular client of Dad's paying his long overdue bill. Each day that Dad arrived with checks for Mom to deposit, I would ask if Mr. What'shisname had paid yet. I don't recall how long we had to wait—a year maybe—and I probably drove Dad nuts.

Not one to lose opportunity, I developed an alternate game of pool while I waited. Using the sawed-off broomstick that we used to secure the sliding glass door leading to the patio, and a golf ball and Super Ball (a high-bouncing, dense ball from that era), I created a way to shoot pool all around the house. We had a strangely colored, tightly knapped carpet that made for a great, smooth surface. With the golf ball as the cue ball—it was white, after all—and the Super Ball as my target, I could shoot pool all around the house, scurrying from one room to another on my knees. I loved pool and would play however I could.

Finally the pool table arrived, and we used it for about ten years. It watched me grow up, and was there for me to teach my nieces and nephews how to play. After marriage and the purchase of our first house, we secured the pool table and used it for a few more years. I then needed the space for a photography studio and we donated the table to the Seaman's Center near the Houston Ship Channel. It provided access and permission for fun to me and my friends for quite a while. No wonder kids loved coming to our house—never fancy . . . always fun.

Ever since we donated the table, I longed to have one again. Space and a growing family did not allow for it, but the dream remained. When Justin was about 12, the time arose for another table. We lived in Albuquerque and had moved into a new home. It appeared that we might be there for a while and the kids were the right age to rejuvenate interest in the fine art of shooting pool. Santa placed "pool table" on his list for the McInnis family for Christmas 1997. Unfortunately, Justin answered the phone when the delivery man called to get the okay to deliver the table. I was furious and raised hell with everyone I could reach at Sears for screwing up Christmas. Santa and his elf (the boys' grandfather) assembled the table on Christmas Eve night and it awaited the boys in the morning. Cameron and his mom still have the table.

Surprise presents that encourage boy-play were not unusual. One Christmas a portable basketball hoop appeared in the driveway, complete with red bow, for Justin. Cameron still has that, too. And when Cameron was about four, a neighbor and I built a fort for Cameron for Christmas while he, his brothers and mom shopped. The neighbor elf drove away as the boys and their mom returned home. Thanks to clever parking of the car, the fort remained invisible and Christmas morning yielded another great surprise. Ultimately, the fort provided access and permission for play.

Thanks to the neighbor's help, and purchased plans, the fort provided stable, secure and safe play. When go-karts were the rage, and push carts an acceptable alternative, Dad built a push-driven vehicle for me to use with my friends. I don't recall there being a good design plan, though I believe he referenced a Scout book for some suggestions on how to make a steering system with ropes wrapped around the steering column and attached to pulleys. We built the cart with wood that Mom and I had collected from home construction sites and leftovers from Dad's projects around the house. It was light, functional and one of three such vehicles on the street.

Though I was the neighborhood lightweight and would most sensibly be in the driver's seat, I also had a low threshold for fear when it came to tearing my body up on concrete. So, usually my friends drove and I worked as the pusher . . . the engine. Even with larger kids in the "cockpit," I out-pushed just about everyone. My closest competitor was Pam. I was faster than the other boys. She lived at the end of the street. She pushed carts fast and tackled hard in football. She was quite the competitor. Our drag strip measured about 150 yards long, and she always made a good race out of it.

Faust Lane bustled with kid activity and just about every other house had a basketball goal, including the McInnises. Our first one sat on the roof over the garage and then, after breaking out one too many garage window panes (I learned how to install window glass, at least), we removed that arrangement and installed a free-standing wood pole on the side of the driveway. That became the hub of much activity until Dad backed out of the driveway too fast with his Camaro car door open. That incident took out the pole, sprung the door and left me without a resident basketball hoop until I married. I installed a backboard over the garage in our first home shortly after we moved in.

Dad possessed good athletic skills according to the stories I heard growing up. A naturally strong swimmer and boxer, he also performed the iron cross move on gymnastic rings without training. He was small-ish (five feet seven inches) strong and confident. In his youth, basketball was played quite differently than in mine. He shot underhanded; my friends and I knew that to be a "granny shot." His game didn't involve much running and dribbling, which was the style of choice in the 1960s, thanks to the influence of the American Basketball Association.

Basically, almost every sport that Dad and I were able to play together revealed the difference between those games in "the old days" versus what some would call the modernization of sports. I learned about the way these games were played by playing with my father who learned baseball when gloves' fingers were not lashed together, and basketball when shots were made underhanded. Some game styles are ageless: pool, dominoes.

I learned a lot about the potential of pool by listening to Dad. He shot a competent game, but it was his attentive eye and real-world experiences that revealed the game to me as a young teen.

Molly dated a guy named Jake for a short time. When Dad and I played Jake and Molly, I noticed a couple of things in Dad's reactions. One, he appreciated the respectful way that Jake dealt with Molly as she learned the game (which was unlike her previous boyfriend who was disrespectful and angry). Two, he saw something in Jake's game that contradicted his appearance.

"Jake, play your real game. Play your best," Dad said.

"I am, sir," Jake replied with a bit of a smile. He continued to play and guide Molly on her shots.

Dad observed. He and I stood side by side, holding our cues similarly, standing on their ends in front of us.

"He's got more than that," Dad said quietly to me. I felt like I was being brought into a grown-up secret. I wondered what Dad saw.

Jake completed a few more shots and then missed.

"Jake, play your game. It's okay. I know you're better than what you're showing. It's okay."

Jake looked toward Molly. She nodded. He had been outed, but in a safe environment. Of course, Dad wanted to see the truth and had enough worldly experience to know that great pool skills frequently come in less-than-desirable conditions.

Jake racked up balls one through nine in the diamond-shaped formation of the game of nine ball. He positioned the cue ball precisely, and broke. He proceeded to run the table. Molly watched. Dad and I remained in our same position, holding our cues like rakes and nodding at Jake's prowess.

"Where'd you pick up a game like that?" Dad asked.

Further conversation, that night and beyond, revealed that Jake began shooting pool at the age of 14 when he left home. Jake had lived a difficult life, fraught with challenges. Stories of his life began to creep out, released by the break of pool balls and Dad's awareness. Dads know things, and they learn things.

You can't grow up in Texas without guns being part of play at some time or another. Maybe not play, in the sense of playing cowboys and Indians with live ammunition, but play in the sense of having fun without serious objective other than good times and good companionship. A .22 rifle makes for good, responsible play.

I learned how to shoot a gun by using a Daisy BB gun in our backyard, shooting responsibly at paper targets secured to paper grocery bags filled with layers of newspaper. Then I began to shoot at things on the excursions that my friends and I would take to Rummel Creek, Buffalo Bayou and other fun places. Kids would be arrested today if they walked the streets openly with BB guns, pellet rifles and wood-handled sling shots. It was all but ignored in the Wonder Years.

When my brother made one of his many job relocations, he left behind some of his guns, also leaving the opportunity for me to learn how to shoot gunpowder-driven projectiles instead of spring-powered ones. My dad taught me how to handle and shoot a bolt-action .22 rifle on the farm land of Hank and Helen Hall in Navasota, Texas. I learned a lot of things at their place; they were some sort of kin to my dad on his mom's side.

It was 1968 or '69 when Uncle Bill died and while staying at my aunt's I experienced a .22 for legitimate hunting. If you call shooting frogs hunting.

Uncle Bill was married to my mom's only sister, Elynor. I didn't remember either of them—I found out later that I hadn't seen either one of them since I was born—but the trip would introduce me to her, my three cousins (their daughters), Missouri, baby pigs and frog legs.

We stayed with Aunt Elynor for a few days on their place outside of Lebanon, Missouri. Bill had chosen the location as a safe haven after nuclear attack. Long story that I still don't fully grasp. But, it was out in the middle of nowhere, which is always a great playground for a kid who loves to be outside. I loved being outside.

Come dusk, we heard the bellowing of frogs, and then we heard about the intentional placement of frogs. There were traditional bullfrogs on the front pond, closest to the house, and some sort of huge frog species in the back pond that was, unfortunately, almost inaccessible. Dad keyed in on Bill's .22 rifles and off we went with a rifle and a bucket. Dad carried the rifle, and I got the bucket.

It didn't take long to use the limited number of long rifle shells that remained in Uncle Bill's inventory and the short shells dropped off dramatically from one side of the modest pond to the other. Day one of frog hunting yielded a few frogs and prompted a trip to Lebanon to buy some more shells. When the clerk asked Dad all the questions that federal regulations required about shells, Dad laughed it off as usual with a comment like, "Don't worry, if I kill someone with these little things, I'll be sure to bring the bodies by." I don't think Dad's humor would work well in today's world.

With the addition of more long-rifle shells, we returned to hunting and plinking. We walked around the pond, watched for frogs and took our shots. If the frogs stayed hidden, we shot cans or whatever else we could find. Dad shot well; I was pretty good. I carried the bucket quite well, and was a good raker. We learned after the first day that a frog can jump into the water even after being shot. On those occasions, I used a heavy duty rake to drag them in for appropriate placement in the bucket. Supper counted on me.

Once enough frogs were "harvested," as they say, it was time for fried frog legs. Dad played chef and relished the role. I always smile just thinking of Dad in the kitchen, which was typical when the menu called for steak or fried chicken or fried fish. He worked the kitchen with a dish towel wrapped around his waist and a highball (bourbon and coke) on the counter. He loved that style of cooking and always seemed happy doing it. He wasn't much for cleaning up though.

My cousins and I played Yahtzee in the living room while Dad cooked the frog legs. Someone let out a shriek.

"Dion, come look at this," a voice called out.

A shriek to a young boy is like a light to a moth—totally irresistible.

Dad stood at the stove with a broad smile on his face. An iron skillet held bubbling fat and a few frog legs. Several others lay on a plate, awaiting their turn to become dinner.

"Watch, watch, watch. The legs jump out of the fat! Really!!"

I don't remember whether it was my mom or one of the cousins who had called out to me, but when I arrived I saw Dad beaming. He then placed another frog leg in the fat and it jumped. We laughed and Dad enjoyed the role of entertainer and cook. I wished I had had the chance to talk to him about how those activities were rooted in his own background and family heritage. Perhaps my lack of information in those areas explains why I am such an open book to my sons.

In 2007, almost 40 years after those memorable times, my Aunt Elynor died after a long bout with dementia. I could not not go to her funeral. She had lived with her youngest daughter and her husband in California for quite some time, but was to be buried in Missouri, in a veteran's cemetery. She served as a Navy WAVE.

It seemed only appropriate that I drove to the funeral, not unlike the drive that Dad navigated for us when Bill died: a 12-plus hour jaunt fueled by sodas and candy. Dad's recipe for a long drive included a couple of eight-ounce bottles of Coke and a couple of Hershey chocolate bars. Dad's route to Lebanon took us through unlit roads in the Ozarks; my route benefitted from four decades of highway developments. Somehow, I felt kindred to Mom's and Dad's memories as I trekked solo to Lebanon.

The day before I left for the trip, I pondered my new life. I would be married again in three months. I felt alive, energetic, optimistic and connected anew to my mom's and dad's memories. I would travel to the cemetery for me (she was my aunt, of course), my mom (she was my mother's sister, which deserves its own brand of respect), and my dad (my aunt and dad were quite fond of each other). My aunt joked about having paid for my dad's education. He took a correspondence course in accounting and had no money for the postage. Elynor lived with Mom and Dad at the time, and he would leave his assignment envelope on a desk and say, "Would you mail this for me, honey, when you're out?" She paid the postage and ran the errand. He ended up owning his own accounting profession for about 40 years.

Anyway, as I sat alone and contemplated the drive that was to come the following day, I felt overwhelmed by the present and the past, like two distinct waves coming from different directions. Instead of drowning me, however, they lifted me and my thoughts. And my memories of both youth and aging.

Cicadas clack and signal
From the height and breadth of trees
Could be they're calling each other
But today, they are calling me

Reaching out to touch my heart
And encouraging my memories
The summer heat closes my eyes
And then I can truly see

Images of my youthful days
Playing in the summer sun
Times of growing and of joy
And of much childhood fun

They've always made their sounds
During the hot summer season
Though for years I haven't heard
And I'd forgotten the sounds' true reason

The boys' mom didn't like guns in the house, and so I didn't have much chance to teach gun skills to the boys. However, I've always loved the .22 and when I re-married, the boys decided to give me a rifle for my wedding present.

A few years later, after Justin became more interested in hunting by gun or bow, I purchased some gear and a 12-gauge shotgun so we could dove and squirrel hunt together. While our take for our first day hunting together only included one squirrel apiece, in terms of "harvest," we had a great time hiking, talking, watching and learning. There will be more trips, and I hope to have excursions with all four of the McInnis men like we do with fishing. Such events become harder to orchestrate as boys become couples and couples become families. But, we're committed to making it happen. There is still plenty of playing to do.

The boys participated in a variety of sports—track, cross country, basketball, swimming, baseball, football and soccer. I served as a coach or assistant coach in all of them at some time or another, except for swimming. Something about a coach showing up in floatees seemed to present problems for the boys and the other athletes. I believe I did set a Houston record in soccer, however.

Dion played soccer and his coach enlisted parents to take the preparation and test to be a referee. Keep in mind that the teams were nine-and ten-year olds, as I recall. The prep and test is pretty much a slam dunk, particularly if one even watches the game. Therein lies the rub.

When I attend the sporting activities of the boys, I invariably am watching only my son. Cameron can ask whether I noticed a move another kid made three lanes over in the pool; nope. Justin could ask whether I noticed another runner who did something or another on the course; nope. Dion could ask whether I noticed another player's hit or throw; nope. I watch my boys, and notice little beyond that. Because of that, I didn't learn a whole lot about soccer in the early years, but had to learn more because Dion's brothers also played. In his era, though, I had little experience with the sport.

Being the dutiful dad and volunteer, I participated in the preparation for the referee training and took the test. I doubt there has been a test score lower than mine since that time in the early 1990s.

Again, except for swimming, I also enjoyed participating in all the sports with the boys. As I got older and my belly got bigger, the pace and intensity of the competition changed. With Dion and Justin, we played competitive basketball though they could beat me by the time they were young men; with Cameron, I play horse in the rare times we shoot hoops. Cameron's only activity of interest is fishing, though for a few years, we played soccer games to a score of ten on a downsized field near the house. By that time, he had developed into a proficient player and a strong high school young man and I . . . wasn't. But he would run and laugh and I would huff and puff until the game came to a merciful end. Sometimes it didn't take very long.

Whether we competed at or merely played a sport, the times always included conversation and laughter. Time spent tossing a ball of any type—baseball, football, tennis ball—always provides a good time. The latter approach worked well for Dad and me. We never competed, except in pool.

Dad and I tossed the baseball and football with enough regularity to know good times were coming, but not often enough to keep Dad in shape. Times were different then, too, because most times there was one kid or another handy for a quick game of some type. In the hall closet by our home's entry door, Mom kept a bamboo basket that held balls, gloves, bats, and other play goodies. Above that, a shelf held badminton rackets. In mere moments my sister could have a volleyball at the ready for her friends, or I could pull together a game of basketball, baseball, football, four-square, kickball, or badminton. Dad was not the only game in town.

The boys enjoyed playing with their friends, but we also relished the chance to play together.

Play began when the kids weren't old enough to talk, and it never stopped.

In Albuquerque, we lived within a reasonable walk of the baseball fields where the neighborhood little league competed. We usually drove the mile or so, but one Saturday we decided to walk to the game, taking the back way out of the neighborhood and across the sandy, sage-filled fields. Cameron was eight, so still small enough to ride on my shoulders. I told him that he was riding to save energy so he wouldn't be too tired to get his first hit of the season that day. An hour and a half later, he got his first hit.

A life with play makes a playful life.

Cameron stood in the doorway of the hall, still sleepy looking but ready for another sophomore day in school. He mumbled, "Okay Dad, let's do this." I held out my fists so we could knuckle up. After that, I replied like a coach at halftime, "OK, MAN, LET'S DO THIS!!" and then I chest butted him. He grinned, raised his hands to position me back a few steps and said, "Okay, okay, let's go. Let's do this." We stepped toward each other and then jumped into the air to chest butt like football players after a touchdown. As we headed out the door to begin our days at work and school, we laughed. "That was weird," we agreed with a chuckle. Playful can be weird.

Playful can also give the neighbors something to talk about.

We own a lot of fishing rods. When they break, we still tend to keep them because you never know when you may need a broken piece of fiberglass tube, right? They stake tomato plants remarkably well. And we have ways of adding to the collection without buying thanks to generous friends and neighbors. The time came to get rid of some of the rod pieces because it was time to clean up the garage. Something about bringing a new wife into the house enhances the urgency of some types of cleaning and making room for new stuff. I recruited Cameron to help. He was not quite 15. Asking a boy of this age to assist with garage duty in a systematic and efficient way borders on insanity. One might as well ask for world peace. My journal entry describes what happened:

Yesterday evening, Cam and I had sword fights in the driveway with old fishing rod pieces. It was a hoot. He commented later, as he often does about such things, that there aren't many 51-year old dads who would do that. "Not many dads of any age," he added. "You think so?" I replied and then cited some of his friends' dads. "Oh no. We can't look strange in front of the neighbors . . . it'll tarnish my image," he said with the accent of a stuffed shirt professional. I laughed—and am proud that we can have fun together, not worried about others.

That doesn't describe, however, the scene of two swashbuckling Errol Flynn wannabes chasing each other around the front yard in sword fights using fishing rod fragments. When one broke, another was scooped up to continue the fight amid laughter.

Dad and I didn't play like that, though I remember playing as a kid, with Dad chasing me around the house, or having towel-popping games and other such fun. Even though Dad didn't play with us as much, he still happily participated in badminton, fishing, volleyball and other things that defied his age. He also allowed us and the neighbor kids to play in our yards, to the detriment of our grass.

When Justin told me about his skim boarding experiences when he was 19, I had to grin at my recollections of that fun. Justin did it the correct way as part of his surfing and skating culture. Mark and I skimmed in our early teens in the backyard after rain.

Pooled water and long St. Augustine grass makes for a wonderful skim board venue. After an hour or so of play, the grass could barely survive and often didn't, but Mom and Dad would let us use the backyard for play of all types, nonetheless.

In the Dark Ages, when I grew up, it was considered normal and okay for little boys (and girls) to "play soldier" with toy guns, running around for hours, making gun sounds, and using the honor system to die when shot until miraculously resurrected to rejoin the battle at hand. There were no projectiles to feel or to mark a shot, so kids would collapse in fast or slow drama to be taken out of the game. Times change things.

When Cameron was about 14, aerosoft guns were quite the rage. When I was a kid, the guns looked real but could do nothing; when Cameron was a young teen, the guns generally looked like toys with clear bodies and red-tipped barrels, but they shot projectiles much larger than BBs at a velocity that makes my first Daisy rifle look like a bookend.

He and I conducted aerosoft wars in the backyard. We'd set the timer for 30 to 45 minutes and whoever got shot the most lost. I lost—a lot. We set up our forts and barricades and then maneuvered around bushes and trees, battling mosquitoes and heat (and sometimes darkness when we were really crazy), all to shoot each other with skin-breaking "toys." Safety goggles were a requirement, as well as a reasonable threshold for pain.

For my 52nd birthday, Kim purchased the opportunity for the boys and me to expand our warfare games to larger fields of fun. We welcomed the chance to play paintball.

Basically, participants wear gear to protect head and eyes while shooting paint-filled gelatin balls that break on impact to mark successful shots. The reality is that not all the balls break, it hurts to be hit by them, and paintball fanatics come in gear worthy of a SWAT team. We wore the provided headgear, along with long pants and long-sleeve shirts. One of the indicators of the day's fun was the number of welts and broken skin bruises. Most were visible by raising a pant leg or removing a shirt. Most, not all. If you're a male who plans to play paintball for the first time, wear a cup. All skin bruises. Enough said.

All the boys have tremendous senses of humor that come out in conversation, entertainment and while playing.

I shared with Cameron some stories of my frustrations with work and several of the people there, and stories Kim had shared about the people that she encountered at work. We were both frustrated. Cameron then vented about coaches, teachers and other equally frustrating people from his week. When I pointed out that our frustrations were quite similar, he replied that we needed a revolution of some sort. I agreed and said, "I'm in."

"We need an organization. We need to start a group that others join so we can do it," he said.

I could almost hear his smile form in the darkness of the car as we were driving home.

He continued. "We can call the organization the Clue-Clucks-Cam." His nickname in the family is Cam.

Play can be organized and equipped or completely random and without implements. There is much to be said for the latter, which is ageless.

One of the places that Cameron and I used to fish with some frequency for the first year or so after his mom and I separated is a county park midway between where we each lived. Free, easy to get to, nearby (low gasoline cost), and no requirement for additional gear like waders or heavy duty rods and reels, it is a perfect place for father and son to fish in such times. My best memory from there does not include either bass or catfish, but play.

Behind the small lake stands a large, manmade hill. Kids run up and down it, despite the fairly steep angle. Less steep approaches allow for hardworking bicyclists to ride to the top. Covered with grass and weeds, it calls for attention though most people spend their time at the water in search of fish.

On one of our trips, when the fishing did little to hold our attention, the hill filled the void.

"Hey Dad, let's roll down the hill!"

I hesitated to consider the invitation more carefully. I needed time to calculate the conditions: 45 years old, no real exercise in quite a while, a mile-high hill with a 45 degree incline. After realizing that I possibly exaggerated the conditions in my head, but not my sense of fun with my son, I said,

"OK, but you better remember how to dial 911!" We laughed and headed up the hill.

We arrived at the top and took turns lying down, starting the roll and then bouncing, bumping, laughing (and moaning, for me) down the hill. Neither of us have a recollection of catching fish that day, but we both remember the day we rolled down the hill. Who says that pre-teen and midlife don't fit together well?

"Slow down booger-butt." Words usually from me, but now from my seven-year old as we raced on swings at the community playground /soccer field. Dad had just taken the lead. To the victors go the spoils: the smiles and laughter of my little one.

The cold air of the post-soccer practice fall blew in our hair, he having more than his thinning father. As we raced higher and higher, faster and faster, the laughter grew more frequent and the smiles broader. We were both being kids.

I could almost relive my own swing set times. None with my father, but certainly with my friends in the "Wonder Years" neighborhood. Somewhere in the photo box protected by my sister 800 miles away rests a snapshot of neighbor Michelle hanging upside down on the trapeze bar. And of forgotten neighbors swinging and laughing as they swung arcs in the air. There are images of backyard playgrounds with grass-less areas below the swings where little feet pushed off to start a ride or dragged to slow down . . . or dragged simply to see how it felt. Images reawaken in memories of that first jump from a high flying swing and that paratrooper feeling it gave as I left the worn wood seat.

Swing sets have always been fun. As a photographer I used them occasionally as props for photo sessions, and there remains the yet-to-be-taken image depicting our first experiences with movement; I envision the photo taken from a vantage point of standing on the swing, looking down at a smiling face—trailing hair and blurred background—as together we re-experience early flight. Now, if I can find a wood-seated swing.

There is movement of time and memories on that swing. It was fun for both father and son on this nippy day when we stole a few minutes for me to enter his world, and to re-enter youth.

The next day we discussed the previous day's play—on the swing set in the afternoon and on the elementary school parking lot hopscotch course that morning—as we drove to school. "I felt like a kid," I said. "You should always feel like a kid, even when you're an adult," he replied. I guess play brings more than exercise and good fun—it develops wisdom.

I think I'll go play.

FISHIN'

Fisherman's Walk

Talking to old fisherman
Fishing families
And fishing alones;
I miss my memories
Of walking piers, jetties and shore line
Learning of fish and men and patience.

I miss my father.
I miss fishing fathering.

March 2000

"To be a fisherman, you have to be a good person." Cameron, 8

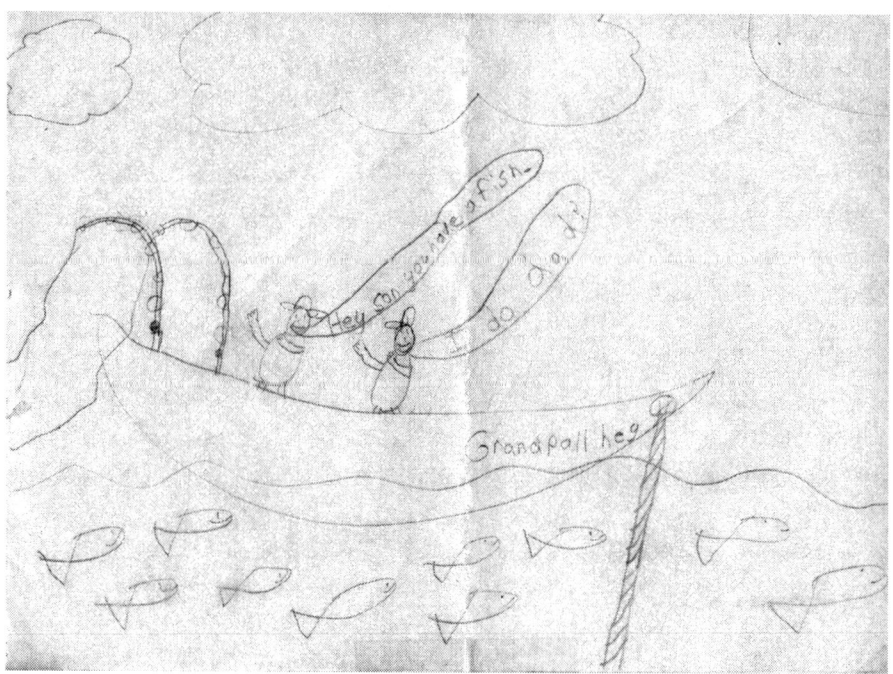

The name of the boat refers to my dad, who we called Grandpa Hey, which is a story in itself.

Fishing as a McInnis father-son tradition predates my memory. It predates me. I'm not sure how much fishing my dad and his dad did together in Mississippi and/or the McInnis property in San Antonio (Medina Creek ran through the back of the property) and/or in their beloved Rockport where granddad built a house, but I suspect that it was not like what happened in the generations to follow. However the fishing trips looked, they certainly created a love for the activity that continues in the lineage today.

My brother (18 years older) and my dad had fishing journeys, but Dad was also a different man then. Family stories share times of when Dad and Jim fished the waters near Rockport, Texas in a rented Jon boat and Dad's five and one-half horsepower Firestone outboard motor. On one such trip, my brother's friend Randy pulled a gafftop catfish over the gunwale and in perfect time and motion swung the fish's infamous, slime-coated spear of a dorsal fin into Jim's rump. About 20 years later, the same type of fish dropped off Dad's fishing line, fin first, and pierced his canvas fishing shoes. Rarely did I ever hear Dad make a noise because of pain. I did that time.

Between those two gafftop experiences were many fishing trips—both freshwater and salt water adventures. Some included his sons and some didn't. They comprise some of my most fond memories of time with Dad and created a lifelong love for the sport without making me an overly intense fanatic. I love the fishing, the time and the conversation; I love the solitude when I fish alone.

My early recollections of fishing started when I was probably four or five years old. Another fishing story from younger than that is part of my memory because of Mom telling the story; I do not recall the incident . . . the infamous snake trip. Though I must have been too young to remember the experience, I vividly recall the story.

Dad loved to fish and Mom was a patient, generally willing participant. The snake trip tested both her patience and her willingness.

As the story goes, I was two or three when Dad found this particular lake to which he could take his family for low-cost fun. The pond had a pier, which is pretty much a necessity when you're taking kids fishing, of which they had two at home—me and my sister who is three years older than me. Around the pier stood trees with low-hanging branches, which usually portend good fishing. Fish like to hang out under branches to catch bugs and little birds that might fall into the water, and to hide in the nearby roots. Fish under branches can be a good thing; slithering denizens in the branches can be quite the opposite. The low, thick branches made great high-density housing for water moccasins, some of which fell from the trees onto the pier where we fished.

Another time the family went fishing together, Mom out-fished Dad with her back to the water. And while working a crossword puzzle. And while smoking a cigarette. Oh, and with a cane pole.

Dad took us to the Galveston jetties for a day of fishing. The jetties—granite barriers that help form a channel for ships and a haven for all types of fish—provided easy access to fish, alternative play for kids, and low cost entertainment. I figure I was six or seven, making Molly about 10, meaning we couldn't be counted on to fish the entire time. We would lose interest and need a distraction. Come to think of it, so did Mom; thus, she brought her crossword puzzle book.

While she and Dad fished, and the kids played, a ship came by, causing good wave movement along the rocks. That happened with some regularity since the jetty is on a ship channel. Something different happened this time: Mom's cane pole was jerked almost out of her hand, requiring her to put aside the crossword puzzle book, and turn to face the water. Dad scampered across the rocks—"Hold your tip up!"—trying to get in position to help—"Hold your tip up!!"—with either the cane pole or with the fish—"Hold your tip up!!!"—depending on where his services were needed. Not long after, with Dad at the water's edge and Mom holding the cane pole, tip up, they had a big redfish ashore. That night, dinner included a redfish that hung over both ends of the largest platter Mom owned.

Mom enjoyed remembering that story and she shivered each time she told the story of snakes falling out the trees and onto the pier near her two children. Thirty years later, my sons began to have fishing stories to share, too. Some involved snakes . . . or worse.

One of Dad's favorite fishing styles was trot lining, which he learned from his father. I was in my late teens before I had the chance to enjoy that style of fishing with Dad in his beloved boat that he purchased in April 1968.

My first recollection of being in a boat with Dad pre-dated his purchase. He rented a Jon boat to use with his Firestone motor. We trekked up and down what memory serves me to be saltwater bayous near the bay, with tall marsh grass on the sides. The flat surface of the water helped Dad, a companion and me to scoot along, though five and one-half horsepower doesn't push anything along quickly when people are in the boat. I don't recall who was in the boat with us, though I believe it was my brother who was in town between his jobs and journeys.

Three people and five horses don't make for speed, but they provided fun. We caught nothing that day—somewhat of a McInnis tradition in itself—but we netted fun which is also a tradition that continues to this day. This trip also provided me my first experience with a boat catching a mullet. I couldn't wait to show the fish to Mom but we forgot it in the boat.

Mullet jump great heights and distances for no verifiable reasons. Explanations range from fish boredom to parasite cleaning to survival. "If a mullet jumps more than three times in a row, it is avoiding getting eaten," the old adage declares. Whatever the cause, they always entertain children, particularly when they inadvertently jump in the boat. Their entertainment value diminishes greatly when they smack you on the side of the head while wade fishing.

The mullet trip is the only one I recall of fishing with Dad in a Jon boat, though I remember him flushing out the motor several times by running it in a steel garbage can full of water. The sound of the gurgling water and the scent of the exhaust blend of burned gasoline and oil always fascinated me. Since he cleaned it several times this way, I figure he had adult fishing buddies, too.

The main adult buddies I knew of included Randall Perkins known as Perk (friends from the days in San Antonio), Hank Whitlock (a neighbor on Faust Lane) and Red Manning (I don't even know his real first name, but he was one of Dad's clients). I frequently fished with Dad and Hank, once with Dad and Perk and never with Dad and Red. The latter trips typically consisted of runs offshore for red snapper and drinking.

The day that I fished with Dad and Perk (Mr. Perkins, to me) was the day that I received my first bona fide, for me only, rod and reel. Until then, I used other rigs that Dad had, particularly a silver-colored Pflueger bait casting reel. But on this day, when Dad and Mr. Perkins picked me up from baseball practice, a brown Shakespeare spincasting rig awaited me in the car. "We're going fishing," Dad said.

The three of us headed to somewhere on the coast for wade fishing. Four and one-half decades tends to dim the memory, so all I recall is the new fishing gear, the stranded school bus on the shore where we fished, wading into the water to fish though I didn't know how to swim, not catching any fish, watching Dad try to open an oyster to eat and gashing his finger, and feeling just a bit more grown up that day because of the experience. I guess that is plenty.

I remained his primary fishing pal from about ages nine to 16. From nine to 12, we fished monthly or slightly less. As an accountant, he was often restricted from fun for the work of the tax season. This period of our most active fishing hooked us on bass fishing thanks to the Halls and Dixie.

Hank and Helen Hall of Navasota, Texas were some sort of kin to Dad, something removed, from my dad's mother's side related to people that raised Grandmom. Or something like that. I never really understood the relationship, but I did understand that they had a farm where I learned bass fishing, lure fishing and shooting a .22 rifle. That was plenty enough understanding for a kid.

The two-hour drives down back roads and farm-to-market roads from our house on the west side of Houston to Navasota combined comfortable quiet and fun conversation. I enjoyed both aspects. Sitting next to Dad as he drove Mom's light blue 1963 Plymouth Fury, complete with pushbutton automatic transmission, provided sightseeing and thinking time. The car had no air conditioning—save for the four-seventy system: four windows down, 70 miles per hour—enabling me to play airplane with my hand outside the window, feel the air blowing through my hair, and experience the scents of cut hay or grass and cow manure in the open areas along our route. It didn't help my hay fever, but it sure was fun.

Even when we weren't talking, I enjoyed thinking while with Dad. I still recall the hypnotic sounds of air and engine while "Abraham, Martin and John" played on the AM radio. Time to think and listen was not wasted time when with my dad. Maybe times like these influenced my belief that playing with your kids is a good thing, but being with your kids is better.

The Halls owned a washateria and convenience store-gas station in Navasota. The store's wood floor had gaps wide enough to lose your change if it fell out of your pocket. Dad lost his favorite pocket knife that way. The Halls were generous and eccentric. Cleanliness and Hall would never be used together in a sentence, God bless their souls. They would offer us candy bars off the shelf—about half the time the candy was white from age and sometimes had a worm in it; they would offer us lunch, prepared fresh in the kitchen at the back of the store—Dad declined but offered that I was hungry. He did that with a grin, even after a Texas-sized cockroach ran out of the sugar bowl and across the table at which we were seated awaiting our lunch to be served. I fell in love with ham and cheese sandwiches there, too. Mrs. Hall (Helen) manned the deli counter and would cut slices of ham and cheddar cheese off the block, then wipe the long-bladed knife across her dirty apron between cuts. She'd then dip the knife into a container of mayonnaise and deftly cover the entire piece of bread in one swipe. When done, she'd lick the knife and put it back into the container for the next use. They both lived to be 1000, or so it seemed to me as a kid.

Hank Hall endorsed the teachings of Edgar Cayce, a famous, if not infamous, psychic who died in 1945. His controversial methods of using trances to discover answers to mysteries ranging from health matters to the lost culture of Atlantis, created strong followers and just-as-strong critics. Hank believed. Part of his reputation included that as the man who would loan Cayce books and tapes like an apostle. Decades later I met an exterminator who grew up in Navasota. She remembered Mr. Hall . . . and the Edgar Cayce books that he loaned her dad.

My dad doubted Cayce's work, but he dutifully brought the materials from Navasota to be returned on his next trip. He dealt with roaches, unsafe food and Cayce apostolitizing because he handled the Halls' accounting (including organizing their "books" that comprised a brown grocery bag full of receipts) and he had a place to take his youngest son for fishing, shooting and enjoying the outdoors. Dad grew up in an agrarian world, and I believe that as he got older he longed for a greater connection to those roots.

Catching fish was always great, but playing and exploring were just as good. Playing on the Hall farm introduced me to Johnson grass, armadillos, king snakes and riding in the bed of a pickup truck. I also learned there to not trust Dad's smile and encouragement when he said things like, "Take a big bite, son. Now is the perfect season to eat those." I learned that there is a right and a wrong season to eat persimmons. I learned about priorities, too.

The fishing had been slow, though the minnows worked their hearts out as they swam around to stay away from turtles, towing red and white bobbers along the way. Dad and I talked, lay on our sides and enjoyed the lunches that Mom packed, Girl Scout cookies, and conversation. One of the bobbers went under. Neither of us moved.

"Should we get it?" I asked.

"Probably just a turtle."

"Yeah."

Lunch and conversation continued.

I still have a few of the lures from those days. A Heddon red head, a red and white Jitterbug, and two generic minnow crankbaits that I bought from an ad in the back of Sports Afield magazine. One of the Halls' sons started us down the path of lure addiction.

We were getting skunked with minnows when one of the Halls' sons drove up to the pond where Dad and I fished. He held a green wire basket of fish equally beautiful green. All the bass had succumbed to the temptation—dare I say, the "lure"—of quarter-ounce yellow Shyster in-line spinning lures with black spots that he cast with a black Mitchell spinning reel. I remember the incident well. Soon thereafter, Dad began buying Shysters and I used my Christmas money to buy a Mitchell spinning reel and a Heddon rod from Oshman's (remember the stories about Ken?). I still have the rod and reel some 40 years later and I still believe in those in-line spinners. So do my boys.

I still have a page torn from a spiral notebook with a poem written on February 10, 1967, three months before I turned 11:

One day in Navasota
We met our fish quota

We caught fish numbered 28
And all of them we have not ate.

Getting hooked on lures opened up new opportunities and ideas for Dad as he sought fishing opportunities for him and his son. Through a client, he had the chance to take us to a 1,000-plus acres property owned by Dixie Brown, a county commissioner in an area south of Houston. Full of pecan and oak trees, it seemed the perfect place for me to learn squirrel hunting, Dad figured. He arranged for us to get access to the property. The experience changed us.

On the first trip, we walked the property for a couple of hours, beginning early in the morning. As we followed the creek that had been dammed up to form four incredible lakes, we saw no squirrels but plenty of big swirls whenever we got close to the water. I took one shot, at branches, just because Dad said it was good for me to shoot the gun. The gun—a 20 gauge, single shot, Springfield—belonged to my uncle who died when he was a young man. And yes, I still have that, too.

After a lot of swirls and no squirrels, we decided to forsake the guns in favor of rods and reels. When we returned to the car, Dad discovered his broken rod tip (evidence over the years has proven this to be a common McInnis affliction) but he encouraged me to "give it a whirl."

I owned a great spincast reel at the time (was it Heddon or Pflueger?). It was incredible; one of the most accurate casting reels I ever had, before or since. Within a few hours I had lost a few nice bass but had also caught a half dozen bass ranging from three to five pounds. Enough was enough.

For lunch, we travelled to the nearest town so Dad could buy a new rod eye and get into the game. By the end of the day, the score was Dad three, me nine. I realized then the generosity required to daddy-fish.

"Daddy fishing" means kids fish and learn while dads unhook lines from trees and bushes, wade into water to retrieve rods and so on. Daddy fishing is about letting youngsters fall in love with the activity, not about dads actually fishing. Each of the boys have stories of "daddy fishing" with children—strangers on the pier, relatives of friends and so on. Teach a boy to fish and he'll gladly "daddy fish" later in life. After we finished fishing on the first trip, we chatted lakeside with Dixie and *his* dad. The dad told us about his fishing experience that included a hook being straightened out by a fish. He showed us the gold hook as evidence.

"Maybe I should go out in this boat," he said as he tugged on the handle of the bow of an upside down green Jon boat. A mouse scurried out from the disturbed housing and the old man deftly kicked the running mouse into the water. The rodent never surfaced. Only a big swirl appeared. Dad and I knew we had to return.

There must have been some grown-up complications that I didn't know about or understand when it came to getting on Dixie's property. For the million times, give or take, that I asked about returning to bass Mecca, we were only able to return twice. Neither trip was as dramatic as the first, thanks to some flooding and damage to the dams. But adventures still awaited us.

On the first return trip, the highlight came after a bass took my artificial pork rind on a pin spinner. The fish hit close to the shore and ran unlike anything I had hooked before. When I brought it in, the fish had something peculiar sticking out of its mouth.

"What is that, Dad?" I asked.

"Beats me. Pull it out," he replied with a common sense answer.

I did. The strange things belonged to a duckling: its legs. The fish had recently consumed the baby bird and already wanted dessert.

The third trip overall, and the last, included my brother. He was in town, between jobs that were, and remain, mysterious to me. I don't remember anything about the fish, but I do recall watching as Jim walked off to explore the property alone instead of fishing with his dad and brother. I didn't understand.

"Why doesn't he want to fish?" I asked

Dad's response addressed my question, but didn't answer it. Based on Dad's response, I had the feeling that Jim had changed over the years and didn't like fishing anymore.

I couldn't understand that because by this time I had been fully addicted to fishing for a number of years. My monthly subscription to Sports Afield had been arriving for a few years by then, and I had become an apostle of the great fishing writer Homer Circle. Not only a renowned fisherman who helped promote the boom in bass fishing popularity, he wrote in a style that informed, entertained and provided comfort. I believe he was known as "Uncle Homer" in some circles, or maybe just in my heart. He helped the foundling BASS organization, winning one of its first Classic tournaments in 1973. His monthly dose of folksy wisdom and insights encouraged me as both a fisherman and a writer.

Thanks to the joy of fishing and the knowledge gained by reading and experiences with Dad at various locations, I became known as a fishing junkie. My friends and I would even fish for catfish with little frogs in the nearby Rummel Creek or Buffalo Bayou. Fishing was fishing, after all. We practiced casting for fun with plastic practice plugs—competing for accuracy—and we'd have distance contests, too. I can't even remember the last time I saw kids practicing their casts in their front yard.

When I first wrote to Kathy Meyer, a young girl I met in the late 1960s on a Winnebago camping trip with Brian Atwood and his family, she forgot my last name when it came time to write back. Her envelope was addressed to "Dion 'The Pro'," which came from her nickname for me on the trip, as in "Pro Fisherman." Fishing has been part of my identity since my age could be conveyed in single digits.

Enthusiasm is contagious. That may explain my love of fishing. Dad always seemed to be smiling when he talked about fishing or was fishing.

On one of the trips to Dixie's—I believe it was the first—I made a precise cast to a stickup in the water about 30 feet from the shore. Fishing with an experienced kid is a far cry from daddy fishing where father has to chase down hung lures and lines because of bad casts and poor judgment. Or is it?

My spinner lure came to an abrupt halt almost as soon as I brought it from the stickup, which is a stick or branch sticking up in the water which may reveal a submerged tree or branch that provides cover for fish. I figured that I had hung up and tried to prompt the lure loose. My line broke near the rod tip leaving a length of monofilament lying across the water. Then the line began to move. It started to head down the creek, proving a fish had taken the lure. Dad ran into the water, hoping to get a hold of the line to retrieve it in by hand. A fish is a fish! The steep drop off prevented Dad from getting far, but I always appreciated his instinctive reaction to saving the opportunity to catch a fish. I fondly remembered that moment just over three decades later when I watched Cameron leap into a pond when the catfish he had broke off the line just as he brought it to the water's edge. Quick as a cat, he leapt onto the channel catfish before it could turn and swim away. Wet and muddy, he stepped onto the shore holding the fish in an arms-wrapped embrace that looked like a three-year old holding a new pet dog. A fish is a fish! (As I completed that sentence, Cameron sent me a text message to state that the fishing trip with Dion at Bastrop Lake has been a success: Dion caught one three-pound bass and Cameron caught three—two, three and five pounds. Dion is regaining his love of fishing and Cameron inspires him with his enthusiasm.)

Dad shared his love of fishing with me, and he shared it with me and my friends. Occasionally, I brought a friend of mine on a trip—although I usually preferred just having Dad for company. Brian and his dad joined us on the boat a couple of times, and Mark joined us on a trip to a sandpit in Rosharon, Texas. The man who owned the sandpit supplied sand to the man who owned the asphalt company who made the contact for Dad and me to fish at Dixie's. As a kid, I didn't realize how well Dad worked his contacts in search of fishing for him and his boy.

Fishing in a sandpit could be compared to fishing in a swimming pool of wild fish. They can see the fisherman before he can see them. Mark and I ran around the lake, watching the large bass swimming around our favorite lures that we tossed at them. They would look and move on. We caught a few fish on that trip. Bass are beautiful, sandpit bass are stunning—emerald green and snow-white bodies with fire-engine red gill rakers.

I learned an important technique on another trip that Dad and I took there. I had cast a strawberry-colored plastic worm out into the lake, across a sandbar. Just as I slowly worked the lure up the back side of the bar to the top of it, clouds opened up and rain began to beat down in a typical Texas summer flash storm. I jumped into the car and kept my eye on the worm, still sitting on the sandbar with its tail floating upward. The rain created enough disturbance on the water's surface to limit fishes' sight of their surroundings, I guess, because a large bass eased up from the depths behind the sandbar, paused to observe the worm, and then inhaled it by opening its gills and sucking water in. The rain had already slowed so the fish fight was on. Years later, I learned that the technique of leaving a worm still like that is called "dead sticking."

As much as Dad enjoyed pursuing bass, catfish or anything else worthy of a fish fry, he longed for a boat of his own. I guess he did for his entire adult life. He and Mom endured the ups and downs of business and life, and in 1968 serendipity occurred. His business and connections enabled him to buy a new boat: a new gold Hollywood, 16-foot fiberglass rig with a 65-horsepower Evinrude outboard and a Lil' Dude trailer for $1,800. Like a kid with a new toy, Dad ignored preparations and instructions before operating. Our first trip was to be a family excursion to San Luis Pass, not too far from Houston. The story that follows represents my recollection when I was about 15 or 16, a few years after the maiden voyage.

Is That Dad's Cap?

Once a family reaches the heights of prosperity that entitles them to have a boat, they usually buy one. When a family was born fishing it usually doesn't wait for such heights. Our family was born fishing. As far back as I can remember, my dad told stories of times when he fished with his drinking buddies. Sometimes they brought fishing equipment. So, being a fisherman, he bought a boat when we were able to handle the price of the boat and seasickness pills.

It was when I was about 12 that we got our 16-foot luxury liner. As any good sailor knows, and consequently no one in our family knew, a boat has a few bugs that need to be keel-hulled on the shakedown cruise. The sailors that took out our boat expected perfection from the beginning; of course ignorance helped in the sacrifice of the boat to Zeus. We knew that the running lights weren't connected but then only novice fishermen are stuck on the water at night. We needed our running lights connected. At least we had our life preservers, which we came to find out would have done us little good in the water we were in. On top of the other qualifications that we possessed, we weren't sure of how all the new-fangled equipment worked. But then it couldn't be so tough that an intelligent group of people wouldn't be able to figure it out once on the seven seas. Could it?

It all started out on a hot summer afternoon. Well, all Houston summers are hotter than hell so it had to start there. Anyway, with boat in trailer and trailer on car (we started out good anyway) we headed for San Luis Pass. Truly a fisherman's paradise, if you don't catch fish you can always try your luck at the trophy mosquitoes. Well, we all got to the appointed location o.k. but the first chore of launching the boat arose. Dad was the vet of fishing but he had never had to launch a boat on anything but a ramp; this was the sand. There really is nothing to launching a boat; just back up and slide the boat into the deep blue sea. Nothing. These salty old fisherfolks backed the trailer into the water and proceeded to launch her. So far so good. Well now we've got the boat in the water and on the trailer at the same time. All we had to do then was pull the trailer out and there she would be, floating and seaworthy, a part of the elite craft of the Gulf Coast fishing armada. The trailer was slowly pulled away and "voila" . . . Oh damn she's standing on her prop, get the trailer back! It seems that it wasn't a bright idea to put the motor down before the boat is placed in the water, or sand, depending. It was a beautiful sight. A 16-foot gold finger sticking out of the sand like Zeus was telling the fishermen what they could do with their boats of leisure. However she was already listing to port or somewhere while she stood up there. We should of known then that she wasn't fit for as capable seamen as us. How degrading. Twentieth century Phoenicians and we end up with a boat that can't even stand in the water right.

There is a theory that fishermen are the nicest sportsmen around and thanks to the truth in that, we are able to laugh at the mistakes and are not still having to be down there pondering a solution to our problem. After the people that watched us had had their fill of comic relief they came to our rescue. Little did either of us know that that was going to be the first in a series of mishaps. We had arrived there just after dawn when the fish bite, but we didn't successfully enter the water until the heat of the day. That is when the fish AREN'T biting. Alas, such is the troubles of the outdoorsman. Now that all the other folks were just coming in till evening we decided that now was a fantastic opportunity to get the rest of the fish. How foolish, that implies that there were fish to begin with. They probably died from hysterics after seeing a boat standing up. Well, in all our enthusiasm and innocence we headed out to bring in the evening's haul. This must have been around two in the afternoon.

All the family climbed into the boat; all gear was ready and water wings attached. San Luis has these currents that change the bottom structure every ten minutes. Dad hadn't been there in two years. And, we knew where we were going. With all the enthusiasm of a 16-year-old that has just gotten his license, Dad proceeded to find out "what she could do." Unfortunately, we also found out how fast she could stop; or rather how fast that bottom could put a stop to our glorious glide across the surface. It didn't take long. At least the water was clear enough to afford us a view of the amazed crabs that were beneath us during our visits. As a matter of fact, a hermit crab and I became very good friends over the course of the weekend. However he thought that we were dropping in to see him; it's probably a good thing that he didn't know that it was not our intention to be with him so often. He was pretty nice, kind of radical though. After about twelve trips to the nearest sandbar and realization that it was in fact getting dark, we decided it was time to hit the sack. On most of the hang-ups it was just a simple procedure of either my dad or sister jumping over the side and pushing us to deeper water while my mother prayed to every saint the church has ever instituted, plus a few. Then at about dusk we had met our match. It was the Great Mud Barrier Reef of Texas. As it grew darker and the absence of a compass became painfully clear we all became a little shaken. Mom was clinging to all four of the life preservers as Sis and Dad were taking turns walking in the ankle-high water. By the time that Dad was a little bit worried it was about ten o'clock and darker than Mom's attitude toward our survival. Stranded at sea and no more than ½ mile from the furthest shore. Another of the fishermen who has built the earlier opinion of them came to the rescue. Mom swore that he looked like a picture she had seen taken of St. Peter with a Polaroid "Swinger." Dad told the man where we had camped and he promptly told us that we had been pushing ourselves to the Gulf. Mom was 100% sure it was Pete then. The man led us to greener waters thru the valleys of darkness and eventually back to where we had camped. We had been saved from everything but ourselves, which proved to be our biggest hindrance.

The original plan was for the two kids to sleep in the boat and the parents to sleep in the car. That was the original plan. Since sleep is essential to all outdoorsmen's plan, we all tried to sleep in one of those cars that "make sense for America." Maybe they do today but they sure as hell didn't then. It wasn't so bad until the mosquitoes began to crowd us out of the car. At first we thought we had been on the water so long that it was already goose season; instead it was the 'squitoes that were flapping their wings. Today we still aren't sure whether we rolled down the window a crack or if it was one of the conspirators of the trophy bugs that let it down. That is still a mystery.

When the morning sun rose again, probably just to see what we were going to do that day, we all looked rather pale. Just like one does after giving a quart of blood. We probably had. The day started out great. The boat hadn't drifted away during the night and that was a consolation. After eating an outdoorsy breakfast of sand coated cinnamon rolls we were ready to depart once again in another attempt at nautical wizardry. This morning Dad felt like he had received inspiration on how to operate the boat. He had his chance to prove it very early in the expedition.

There was an air of determination to prove ourselves this day. Simply an air, no doubt. With the keen fishing eye of a Gila monster, Dad selected a place where the fish would come to us. After we had parked the boat at this aquatic Eden, Dad decided it was time to jump in the water; maybe to verify the fish were actually there. His jump wasn't particularly scary since from one side of the boat we could talk to our new-found friend, the hermit crab. Dad went over the other side. Never knew that the Marianas Trench was in a bay only a few miles from Galveston. There was a big splash when Dad went over but long after the ripples had died only a cap was to be seen on the surface of the green water. After Mom had declared herself to be a widow a face popped out of the water. Sure enough, Dad had managed to make it back to the surface. The sight of help was encouraging to him I'm sure, too bad he didn't see his cool, and collected wife. "Toss me a rope" he said rather gurgly. "Ahhhh, you want this one dear?" Mom asked as she handed him the rope, anchor first. She was almost a widow twice. The lifesaving worked so Mom only had to worry about the trip back to the car since Dad declared it was time to go. There were no unexpected occurrences on the way back to the car. Well there was one: We made it without a hitch.

Once back to terra firma it was time to bid all our friends and saints farewell. Thus we did by loading the boat back onto the trailer all by ourselves. Boy were we proud. And then we quietly drove into the sunset, just another example of civilized man making it in the wild on pure cunning and intelligence.

Our second family excursion was delayed when we realized many, many miles from home, that no one remembered the keys to the boat. We eventually found a boat shop that could make a new key, but we didn't get into the water until hours after originally planned.

Eventually, we got the kinks worked out of the boating process and it became a great source of fun fishing and an occasional water skiing trip or two for Molly.

Years of adventures followed, though most were compressed between 1968 and 1972. In September 1972, I got my first job which cut deeply into the times that Dad and I could spend together on the bay. There were many fond memories. Luckily we lived through them.

For most of our bay fishing, we launched from April Fool Point out of San Leon, Texas. From there, we could easily hit many of our favorite spots including Dollar Reef, a barge stuck on a sandbar or oyster reef and various hotspots along the Intracoastal Waterway. The waterway used to run about 50 feet deep, allowing the passage of huge ships as they made their way to the various ship channels along the way—Houston, Galveston, Texas City and Freeport. This deep water also enticed fish to navigate them. Most fish that use the channel are like the boats that do: large. It would not be unusual to find rows of boats lined up alongside—but not too close—to the channels to haul in the moving fish. And sometimes, one would find themselves alone. No matter the nearby company, it was critical to be able to move away quickly because the huge swell from a ship passing through the channel could easily be large enough to surf or to swamp an anchored boat without the freedom of movement to ride the large wave. It was those conditions that twice made me wonder if we'd make it home alive.

Keep in mind that the typical assignments when leaving a fishing spot included me lowering the motor and pulling up the anchor while Dad secured the Bimini top and started the motor. I weighed less than 100 pounds until after 1971.

On one beautiful fishing day, with calm waters and a gentle breeze, we found that somehow we had anchored in the channel instead of alongside. If the anchor doesn't hang at first, the boat will drift. Later, we figured that the boat moved, dragging the anchor along until it caught hold in the channel as we drifted over it. We hadn't really noticed until we heard the sound of the huge ship in the channel heading our way. Ships don't have brakes.

My efforts to pull up the anchor proved fruitless. The motor was running, the ship was honking its horn and we remained in the channel. I wrapped the rope around a cleat and Dad used the power of the motor to detach the anchor from its hold. Nothing doing. Eventually, that strategy worked as Dad moved the boat on the end of the rope in order to change the angle of the pull. We struggled as the ship honked and we swore we'd be more attentive in the future.

Paying attention is always a good thing in a boat.

The same venue where I learned to play Mexican dominoes provided me a laughable, scary lesson in how drinking and boating don't mix, particularly during thunderstorms that destroy all visibility. But, at least the mosquitoes weren't biting like they usually did when we ran trotlines on Chocolate Bayou out of Liverpool, Texas. When the conditions were good, we couldn't see at night for the thick clouds of mosquitoes that I scraped off Dad like putty as he checked the lines; the conditions this particular night made mosquitoes look welcome.

My dad and his friend, Mac, had set trotlines earlier in the day and dominoes games began and then the highballs joined the party and time passed and the weather began to change and the games continued and finally, Dad and Mac decided it was time to check the lines "before it got any worse." I believe we headed out about midnight for what should have been a one-hour, out-and-back race to the lines and home. With good light and clear heads, the trip might have been only an hour, but one of the major challenges of Chocolate Bayou is that it hides many offshoots from the bayou that run back to petrochemical processing plants. They look exactly like the main waterway except for the log barricades and security patrols to prevent trespassing.

Once we left the pier, the rain worsened. Once we were well along our way, the rain became torrential. Mac and Dad were a few sheets to the wind, and the wind blew the rain such that the visibility could not have been more than 50 feet, which is not a long way when clipping along in a boat driven by an intoxicated captain encouraged by an intoxicated navigator. Only the ship's mate, me, had not had a drink. I was only about 16.

As we tried to find our way, Dad called out to me to "Stick your head out the side to see if you can see something." There, without the protection of the windshield, my skin and eyes stung from the pummeling rain. To think I could see better by sticking my head out the side was pure folly. I grew concerned.

Up and down we travelled the waterways, looking for where the trotlines awaited us. Landmarks were impossible to see; it was midnight, after all, with dense cloud cover because of the torrential rains. Dad plugged our extra light into the cigarette lighter and told me to shine it ahead. Bright lights shown into heavy rain or fog only bounces light back into the driver's eyes. That was not a problem with our goofy little "spotlight" that used a flashlight bulb for illumination. A few minutes of that proved fruitless, too.

As we continued to get lost in the dark and the rain and the comedy, Mac called out, "Sharp turn, Russ." Dad turned. Then, "Sharper turn, Russ!" Dad turned some more. And then, "Dammit Russ, turn the damned boat, we're gonna hit the shore." Dad turned the boat on a dime, and I remember seeing the shore just a few feet away, lit by the orange glow of the flames coming out of the refinery stacks.

Eventually, we made it back to Mac and Edith's house. I had no idea how long we had been gone, but as we walked up the stairs to the beach house, we saw a neighbor at the door. He worked for the Coast Guard. He suggested to Mom and Edith that the Guard send out a boat to look for us because of the weather and how long we had been gone. I've never had a drink while driving a boat, much less with my kids in it. Fishing can teach many important lessons.

Sadly, we weren't able to keep the boat. I tried to find it in 2008, requesting from the state a list of its owners. The last names were not uncommon and many phone calls yielded nothing. I believe that finding the boat could have been hard if it had not been maintained well and showed its age—40 years. Fond memories are best left unchanged.

By the time I could buy a boat—a used Jon boat with a modest trolling motor and a trailer with two flat tires—my boys and I had spent a lot of time fishing, particularly in fresh water. We tackled carp in drainage ditches; bass in small lakes and golf ponds, creeks, bayous and streams; catfish in all the above; and, more. I was about 40 when we purchased the boat. Not long after, we moved to Albuquerque where it went totally unused for four years and the separation of me and the boys' mom came before we had a chance to use the boat in Houston. My ex-wife got the boat for Cameron to use and it has brought him much joy. If he writes a fishing book when he is 54 like his dad is today, he will likely be able to say "Yes, I still have the boat." McInnis men tend to keep things that are meaningful and important to them.

All the fishing trips have one thing in common. Unfortunately, that is not fish. We always have good company and random incidents, laughter and conversation. Cameron summed it up well after a wade fishing trip: "We have more fun not catching fish than others do catching fish."

Depending on whom you talk to—me or my oldest son, Dion—he either experienced the cruelty of his father or was simply part of a misunderstanding. Of course, the latter is correct because I'm telling the story. You can decide.

He, his mom, and I went to Brazos Bend State Park for a day of fishing. He was about four, I believe, and it was a beautiful day at the park southwest of Houston. The weather was perfect, bringing out park guests and park residents—gators. The park, although fairly new, already had a reputation for its alligator population. But, we were watchful and set about to bring in a few bluegill, crappie, bass or catfish. Dion swears that I actually aimed to catch an alligator, using him as bait. You can decide.

The three of us scattered along the bank of the lake. I fished from a bit of a rise, looking down to my fledgling fisherman and his mom. Norman Rockwell would have been inspired.

We caught a few bluegill or crappie—I don't remember which and it doesn't matter to either version of the story—and they swam at the end of a stringer. Dion stood near it, attempting to catch more while dutifully watching over, and playing with, the fish. At one point, his mom started calling out to me and waving. I waved back, but couldn't hear anything but "Dion," which could have applied to "I'm calling you" or "Look at your son." Soon she began to point to Dion while yelling so I assumed it was the latter. I waved back and continued fishing. I saw my boy fishing and smiled.

This is where his version of the story and mine begins to part ways. You can decide which is true.

Granted, it took me a while to catch on, but eventually I moved my adoring gaze from my son to a wider angle of view that revealed the large alligator in the water, just a few yards from him. At that point, I dropped my rod and reel and rushed to the rescue. The gator had been attracted to the area by the fish on the stringer and Dion stood by it. I moved Dion out of harm's way while the gator moved on, making way for the non-event to become family lore.

If Dion were telling the story, it would be a bit different. He would say that I looked from my position with barely a glance as I focused my attention on the fishing. Only after the gator ate our fish and then moved on shore did I respond out of anger for having had the fish consumed. By the time I arrived, the gator had Dion by the legs and my yelling about the fish enabled me to rescue Dion from the gator's grasp.

You can decide.

We lived in the Mission Bend area on the far west side of Houston from 1979 to 1994, leaving when the boys were 13, 9 and 2. During that time we fished at Brazos Bend, crabbed at the Galveston jetties, and fished wherever our activities took us. We even tackled carp in the drainage creeks that ran through the subdivision. A light rod and bait of crushed bran flakes soaked in Big Red soda made for fun trips within walking distance of home.

In 1994, we moved to Huntsville, Texas when I began working at Sam Houston State University. We lived in the Elkins Lake development that had three lakes, abutted Huntsville State Park that holds Lake Raven, and my job gave me access to the university's ranch and its ponds. Fishing was not hard to come by.

We fished the three main lakes of the development and a couple of the golf ponds when we could. The largest golf pond bass weighed just over six pounds, but I caught him by accident.

Justin and I went to one of the ponds to try out his new rod and reel. We intended to catch a few bass, and then he decided to try for catfish. He rigged for whisker fish, cast out his line and left it. Before too long of a time, we noticed his rod-and-reel was missing. Something had dragged it into the lake—a catfish or a turtle. At any rate, it sat on the bottom of the pond somewhere and not on the shore where it belonged.

Fall in Huntsville: not cold, but the water was definitely not wading or swimming temperature. But a new rod is a new rod, so I donned waders and grabbed a heavy rake with the intention of trekking into the pond and raking the bottom until it snagged the rig. The journey did not last long thanks to the very steep incline. Only a few steps into the pond, and water already flowed over the top of the waders. The chest waders. Never mind that I didn't know how to swim . . . the water was cold! As I stood in the water, with Justin and his mom on the bank, and residents and passersby watching in amusement, I had to laugh at the sight. It appeared that I was wade fishing with a rake. Talk about optimism!

The rake solution attempt lasted mere minutes. My next solution consisted of tossing a half-ounce slab spoon and dragging it along the bottom slowly in hopes of it snagging something on the rod—eyes, line, reel handle, anything. As I reeled in the spoon, it seemed to catch on something that was still able to move—meaning I didn't have a tree stump or rock—and I felt confident that the solution would yield results. The lure then began to move more quickly on its own, not like a snagged rod at all. It continued to move until I brought it ashore: a six-pound bass. We had a story, but never found the rod.

The golf ponds served us well, even if one of them ate a new fishing rig. As many days as possible, Justin and I would stop at one of the ponds for 10 to 15 minutes of fishing on the way to school and work. Most people were amused—if not also a bit jealous—at the sight of a man in a suit and cowboy boots with his 13-year old son at a pond in the morning.

Fishing before work provided a great way to start the day. Sometimes, it provided remedy afterwards.

After one particularly frustrating day, I drove straight from work to a walk-in spot at the second lake in the development. I took off my coat, put on waders and headed to a good casting spot. Half an hour of casting put the day back in good order.

The next morning, my assistant director, Beth, asked if I had fished after work the day before. "Yes," I replied.

She explained that her husband had seen a man in dress shirt, tie and waders head into the lake and he thought it looked like me. I believe he wanted verification of my sanity, or insanity.

Elkins Lake provided many great fishing experiences and stories, all of which expand over time. You can count on the truth from me, of course.

A creek joined lakes one and two, and a dam separated lake two from three.

In our first week in our house there, I took the boys to the dam to fish. We cast lures along the shoreline and I hung up on some weeds. A quick jerk of the rod proved too much for the weeds. The lure came free. It came free, flying toward me at mach two. Almost instantly, I had a lure with two of its three treble hooks in my arm. This concluded our first fishing expedition. We went home.

"What did you catch?" their mom queried as we drove up to the house with car windows open.

"A hundred fifty pounder. Me."

I extended my arm so she and the neighbor could see the lure attached to my arm.

Luckily, the emergency room doctor understood the importance of not ruining a good surface lure and removed it without having to destroy the hooks or barbs. It appeared that he had much experience in hook removal and fish-story telling. He ended up being my physician for a couple of years.

The lakes held bluegill, crappie, bass, catfish, white bass and carp. And plenty of water moccasin snakes. It was a great place to raise kids, fish and play. Little did we know why some of the hot spots were thus.

We learned early on why some places yielded good size crappies—sunken Christmas trees served as cover for crappie and their forage, a successful strategy in many lakes. The boys also found a catfish honey hole only a short walk from our house.

We had about a year of successful fishing at the magic spot when a city employee knocked on our door. He requested access to our bathroom. It seems there were a few houses on the street that were never connected to the city's sewage lines and they needed to run some tests to confirm their suspicions. He only needed to put some dye in our toilet and flush a few times, he said. We agreed and the evidence proved that the houses in question had become fish feeders. With each flush, the water ran into the storm sewer system and then eventually found its way into the lake. The water and all its contents flowed into the lake where the boys found their great catfish successes. We sought new locales afterwards.

The environment of lakes, creeks, trees, wildlife and fish held the boys' attention. They would disappear each morning, returning for snacks or supplies, and then come home to roost in the evening. Dion rode his bike to explore every inch of shoreline for possible fishing opportunities. Justin would sometime fish alone or with his older brother, and would often seek adventure in the woods, including climbing trees. Cameron played outdoors, in the yard, sandbox or neighboring wooded areas.

One day, Barbara and I returned from errands to find a black metal garbage can with a plywood board for a cover, sitting in the middle of the driveway. We didn't own a black metal garbage can, though the wood looked like something from my stash in the garage. Dion stood next to the can with a broad smile, seams bursting with pride.

He removed the plywood to reveal a by-then-dead carp that weighed a verifiable 15 pounds. As he revealed the details of his adventure, we learned that he caught it on his microlight spinning gear and the tail of the catch dragged on the ground as he rode his bike home with the catch, and everyone looked and smiled, and he didn't think he was going to be able to catch it but he did, and he didn't have any place to put the fish to show us, and he contrived this solution so he could keep it but we wouldn't see it before he was ready to show us, and . . . And that's about it.

Not all solo adventures got the same encouraging response from the neighbors. I can only imagine that the boys' fun sometimes met with bewilderment from others, about half of whom were retired.

During one of Dion's outings on the first lake's dam, he snagged one of my lures that he borrowed. It hung on a submerged tree that invariably provided a nice fish or two. He believed the lure was one from my youth. Remember, McInnis men value memory items. Dion felt the need to recover the lure at almost any cost; he opted to step out onto the tree trunk which laid out into the water like a slightly submerged bridge to nowhere. After a few steps, he realized the lure was too far out, and then stripped to his "tighty whiteys," enabling him to walk further out onto the tree. More than a few nearby neighbors witnessed the rescue.

He shared the story of his heroics upon returning home. Being the storyteller that he is, we received a full, dramatic telling of the adventure to save the lure of his dad's youth. I thanked him for his efforts and concern, and then clarified that the lure was *like* one that I owned as a kid. The lure was not the memory-invoking antique that he thought it was.

When neighbors watched McInnis fishing antics, it didn't always involve just the kids.

A friend gave me a small outboard engine to use on the Jon boat if we wanted to repair it. The motor didn't run, but he felt confident that it could be brought back to life. The old Sears engine, reminded me of my dad's Firestone that I recalled from my youth. Keep in mind that one of Firestone's claims to fame in outboard motor history is being the first producer of a line of shiftable engines. Anyway, I took up the friend's offer.

I ordered a manual from Sears and the necessary parts to begin repairs. I disassembled it, cleaned the parts, replaced gear fluids and reassembled it. I tested it in the black metal garbage can that Dion had used for his carp. The engine ran smoothly, accelerated well, and the exhaust blew strongly into the water.

The day came for us to test the motor on the boat. We chose the second lake. As I recall, it was Justin, Cameron and I who attempted the maiden voyage of the repaired motor on the fixer-upper boat. Everything went smoothly, from backing the trailer down the ramp, to releasing the boat and holding position while I parked the car and trailer. I returned to a boat that was ready to prove itself and two young boys eager for a ride at something faster than our modest trolling motor provided us. Their smiles broadened when the motor started quickly, easily. It ran well, the exhaust gurgled and a robust water stream revealed that the cooling system worked well. I shifted gears to back away from the shore. It popped back out of gear. The breeze blew us slowly away from shore as the motor ran smoothly, and revved ferociously in neutral. It couldn't shift. So much for being reminiscent of Dad's Firestone and Firestone's legacy to outboard motordom. It was pretty embarrassing, and got worse.

As I contemplated the clutch problem, with the engine running magnificently, the boat began to move against the wind. I looked up to see Justin—ten years old and slight of build—paddling the boat. The McInnis nautical wizards were being paddled by a lad while the motor roared with confidence. The irony and embarrassment became too much to bear and then became another laughable McInnis fishing moment.

I killed the motor and used the trolling motor to get us back to shore where we belonged. We still have the Sears motor in parts in two boxes, but we never got it to stay in gear. We moved to New Mexico before I reassembled it after the second or third try to fix the clutch mechanism.

The location of the laughable boat launch also served as the site of my greatest "one that got away" story while in Huntsville.

It was late afternoon when Cameron, Justin and I took to fishing for carp from the bank. We had seen monsters moving through the creek and in the lake where the creek flowed in. Fishing didn't go well, so the boys set about playing, throwing stones, climbing trees and doing other boy things. Well before sunset, a solid hit on my carp bait provoked mental images of bringing in a big one. Hanging a large carp is akin to snagging the Space Shuttle crawler that transports the shuttle to the launch pad—powerful but slow. There's no need to be in a hurry when you're the strongest thing in the lake. And being hooked is not that much to worry about. The long, slow fight was on.

Eventually, daylight became dusk and Barbara came to get the boys after I called to say that I couldn't get them home on time because of the situation. Justin returned home and Cameron hung around for the activity. I had asked Barbara to bring my MagLite flashlight, a five-battery wonder. As I held tight to the rod and watched the line move from open water to lily pads, at one point coming straight toward me which enabled me to gather a lot of line,

I occasionally shone the light to where the line disappeared into the water. Every time I doubted that I could actually have something on the line, it would begin to move slowly to a new spot. After a few trips from the lily pads to the open water and back, it settled in at the pads. I again begin to doubt that anything would stay on the line for that long—it was over an hour at that point—and asked Cameron to take over flashlight duty. He was five and proud to be part of the adventure. Just beyond where the line entered the water, a fish tail moved slowly, not unlike a tailing redfish in the bays. It moved slowly and Cameron tried to keep the light on the target. It moved a bit; I hung on. It moved a bit; I hung on. The process continued, straining the 12-pound test line and my patience.

This continued for another 30 minutes before my impatience overtook my decision making, and I put too much additional strain on the line in hopes of "encouraging" the fish to move from its nose down, tail up position at the bottom of the plants. Snap.

Throughout the ordeal, Cameron occupied himself while waiting, except for the times that I needed him to help with the light. He talked at times and left his dad to the dilemma at hand other times. Again, we had no fish, but a good fish story. At that time, he had not yet fallen in love with fishing.

One of the benefits of being an administrator at Sam Houston State University was that of having access to the university's ranch and its five lakes for fishing. We had many good times there.

Dion never objected to going to the fish if they wouldn't come to him. The largest bluegill that any of us has ever caught was Dion's at the ranch's "big lake," the favorite spot of the former owner who donated it to the university, and her deceased husband.

Dion again used his microlight rig to ply the open spots of a sunken tree that had been felled on the dam. It provided perfect structure for all types of fish. As Dion worked his lure amidst the complexity of branches and twigs, something big took hold of his offering and soon entangled itself on a number of the wood obstructions. Somehow, he kept sufficient tension on the line as he walked out on a tree trunk, kept his balance and encouraged the fish's movements until he had led it to freeing itself. Minutes later the fish was in: a beauty! I witnessed the action from about 50 yards away and marveled at his patience, persistence and ultimate success. Watching one's sons fish reveals a lot about them personally and how they live their lives.

The ranch had a reputation for water moccasins—in fact, one pond was affectionately known as "Moccasin Lake," but that's another story—so walking out onto the tree may not have been the best plan of action, but the move was thought out and executed carefully, and proved successful. Besides, smart and fishing don't always go together. Such is life.

On one trip to the ranch with the boys, I decided to drive our Taurus closer to the pond despite possibly soggy conditions from recent rains. The lake could not be accessed by road, like the "big lake," and I wanted to get as close as possible. "As possible" and "as desired" were not the same.

I managed to get the car stuck deep quite quickly. As the boys laughed, I pondered. I walked to the dirt road that ran the mile-plus from the front of the ranch to the back. As I headed across the pasture to the road, I wondered how I would explain my predicament to whoever came by—one of the paid staff or one of the university students who worked the ranch. I needed an answer quickly; I saw dust coming up from the road and heard the rattling sounds of a truck pulling a cattle trailer. The clatter and dust drew closer, and I arrived to the side of the road a minute or so before the truck came by. The driver stopped.

"Yes?" he asked as I stood with an obvious look of someone needing some assistance. He smiled as he waited for an answer.

I smiled, pointed to the burgundy colored car somewhat visible in the tall grasses, and then to my t-shirt. Across my chest were words that needed no explanation: "Stupid is as stupid does . . . . Forrest Gump." He laughed and promised to get us out after he returned the trailer. Eventually, he got us out, I gave him the cash I had—which was probably enough for a case of beer—and the McInnis men had a new fishing story.

Most everyone knows that fishing matters to me. In fact, when the University of New Mexico worked to persuade me to leave my beloved Texas for a job there, a former colleague who worked there gave me a book to help plead their case. The book was "Fishing New Mexico." The dean also tackled the challenge by encouraging me. "Perhaps you're not familiar with New Mexico," he said. "We have a lot of beaches." Pause . . . "Just no ocean." I accepted a job there in 1997.

Fishing in New Mexico failed to catch my interest and attention like it did in Texas. One of my colleagues tried to cheer me up with stories about his wife's fly fishing trips. "There are some great 9-inch rainbows up on the Jemez (River)," he said with a smile of encouragement. I explained that on my last fishing trip at the university ranch in Texas, I used 12-inch artificial worms so a nine-inch fish didn't entice me much.

The boys and I tried fishing drains and lakes in New Mexico. The former runs throughout the area, bringing water to areas for irrigation and they hold small bass and an occasional trout. We gained a lot of laughs and a few fish with our fishing adventures in the Albuquerque area. Justin proved, too, that the elegant cast of a fly fisherman can sound like the crack of a bullwhip worked by a cowboy. Of course, it's not supposed to.

Our first fishing trip in New Mexico occurred before Cameron was born and long before we lived in the state. Justin was about two, meaning Dion was five or so, when we took a trip to stay in a cabin in the Sangre de Cristo Mountains. All comments about small trout aside, New Mexico provides incredibly beautiful terrains and magnificent light to see it (or photograph it). It is because of this trip that the offer to live in New Mexico was actually well received.

The cabin was rustic, the trees were lush, the air was clean, and a stream ran outside our back window. There is no more beautiful or natural a sound to wake up to than that of horses clopping across the stones, blending the sounds of water, hooves on rocks, and splashing. We awoke each morning for a week that way. And each day, I spent at least some time fishing. With no results. When I sought advice before we left from the associate dean at the college of engineering where I worked, he said, "Just remember, fly fishing is really just fluid mechanics." That's all he shared.

Each time I asked the landowner what I should be using, he replied with "Use what you think they want. Think like the trout." That's all he shared. That is, of course, a very wise version of the fly fisherman's credo, "match the hatch." In other words, use bait that matches what the fish are eating.

I tried all the traditional baits, since I had a spinning rod and was not a fly fisherman. The fluorescent red salmon eggs and soaked corn kernels provided me nothing, day after day. Each day, I reported my status to the landowner and each day he smiled and nodded.

On the second to last day, I walked the high grass by the stream early in the morning. Grasshoppers jumped with every step I took. They moved slowly because of dew on the grass, which made for easy catching. A light bulb came on and I changed strategies, blending the two pieces of advice I received: "Think like a trout," and "Fly fishing is really just fluid mechanics." I soon had grasshoppers impaled on small hooks riding the water flows and disappearing into vortices that brought the morsel to a waiting trout. And I caught trout. I revealed my catch to the owner and he smiled. "Nativos," he said. "They have been here even longer than my people, and we came before the Indians." Years later, when we moved to New Mexico, I learned that those were cutthroat trout. I liked his name better. I also learned that live bait is illegal.

I doubt Justin has much memory of that trip, though Dion has some recollections of the moths in the cabin when we arrived. He hates moths and butterflies. He didn't care that much about fishing then, I believe.

Anyway, when we relocated to the Houston area from Albuquerque, we lived not far from where Dad and I fished. The appeal of saltwater is strong. While Dion lived in College Station and was unavailable for most family opportunities, Justin was the age of adventure and Cameron that of curiosity. The waves and its denizens beckoned.

On one of our first wading trips in Texas, Justin and I walked the surf at Bolivar Peninsula. Justin, with shaggy hair and tanned body, looked like a cross between a surfer and a homeless beachcomber. The sharks that he caught that day made for good eating and for re-lighting his love of the ocean. Before long he *was* a surfer, carrying his board into class at College of the Mainland so he could return to the waves after lectures.

Shortly before we returned to Texas, the family took a vacation in Corpus Christi, Texas. That helped stimulate our interest in the ocean. Again, few fish were caught but there were plenty of stories. I wrote this after the trip.

The packing for the family vacation could easily have sounded something like this: socks, underwear, fishing equipment, camera, food, drinks, games, maps, swimming suits and humor. While many family vacations are organized to see the world with wide-open eyes, this trip showed us our home of Texas through eyes squinted in laughter.

Timing, as they say, is everything. It is not the words that are necessarily the seeds of laughter, but the time and place. Perhaps the greatest thing about the trip is recalling laughing so much. Not that I recall all the circumstances, but recalling laughing at every location, every site and every activity.

It's a big day for the older McInnis boys, me and my two oldest sons. We're booking an offshore trip on one of those charters where half the people are going to get drunk and the other half are hoping to be part of the vacationer carnage to the fish population. Us? We're just trying to have an inexperienced experience. We've completed booking our excursion for two days hence and are set to proceed out the door. Son number two lags a bit behind to ask questions regarding what types of fish we can expect to catch. "Kingfish, mackerel and ling," the polite coastal woman replies. The mumble off my shoulder responds, "Yep, we're gonna catch little Chinese guys." My oldest is in fine form.

The cascade of thoughts and collaborative humor begins: the boat freezer plate full of short men in white coats, the fisherman dockside on one knee with his arms outstretched over a little guy as they pose for a Polaroid, the technique of "tlolling" to make the catch, and more.

Things continue to degenerate amid laughs, snorts and dry jabs at any and everything. Words stand alone as triggers to the funny bone, as do actions. Crabbing on the jetties by one of many marinas in the tourism town of Port Aransas has yielded precious little in the way of crabs. DC (Dion) decides to fish for seagulls, "casting" the crab line onto jetty rocks, waiting for a hungry seagull to hop along to the soaked meat and then "battling" the prey as it flies off with bait in beak. There is nothing to hook the birds, and the patience of traditional bobber-and-bait fishing applied to seagulls defies description. There's the waiting, the holding of the line and the muttering to the prey in hopes of coaxing them to a "bite." Then I hear a "bait voice" squeaking a tantalizing "don't eat me, I'm just a dead chicken."

Others don't understand us, for some reason. I can hardly imagine why. Perhaps it is the style of humor, or simply the candor of everyone's comments. As we all pile out of the van, we line up for sodas from the cooler in the back. I dispense Dr. Peppers to the clan, then hug Barbara to the sound of fitzing can openings. A hug and a kiss are interrupted by "Hey, don't put your hand on her booty." The six-year old then giggles to the sound of his own warning.

Maybe everyone laughed at his comments because of the activities beforehand. The bait fishing for seagulls. The appointment to catch ling, or was it Ling? The trolling for kids.

We left the crabbing site and proceeded back to the beach in hopes of a few more rays and waves before heading back to our vacation home-away-from-home. As we're driving down the beach front, in the appointed car lane of packed sound, we hear a tapping sound out the back window of the van. Trailing the van in the wind are a kite, its string and the fluorescent pink plastic string holder. Just as a teaser works in offshore fishing, using a hookless surface plug to attract game fish, the kite and string have no chance of snagging anything, but behind us lurks two kids as they race down the beach trying to catch the van that caught their kite.

Did I mention that this vacation of family laughter began on Father's Day? It doesn't get better than that.

There was a time when Justin believed he wanted a naval career. He would talk to anyone who had experience in the Navy to learn more about the experiences. He learned much about life on submarines, aircraft carriers and battle. His interest grew every day, until that fishing trip in Corpus. This was my take on the outcome:

Justin, Dion and I took a once-in-a-lifetime offshore fishing trip while the family vacationed in Corpus Christi. We launched from Port Aransas, one of Dad's and Grandpa's favorite spots while they lived in San Antonio. What looked like a very private charter for 10, turned into a three-fourths capacity group of 45 comprising primarily what appeared to be a church youth group. A dock full of young female fishers (of men?), suggested a pleasant trip of different types of trolling for them and my sons. Twenty minutes into the trip, the designated meeting place became the back of the boat, chumming with chunks from heads leaned over into the rich diesel fumes of clacking engines.

From his view, Justin was able to track the successes of his father's fishing. He saw several trailing ribbon fish, seemingly attached to the boat. They were. In the prop. I had lost three or four (it is hard to remember details in the utter excitement of offshore fishing) in the props. One time, the pull from the prop was so violent that a fisherman, two down the rail from me, called out the much awaited cry, "Fish on." I looked back at him, wondering what the heck he was talking about. "Haven't you ever seen a fisherman in pitched battle with a propeller before?" I thought. Tyro.

It has been several days, and I'm still waiting for the crew member to bring me another rod. Or another rod. Or another rod. (I told you, I lost at least three terminal rigs loaded with ribbon fish for bait in that darned prop.) So, I would go to the growing stash of unused rods and locate bait, usually placed on the benches where the nauseous would return to, and then get back to fishing.

Very little was caught that day, but much was lost: opportunities for two young, handsome, charming, chips-off-the-old-block to enjoy the pleasure of pleasant young women, and . . . a naval career.

Justin has long looked to the Navy as his dream. He has patiently pursued active and retired military types to get the low-down on each service. Navy was this young seal's call. On the fishing trip he learned a new call: "Dramamine please." Time will take him past the memories, but as of June 1999, Justin and the Navy are no longer bunkmates.

After I separated from the boys' mom, time with my sons was called "visits." This presented a profound change in concept. Fishing remained a way for us—particularly Cameron and me—to have fun together, discuss whatever was on his mind, and find reasons for laughter. We both needed all those things.

Humor comes in sublime moments. During a short fishing break on a trip with Cameron, Justin and me, Cameron snagged a floating branch and uttered words that are now legendary in our family: "Look, I caught a tree pounder." Laughter is on the line even when fish aren't.

Justin moved to college in 2006, leaving Cameron without any ever-present male companionship. Once a week and alternate weekends with a month during the summer does not a presence make. Unless you make it so—which Cameron and I did.

With separation and divorce debt still looming, I was unable to accomplish what Cameron outwardly wanted and I did, too, though more secretly: buy a fishing boat.

Being the creative problem solver that he is, Cameron explored boat options including inflatable catamarans. That discovery launched a series of possibilities. We found a new nine-foot inflatable Aztec boat and six horsepower motor that would serve our purposes, i.e., would allow us to get to fishing spots, didn't need to be towed or put into storage, and could be easily managed by either of us, or the two of us. It provided a good start.

Think of a nine-foot, propelled cork and you have a picture of how the boat performs in water. It has a carrying capacity of about 900 pounds and floats atop the water instead of slightly in the water like a boat that has a draft. The good news is that it can handle fairly challenging conditions, but the bad news is that it doesn't cut into waves—it rides them. Up and down. Water over the sides and into the boat. Did I mention the up and down part?

The break-in period for the Daihatsu motor required ten hours of running time. Until that is completed according to the instructions, the motor can't be run at full throttle. We decided to complete much of the running with the motor lowered into a garbage can of water, just like my dad did with his Firestone when cleaning it after trips. We used the black metal garbage can that Dion used to hold his carp a decade before.

While neither Cameron nor I have gotten completely seasick in the boat, we have been completely entertained.

We have explored bayous and creeks in our area; pursued bass, catfish and alligator gar. Our favorite use of the boat challenges us while bringing us to deeper water. We launch off the beach—preferably in Surfside, Texas—and have learned the most efficient ways to follow birds (at low speed, considering our modest horsepower) for sharks and whatever else we can muster. While speckled trout and redfish served as our original prey, we discovered that our equipment seems more consistent with shark fishing.

One of our first trips yielded several firsts, including first fish tale for the new boat.

Nine feet provides little space for two men, cooler, tackle box, net, two rods and reels, anchor, food bag, two boxes of sardines for bait, gas tank, and boat emergency gear. But we make it work.

The water was beautiful on our first trip to Surfside. Trout green, flat and accessible—that's about as good as it gets, particularly for a small boat. Launching always provides an adventure, a mix of Navy SEAL and McHale's Navy.

All coastal fishermen look for diving birds or bait balls. The latter occur when schools of bait fish explode to the surface of the water because of predators below. As the bait explodes out of the water, seagulls swoop in for a meal, too. These moments of frenetic activity present perfect opportunities to drop bait or retrieve a lure in hopes of catching one of the large fish below—trout, mackerel, shark or other speedy eaters.

During one bait explosion near us, we saw a shark fin move by the boat and into the bait activity. For all practical purposes, we sit on the water with just a layer of boat material between us and the surface. The fin stood as high as the side of the boat. Cameron and I looked at it, then at each other.

Shortly after that eye-opening experience, we encountered another bait ball. I sat at the front of the boat (too small of an area to describe as a "bow" with a straight face), while Cameron manned the motor to get us to good spots and keep us in the vicinity of the action. His job soon included "miscellaneous duties as assigned."

After a retrieve, I noticed that one of the two hooks on my leader had no bait and the piece of sardine remaining on the second hook constituted barely a morsel. In seconds, I talked myself out of re-baiting and made a cast with my surfcast spinning rig to a point less than 30 feet away. Another bait ball exploded as my bait hit the water. Almost instantly, I had a fish on. Or the fish had a boat on. Remember me saying the boat is like a propelled cork because of how it sits on the water?

The fish took off, stripping line from the reel against the tension of the drag, the bow of the rod that I held upright, and the added resistance of my hand on the side of the spool. Nothing that I tried could slow the fish and quickly I could see the end of the line nearing.

"You're going to have to get us going," I said to Cameron.

He started the motor, and retrieved the makeshift anchor of barbell weights. He then set a bee line to the fish, enabling me to recover much needed line. His straight path became complicated by the fish's decision to make a long, slow arcing left turn.

Dragging the boat, its tenants and gear, the fish's turn headed to a nearby boat. A woman fished from the (real) bow of the boat and watched as we were pulled by, or in pursuit of, whatever had taken my measly piece of bait.

"Sorry!" I yelled out as the fish's path soon entangled her line and broke it. I continued my drop-reel-pull cycle to gain control. The fish's left turn continued; I continued my retrieve cycle. As I recovered line, I saw the woman's leader and bright orange beads ride my line toward the rod tip. It looked like a monofilament bird nest.

The jumbled mass of hooks, bait, leader and weights collected at the tip of my rod. My line would no longer pass through it. I called out to the woman that we'd return her leader as soon as we were through. Then I said to Cameron, "Can you do anything with that?"

He stood in the ever-smaller-feeling boat, trying to reach the rod tip to untangle the leader mess while also keeping the boat on track. The latter proved tricky enough as the boat turned in circles with the fish's path. The circling pattern had me humming the musical score to "Jaws" in my mind.

"If this is a big shark, we'll need to cut the line. After you fix the other problem," I said. This serious fishing effort also carried humorous overtones.

I watched as Cameron reached to the rod tip to untangle the mess enough to allow my line to pass through. The bare hooks of the woman's leader swung to the motions of the boat. I tried to put out of my mind the prospect of Cameron embedding a hook or two in the heel of his hand or fingers.

He completed the un-entanglement without incident; the fight continued.

Now clear of any other boats and the fish slowing its run, we let the fish continue circling, each round slightly smaller as I brought in line. I again cautioned Cameron to have the knife ready, and put aside my thoughts of cutting at the line and accidently hitting the side of our inflatable boat. The mind can carry a lot of simultaneous scenarios while also working on a problem. All this and we had yet to see the fish.

Smaller and smaller the radius became. A light-colored flash in the green water reminded me of the underbelly of a shark.

"Knife?"

"Yeah, Dad."

Again I thought of the inflatable nature of our craft. Though the salesman and promotional materials promised great puncture resistance, we had no desire to test their claims in 30 feet of water with sharks swimming around. Nowhere in the literature did it clarify the differences between punctures from wear and tear versus knives, shark's teeth or hooks.

Closer and closer. Glimpses of white began to reveal more, eventually enabling us to see a splash of yellow. After a couple more circles around the boat, the fish surrendered and I brought in my first-ever Jack Crevalle.

The photo that Cameron took of me holding the fish now sits on display in a wood frame in our living room. He stuck the hook, bent from the fight, into the wood.

A year or so later, we pursued black tip sharks thanks to lessons learned from other beach trips into the gulf. We learned a lot, except how to take less gear with us. We learned to take a large landing net though the one we had showed signs of age, rather than wear.

One of the tricks to effective fishing with a motor that consumes so little gas and produces a top speed of about 10 miles per hour when loaded down, is to always keep the motor on and the boat moving to opportunities as they present themselves. Ever on the lookout for bait balls or diving birds, we travelled along the shoreline and then across a channel between jetties to get to where we saw bait being disrupted. Traveling across the channel epitomizes risk taking.

The channel exists to enable boats and ships to leave inland areas for the Gulf of Mexico. Tug boats, yachts, Coast Guard boats and recreational craft of all sizes shoot through this passage. Though they have to watch their wake when between the jetties, they are free to run fast and hard once clearing the end. We are obviously beyond the end of the jetties when trying to cut across the channel. We chug across the channel when we believe we have the chance, and hope that oncoming boats—either those accelerating hard after clearing the jetties or those racing as long as they can before entering the space between them—see us as we ride close to the water. Occasionally, we must abandon our attempt, circle around and away from another boat's wake, and then try again. The challenge of crossing makes for greater joy when we catch fish on the other side.

The reward for surviving the passage is usually access to reasonably good fishing. This particular day evidenced the value of the risk.

Chasing disturbances on the surface put us close to sharks time after time. Cameron caught the first shark, which we intended to keep for steaks. About three feet long, the blacktip was not huge by shark standards, but it did exceed the capacity of the net. The strategy to scoop most of the catch in the net head first and then drop it tail first into the cooler seemed foolproof. All things are not as they seem.

I placed the net in the water after Cameron fought the shark to the side of the boat. The shark showed no signs of being tired. It lunged forward, into the net. So far, so good. As I swung the net over the 12-inch high side of the boat, the shark broke through the aged net. It tried to get out. If the shark succeeded, it would be on the floor along with the cooler, gear and two fisherman's bare feet.

Cameron's creative thinking changed from "how to land the shark" to "how to avoid a shark without jumping out of the boat." My thought process shifted to how to guide its head through the net's hole without encountering shark teeth. Rusty pliers made smooth de-hooking impossible. The antics of de-hooking, guiding, pulling net web off shark fins, and avoiding the leader's extra hook became a comedy of errors.

The shark, pushing its way through the net, when viewed in such close proximity, conjured up images of scenes from "Jaws" when the shark lunged into the boat, chomping for its next meal. Something about being in a small boat exaggerated the size of the shark.

Guiding an upset shark of any size through a net that is snagging its fins while rocking in a cork-on-the-water makes for memorable lore. I wonder how the story will sound 20 years from now.

Cameron and I prefer the Surfside area because our luck on our own trips and the bull redfish caught on a couple of guided trips to the same area. It only made sense that when I thought of an appropriate bachelor's party for me when I married Kim in 2007, I would pick a guided fishing trip to pursue redfish. November is a pretty good time for that sort of excursion if the weather and winds participate. I booked a trip for the boys and me, and Kim's uncle, Hal, and her stepfather, Joe. All of us looked forward to the chance to hook into something big.

From the moment we boarded the boat, Joe felt queasy. By the time we cleared the protection of the inland water, seasickness became Joe's companion. And when we cleared the protection of the two jetties, we faced three-foot waves. The largest thing that Joe caught that day was a wave that came over the bow of the 24-foot fishing rig. We rode the waves, fought some fish and laughed until sore.

Dion has always been less confident with his balance and footing, and has taken a look before you leap approach while Justin has, since his youth, felt that looking while leaping provides a fantastic view. Cameron stakes a middle ground between his brothers' positions.

The wave-riding adventure provided a great opportunity to witness the boys' different styles. Dion moved from observer position to rod when it was his turn to bring in a fish. He moved with the security of grabbing the sides of the boat and the structure supporting the roof. Justin moved directly when it was his turn. Cameron blended the two techniques.

Unfortunately, Joe never made it to a rod, but Hal managed his way to fish-fighting position despite wearing a knee-high boot because of a foot injury.

Eventually the waves became too much to navigate safely. The guide said we had to return to the dock. On the trip back to the marina, riding four-foot swells, Dion held onto a rail and leaned over the side of the boat so his face could catch the spray of the waves as the boat cleaved them. He looked at me, his face dripping salt water, and said with a big smile, "I feel so allliiiiiive."

The guide allowed one last stop near the opening of the jetties. Dion hung a huge something but was unable to turn it from a long, steady run. After the line broke, we headed to the marina. Cameron and I held the last stop in our memory; it has become a fishing spot for sharks.

All the verbs of fatherhood are complex: combinations of verbs that form a single meaning—being a dad. Laughing, living, learning, loving all combine to form parenting.

Fishing is one of those verbs that combine many verbs of being an action. And it passes from one generation to another. That is why it earned its own chapter in the book.

For Christmas 2009, I gave each of the boys something from my father or grandfather. Dion and Justin received a woodworking plane and Cameron a wooden tackle box that my grandfather made. (In the interest of fair reporting, they did not receive them on Christmas—they received the promise that I would clean them up enough to give them a tool in their area of interest . . . they took longer to clean than I had planned.) It only made sense for Cameron to get the tackle box.

Fishing has always been part of the bond that connects the boys and me. Others have noticed.

In 1997, I departed my employ at Sam Houston State University. At the going-away event, my newest employee came to say that she wanted to bring by a present later in the week. I expressed my appreciation.

Robbie came by a few days later with a gift bag and a message.

She sat in the chair across from my desk and began to explain.

"I wanted to find the right gift for you. It had to be the right one."

"But the gag store was closed?"

She deflected my humor by simply shaking her head.

"I wanted to give you the right gift . . ."

She went on to explain that she recognized how much I enjoyed fishing with the boys and that she and her sister grew up fishing with their dad in the western United States. The trips included the three and a pet dog.

"We had to be quiet since we fished from a boat—all of us together."

She continued that her father never had a chance to teach a young boy how to fish. She and her husband hoped that their first-born would be a boy so her dad would have the chance to teach a boy his love of fishing. When their first child was born, they were excited at the prospect that her dad could teach fishing to his first grandson.

"I bought a special statue that exemplified those times fishing with him and the hope for the future of him teaching a young boy. Unfortunately, Dad died before he had the chance to take our son fishing. We kept the statue in a very special place in our home and each time I see it, I think of you and your sons."

At this point, I was silent and uncomfortable, though proud and pleased that the relationship between my sons and me was so obvious.

She lifted a gift bag from the floor, placed it on the desk and slid it to me.

"I want you to have this."

I was speechless. I reached into the bag and under the crumpled tissue paper as if easing a trout out of a net.

From the bag I removed a statue of a row boat with an old man and young boy aboard. In the bow of the boat, a happy dog looked out. A creel awaited the day's catch. The statue captured the complete scene of fishing. It also revealed a bond of time and love that transcends the years. The piece conveys the everlasting verb of daddin'.

To be a fisherman, you need to be a good person.
Cameron at 8, affirmed by him at 17

GROWIN'

Chubby hands
Too soon become
The hands of a man;
Son's touches
Become man handshakes
He's growing faster than planned.
Soft little hands
Once fit in my palm
And now they labor and play.
My son's hands
Reach out to their dad
And touch me in so many ways.

2004

As I put together the years of notes, clippings, drawings and materials that served as the basis of memory joggers for this book, it became clear that one verb describes what happens each moment, day, month and year of being parent or child: growing. Growth comes in stature—physical and integrity; in voice—tenor and message; in ideas—simplicity and grandiosity; and, in heart—spirit and love. Pausing to write now amidst the thousands of short pauses over the past 28 years used to observe the boys provides me a complicated vantage point.

After I had been out of the home for four years and was a half-year shy of remarrying, I contemplated how far the boys and I had come, both individually and together. I wrote in my journal:

My greatest job and responsibility is to get the boys on their feet and in possession of themselves for their lives ahead. They are the product of their environments—which will serve them well over time—but I also need to help them find, see and own their gifts and abilities.

Watching them grow over the years, has provided me great insights, and caused me to believe optimistically about their futures. Each step, each action provided more evidence of their development of children to men.

I feel like I am looking at the door jamb of the kitchen, with tick marks showing the ever rising height of the measured one. Is that the door at the house I grew up in, or the doors of the homes in which the boys have grown? I feel like I am looking at the rings of a tree trunk, each marking another period of growth in which the tree witnessed events (turmoil, fire, pruning) and circumstances (rain, draught, cold and heat) that change the shape and width of each concentric circle. I feel like I am looking at the tree from a distance, observing an embodiment of time's passing, though the details of growth are contained invisibly within; I see the roughening bark, the scars of life lived, and the fruits of labor, but the stories of growth's changes are buried within.

Growth comes from direct action: care and feeding; growth comes from intangibles, too: light and dark. With kids, they grow from the things that parents do as well as the things they observe about the parents' actions, attitudes and beliefs. Whether they choose to use their observations as examples of what to do and be, or as warnings of what not to do and be can only be determined by the passing of time . . . by growth.

Dad isn't around anymore, but it doesn't stop me from seeing him in me and me in him. The reflections from the mirror of time startle me. The images yank me back and forth across time and emotion creating an experience akin to that of a stuffed doll's arm flailing while a dog plays roughly with it: No harm intended, but a difficult ride at times.

Age creeps up on me like a cat creeps up on a young bird: Silently, unknowingly to the unaware, and with deadly intent. I see things in my aging body that I hope to stop and things that I must sacrifice to the tides while I scurry to move the things that I can take from harm's way . . . like my waist. And in those moments I see my dad and his feet, his belly, his balding head and in his neck that I liked to rub as a way of saying "Sorry you're stressed . . . I love you, Dad." I see wrinkles, gray hair in whiskers and hands that cut easy, like his as we worked together on a car, in the yard or on the boat.

Growth and the passing of time have always fascinated me, particularly how growth toward strength continues to become growth to weakness and frailty. While in high school, I wrote the following poem. My dad cried when I showed it to him, but we never talked about why. Seven and one-half years later, Dad died at the age of 69. Cameron has declared several times that he fully expects me to live to be 120. I will hate to disappoint him, particularly since my male lineage tends to die before they're 70.

Old man can you manage
With that cane in your hand?
Can you continue watching
The dropping of the sand?

Do memories plague you
Of the days in the street?
Do memories haunt you
Of the people you did meet?

So slow to walk
And feeble to stand.
Old man do you need help?
Can I lend you my hand?

Those arms that hang and shake so
Were once trunks of power
Does the loss bother you?
Has your life become sour?

Your steps are now in inches
Yesterday they were in miles
How come? What is it old man
That continues to bring you smiles?

Old man you make us wonder
Is old age such a sin?
Old man my eyes water for you
But, remember, here's my hand.

February 15, 1974

It is this fascination that draws me to books like Shel Silverstein's "Giving Tree." While some interpret the book as a horrific story of the boy's selfishness, I prefer to see it as a story of unselfish giving. Central to the story, however, is that change happens and it affects relationships. However, what remains throughout time is both love and need.

From the perspective of son, I see how important ever-present and ever-ready love is to one's growth, development, risk-taking and leaving the nest. It doesn't assure a perfect adult, but it sure helps. I never doubted Mom's and Dad's support of, and belief in, me. It made for fertile ground for growth, and when I see the emotion rings of my growth, I can tell those were good years for growing. I've tried to provide the same to my sons.

Watching the boys' development from baby to adulthood provides me as much insight into myself as anything that I have access to. Many of our concerns, passions, and other elements of our core are similar. Thanks to the good fortune of lives spent sharing with each other, I have seen them grow, and I understand better my own navigation from youth to midlife.

The seedling believes the oak is a huge impediment to its own growth because the aged one blocks light, takes water and catches the attention of others, until the day that the seedling becomes a substantive tree that shares in the abundance of life, now able to give shade, rest and resource to others. It all makes much more sense now at midlife with my sons who have grown from acorns to become strong oaks.

Some of my earliest memories of Dad involved his walk. I watched him come across the driveway and onto the front porch with a vibrant step, carrying a suitcase and a smile. I strived to replicate the walk, trying to figure out how to swing my arms the right way and in proper coordination with my steps. Perhaps I realized early on that boys wonder how to follow in father's footsteps, but must have their own walk. Many years later when my boys and I were chatting and I said that I was lucky to have the dad that I had, Justin replied, "We're luckier." I've been lucky all my life in the parent and child lottery of life.

Perspective changes the realities of observations, too. I remember vividly my dad's chubby little fingers which were so different from my skinny ones. After he died, my mom gave me his wedding ring that I wore for 20 years before it started showing too much damage. It fit perfectly. Without adjustment. I still think my fingers are skinny, but they are the same size as Dad's. Growth to adulthood changes one's perceptions about parents. No longer are they as big, as perfect, as larger-than-life as when we are young. And so it should be. Within reason, I have always tried to let the boys see the reality of my capabilities and inabilities. I figure it might help them be honest about themselves with themselves and others (friends, spouses and children), which can be a priceless gift to all involved.

Fathers are about hands. In high school, a girlfriend showed me a poem or story about an angel talking to a man about his hands and how important they were. Indeed. Pudgy or skinny, smooth or scarred, nails manicured or chewed, so much of a man's existence is lived out through his hands. As a youth, the middle finger acts a sign of rebellion, challenge or disrespect. If the gesture was deemed unacceptable by the recipient, the offending hand may be needed for defense. When older, the hands support little children's bottoms as they doze off on broad shoulders, or they may catch a little one's attention with a pop on the rump. Experience or good intentions direct those hands into hot crevices near manifolds to help a woman with her car troubles, burned knuckles being the brand of the attempt. Or they adventure into unknown mechanical realms with beer-drinking buds, bringing back to life a vehicle found in the classified ads. They tie fishing knots, dry tears, glue together broken toys and break unbreakable items. All along the way, the children watch.

Dad had healthy self-confidence, but could admit to flaws and mistakes, though sometimes grudgingly. It took the directness of a friend in San Antonio to persuade him to join Alcoholics Anonymous; he didn't stick to the process and fought that demon throughout his life. He didn't like losing, but he wasn't a bad sport. He was more gracious with fallibility in his years after my birth than before. I was lucky to witness enough of his mistakes to know his mortality and fallibility. Dad believed he would live to be 100, at least, but years of smoking and drinking stacked the deck against him. Dad was not a mushy guy, but he was not devoid of emotion either. He cried at two of my poems—the "Old Man" poem in this chapter and "There Are Two Stones" in the Lovin' chapter—and I saw him cry as he struggled with what to do with his mom living with us and being a burden and torment to his wife: "The two women I love the most are driving each other crazy. What do I do?" A few glimpses of humanity helped me realize that Dad was, above all, just one of us human beings.

Part of growing is growing together. It happens at all stages of development. And different wisdoms, insights and bonds come along the way.

Dion couldn't have been as old as nine when he shared an observation that taught me early on in fatherhood that coachable moments—for dads and kids—come at the most surprising times.

He and I returned from a Scout meeting, driving deep into the subdivision that was still being developed at the time. As kids sometimes do, he perceived that we were being followed and called it to my attention. I said, "Okay," and continued driving until we stopped in our driveway. Before we had a chance to exit the car, he said, "Dad, the other day Mom thought she was being followed and drove a long goofy way home, but when I told you, you just drove home. Does that mean Mom's a coward?" I said, "If you're old enough to notice, then you're old enough to understand." I went on to explain that a man's world and a woman's world are different, though neither is safe.

Children's observations can be about their world, or themselves; in either case, they indicate growth.

Cameron, who proclaimed as a youngster "I'm using my good brain," has always been willing to share his wisdom, just as his brothers have. In 2000, I began looking for a new job and sought the boys' input along the way. They appreciated being part of the grown-up process and I value their perspectives.

As Cameron and I drove home from a Scout meeting, I asked for his thoughts about offers in New Mexico, Vermont and Colorado. "I'd like your advice because you're a wise boy." What he offered could have come from a book authored by someone with doctorates, certificates and years of private practice. But his came from a caring, insightful soul, well grounded in common sense. He said that I should consider a few points:

"Will you have friends there like you do here to help you? (He was talking about having employees). Do you trust the new people and do they trust you? Do you like the new people and do they like you? Is there a place to fish? Will you be able to do the things that you want to do? Will the work make you happy?"

Cameron was eight years old. The following morning, as he, Justin and I prepared for school and work, Cameron said, "Dad has already talked to me about the job." I've had good advisors all along.

Cameron's input was particularly important to me because he's the youngest. If a job change was to come, I didn't want him feeling left out or that his concerns were not considered. When a formal offer came for a job in Vermont, I asked his thoughts about me taking a job where he would be able to play and fish safely outdoors, but that would require me to be out of town fairly often for work.

He replied that he could be happy there, but that I should be primarily concerned with enjoying the work because the family would be okay. A friend had told me that my family knew that I would make decisions that were good for them and that they knew they would be loved in whatever new situation they found themselves. "Anything else is gravy," she said. She was right. And so was Cameron.

From then on, he excitedly offered his thoughts whenever he heard me talk about the job search.

No matter where we ended up, I knew that we would be playing together in some way, shape or form.

Mom and Dad said that my coming late in their lives kept them young. While they helped shape me as a child, I re-energized them. I didn't know how what they did would affect me, and certainly didn't realize that my presence had a benefit to them, too. Even being young minded doesn't stop the body from changing however.

When I was a runner without a team because I got kicked off the track team in high school, I worked out with a buddy or two, or alone. Dad joined me for a couple of runs and though I laughed about his running style—short curt steps with arms held close to his body while I had long, fast, limber strides—I realized that I witnessed age, not inability. I knew, thanks to his stories, that he was an accomplished fighter, a great swimmer, and was capable of a variety of physical feats. The sight of Dad running amused me, but also informed and enlightened me: never give up trying, and accept gracefully the changes of the years. I believe that I am good for the former; I have my doubts and fears about the latter.

While I never forced the boys to follow my favorite sports, Justin became most attached to running. He ran track, though now confesses that he hated it. Track was part of the deal in school: cross country runners ran track. He loved and loves cross country. When he stood at the waterfall start for an 800 meter competition in eighth grade, I saw the similarities and differences between us through the lens of track. The 880 (yards, in the old days) stole my heart in spring 1971.

Now, Just as Then

Similar to then are the faces now,
Experienced, a little nervous, but ready,
As they stand at the tartan waterfall line
And their coach's last reminder is "Run steady."

Vibrant colors adorn lean, poised bodies
As final instructions are delivered,
The man with the pistol and the experienced tan
Smiles kindly, backs away, finger on the trigger.

Now, just as then, butterflies rumble
In stomach and knees and heart.
And now, just as then, all focus begins
When the man boldly calls "To your marrrrrrrrrrrrks."

Work-shaped muscles, sculpted by hormones
Bulge at the ready . . . desiring to fly

Tilted around the curves, on into the straights . . .
"Pull the trigger man, it's time for a ride."

Now, not then, the scenario captures
My eyes, my ears, and all my attention,
But I won't be running this 800 meters.
That blonde in the blue is MY runner, MY son.

"Sehhhhhht" comes now to the eleven runners.
The tell-tale rise in the starter's voice,
Is quickly followed by the order
That compels them, fires them . . . GO!

The blast of the gun makes everyone feel
At least somewhat like the exploded charge.
Groans accompany the driving of muscles.
Arms pump. Spikes grip. They stride with their hearts.

A gross of seconds later the young leader crosses,
A second for each month of his life.
He struggles and stumbles and smiles in pain,
Now, just as then, the race is the why.

Just to race was a sufficient reason why. What once empowered me, now blocks me. As I try over and over to begin jogging to get in shape and lose weight, I fight the reason. I cannot accept that I am running for conditioning; I have to run to prepare for the race. And that defeats me with pain and injury every time.

The 880 held my hopes and dreams, and it also vexed me. I had the speed and ability to run my goal of 1:58, but I quit the high school team over a war of wills: coach wanted me to cut my hair before putting me in meets, and I said "Put me in a meet and then I'll cut my hair." The standoff led to me training myself. I loved the race. "1:58," complete with split times for each of the 220s in the race appeared on the outside of my binders, notebooks, on scraps of paper. I had the desire, but apparently not the will. My sons possess will.

Justin chose to run cross country during his freshman year in high school. Houston area cross country meets are run in fairly benign conditions; in

New Mexico courses are much more challenging. The thin air of 5,000-foot altitude doesn't help much either. In one of his early races of high school year, the course took the runners through rough terrain invisible to the spectators and then along a road where family and friends could cheer.

The hidden part of the course went up steep inclines, down sharp embankments, and on sandy river bottoms where each footfall landed on sliding surfaces. After the runners came out of the most challenging part of the course, they hit the road of long, slow inclines. As I recall, they ran the course twice for the required distance.

At the juncture where the runners turned off the road and back onto the course, Justin described the event: "This is hell, Dad." Nearby spectators laughed, holding cups of coffee and reading materials as they waited for their team members to run by. Everyone understood. Those very same conditions that caused him to fall in love with the sport; it challenged him, made him grow, and pushed him.

He ran cross country in Houston, beginning in fall 2002. His junior year season did not go very well. At the district meet, he choked. There is no other way to describe what happened with his ability and competitive passion. Anyone near him after the event could sense his anger, but many may not have known that he directed it all to himself. We chatted briefly—whether this was to be a growing moment to set the bar for the following season, or a reason to give up on himself and the sport—and then I left him to himself. No one could challenge him as much as he could . . . not his coach and not his father. He ran at the state-level competition the following season.

A few years later, Justin encountered another 880, of sorts. While working for the Student Conservation Association, he came upon a large, dead tree that needed to be chopped down. He told the story with great pride, emotion and introspection as Cameron and I drove him home from the airport in Austin.

The tree needed to come down, and Justin had the will, determination and strength to do it; he also had the need to express through physical dominance and exertion his frustration and confusion that comes at that age, and exacerbated by his parents' divorce. Each day for a week, he chopped on the tree for hours and hours when not performing the duties of the job which included teaching high school kids about the environment while building trails and other projects that the park needed completed. When the old, sturdy tree came down, it took out a few young trees in its path. Justin felt badly about the unavoidable destruction and philosophized around the entire experience. He could have backed away from the challenge when the going got tough. He could have cut in a manner that would have destroyed even more trees with a different fall direction. He stuck with it, the right way, and still has a chunk of the tree as a reminder of exerted will.

As I watched the boys grow, I observed their various other "880s," things that they wanted and had the ability to complete. I watched whether they sacrificed to achieve it or realized that on their personal priority lists, other things would place higher. Over time, I'll see whether those things become part of their stories of joy or of regret. The 880 (now called 800 because it is measured in meters) continues to be a source of joy and enjoyment from my past. It also blocks my attempts to run again. It has presented another challenge for me. Time will tell how I respond.

Time tells a parent much about how their children respond to adversity, whether a short-term experience or a long-term challenge. Do they seek advice of others, expect others to resolve their issues, or refuse the wisdom and guidance of others? Of course, ideally there is a blend of wisdom seeking and independence, but always responsibility.

I've enjoyed the conversations that the boys and I have had on matters ranging from how to deal with a kid in school to how to deal with a punk on the job, or how to work a child's camera to how to prepare prints for an exhibition, or how to understand a crush to how to understand true love. My nature commands me to assume that they are asking for help though more often than not, particularly as they grow older, they are looking for advice and not action.

A few years ago, Dion called to vent about some situations related to cash flow, customer relations and negotiating the intricacies of managing his business' finances. In short, bills were due and money wasn't coming in and clients were slow. I listened for quite a while and replied, "I'm not sure what I can do to help right now, at the end of the month and all." The boys know for years that more than half my income went to child support (which I don't regret for a second) and paying off separation/divorce debt, but they also know that I will help however I can financially, too. It is easy to forego some personal things when your kids are having troubles.

A long pause followed my comment.

"Dad, I don't need you to fix it. I just need you to listen."

Moments like that remind a dad that young boys become young men in experience after experience.

Such moments of growth can be either subtle or bold, poignant or sublime. But they all add up.

Within a few years, the boys lost both their grandmothers. They exhibited great strength, generosity and thoughtfulness.

The death of their mother's mom came as a surprise. Her husband found her unconscious on the floor and the ambulance team revived her. As she laid in a hospital bed in ICU, Dion underwent an interview that would decide whether he would be able to spend his junior year in high school in Germany. He completed the interview and then came to tell his grandmother goodbye. The family agreed to keep her on life support until Dion made it to the hospital. We found out later that he impressed the interviewers and was accepted into the program. He declined it, believing he belonged at home with family during the time after his grandmom's death. About ten years later, he went to Germany . . . on his honeymoon.

All the boys grieved, and they had different perspectives. Cameron was young, and certainly saddened. A year or so before her death, she had had a tracheotomy because of treatments for throat cancer brought on by decades of smoking. Rarely would you see her without a cigarette in her hand or one burning in an ash tray. Cameron said a few months after her death, "I don't have any more grandmothers. They smoked."

Justin was fairly proficient on the piano at the time his grandmother died. She enjoyed coming to his recitals in Huntsville, Texas and had a favorite song. He offered to record his playing of that song and have us play the cassette at her vigil. He did and we did.

When the family asked if I would prepare and deliver a eulogy, I was honored to assist.

It was late in the afternoon this past Saturday. Things weren't going well at the hospital. Heidi Williams—our mother, mother in-law, sister, wife, grandmother—wasn't responding. The procession of good byes was beginning, each of the family and friends taking their turn to look in disbelief. I held our four-year old next to her bed in ICU. Barbara asked him if he would like to kiss grandma on the forehead. "No," he said, "I don't want to wake her up." Oh if it were that easy. Were it that easy, a long line of family and friends would have formed around the hospital, each of us waiting our turn to give the awakening kiss.

How could she create such a line? My perspective as son in-law is more than a tad biased and a tad under-informed. I knew her for only half of my life. But I never felt like the "in-law" part of my title applied anyway. Just like everyone else in her life, I was truly part of hers, and she a part of mine. She was generous to all; the only thing she didn't give me was an excuse to tell mother in-law jokes.

But don't we all have part of the story to tell? Each of you here today is part of this eulogy, in what you're thinking, in what you've shared and in what you'll share with each other later. She lives forever in our memories of who she is and what she has done, and we can offer her no greater honor than that.

We all have our stories to tell, images we remember and sounds that still echo in our ears. It would be an insult to the wonderful friendships each of us had with her for me to try to convey them all. We can only find out through each others' stories how it is that we all loved the same things: her feisty smiles and her joy-filled smiles, her laughter, her hard work, her . . . cooking!

Today she is cooking while Oma and Butch stay underfoot, and she loves it. And we're happy for her. Happy is what she always wanted each of us to be. She was much to many: generous, loving, hard working . . . hard headed. Always doing for others like her kids, husband, family, friends, friends of her kids, grandkids, neighbors, police officers, bowling buddies, bridge partner, woman's club and garden club pals . . . she loved to be around her friends.

All those groups are represented here today, and the family truly appreciates your being here. Sorrow is dampened and happy memories extended because of all of us sharing. Sharing the legends:

- *The hands and arms that could wring dry a towel that most of us thought was already dry. The same arms with the "love you" bear hugs and the warming wave as she said good-bye;*
- *Her feast-or-famine approach to raising rabbits as a child in WWII Germany . . . a style which resulted in a lot of dead and inedible rabbits.*
- *Cooking that was modified over the years—a pinch and a schkoop at a time—to be some of the best that any of us tasted.*
- *Her grandmothering style that can serve God in His programming of future grandmothers. She always provided all her grandchildren with attention, love, goodies, affection . . . She would do this quick, staccato steps feigning pursuit of the little ones. Who giggled more, her or the kids? And no holiday ever went less than fully recognized: Valentines, Easter, St. Nicks and her favorite, Christmas. Holidays weren't days, they were celebrations. She loved reading to the grandkids and the dream of doing that again inspired her hopes for once again being able to read aloud in the future. She can do that now. This woman who once wanted to be a kindergarten teacher is surely reading to a bunch of little cherubs now . . . and I'm willing to bet that they have heavenly streusel crumbs on their wings already.*
- *She was tough, durable and strong. Growing up in WWII Germany with her sister while her mom put in incredible hours to take care of her children while her father was lost in Russia, was not easy. Yet she was always spunky. Full of mischief. She never let her child inside die, and we all benefited. She was a model for "keeping your chin up." So much so that many thought she would pull through this recent trip to the hospital like she had done on so many trips to the emergency room, and as she battled cancer.*
- *She loved to share the child-like wonder she held for fun gifts, holidays, cold snaps and the slightest hint of snow. Mr. and Mrs. Claus were put to shame by the fun she brought to Christmas day and Christmas decorating. She built a sanctuary of laughter, aromas, tastes, and images that made us all feel young and kid-like again. I still wear the Charlie Brown sweater she gave me many years ago. My sons know the sweater goes on when my employees are getting too grumpy and they need a smile.*

- She liked the company of friends. Especially at a party! Two that stick in my mind are her 60th birthday some 22 months ago and the 25th anniversary for Henry and Heidi. How many of you always thought that was one word? One. HenryandHeidi. Neat. The anniversary was held at Barb's and my first house, largely made possible by the office studio conversion that half of HenryandHeidi built while the other half supervised. I was chief gopher. Anyway, I remember the surprise, the quick "Achhh" and the laughter as the balloons popped and friends cheered. And many of those same friends were at her 60th birthday. Forever friends. She didn't mind working hard to maintain those friends as they moved away or as the relocations of US Air Force life separated the Williams family from others. She worked at those friendships.
- And don't we all know the legend of the housecoat worn until noon and the shorts and open toe shoes she wore while messing around with her plants? Or of coffee brewing, slippers on, newspaper spread out . . . the hominess of the kitchen was in full effect before anyone else woke up.

She gave us much. And now we have our memories. Those will keep her alive forever. And we thank you mom, grandmom, sister, and wife for all of it. Frederick Faber said, "There are souls in this world which have the gift of finding joy everywhere and of leaving it behind them when they go." She is gone, and we hold on to the images of her waving hand as she played good-bye games with the children, to the sounds of her laughter and raspy whispers as she got tickled with the cold weather or mad at the ill-mannered people in the restaurant, to that big hug that said . . . "I love you." Well, Mom, we love you, too. For you, and selfishly for ourselves, we'll keep you alive in the memories you left us. When Santa comes, or lentil soup brews, or grandkids play in the sun at the cemetery . . . we will have kissed your forehead and you'll awaken.

We miss you.

The boys had more interactive time with their mom's mom than with mine. Long story. So when my mom died, the greatest of their pains, I believe, was for the pain it caused me.

Mom's health had failed slowly over time, and a few days before Mom passed away, all the family came to her bedside for prayer and the last sacraments. We had a chance to find a peace in the process before she died, which took some of the traumatic effect away. She melted my heart with two particular comments on one of my last visits. As I leaned over her bed to hug her, she said, "You'll always be my baby boy." I cried and held her. A few minutes later she said, "You and Molly are going to be orphans now." There was a peace, grace and honesty in her words that brought strange comfort, like when you aren't sure what is around the corner but you have a sense of what is coming. I suspect that the boys felt and understood that gift.

We cried at the loss; we hugged after I gave the eulogy that I hoped would help everyone in the church realize why we would miss Mom. And then we drove to the cemetery. After the service, as we drove away, Cameron asked us to stop. "I want us to watch as they lower her," he said, "so she's not alone. She knows we're watching." Once the coffin lowered beyond ground level, he calmly said, "We can go now." And we did.

Here is the eulogy that I wrote at 39 on behalf of all of us:

A week ago today, I wrote about my mom. I had visited her on Sunday to talk to her, my dying mother. On Monday I had to discharge a bomb of thoughts and emotions. The first sentence read "She died with poise." Mom's life was one of poise—calm and class in the adversities of living. A life developed during the Great Depression, continued through forty-plus years of marriage to a loving, adoring man who was a pretty damned good father but sometimes a difficult husband, and all the way to death.

Only once did I see Mom "unpoised." Is that a word? Anyway, Dad had just purchased a fishing boat. It was April 1968 and Dad had fulfilled a lifelong dream by buying the boat which would take us onto one of Mom's most dreaded enemies: water! We spent the first day on our expedition at San Luis Pass getting stuck on every sand bar in the Pass at least twice. Mom hated the water and feared it, never mind the two lifejackets she had tied securely around her. The responsibility of pushing us off of the bars belonged to Dad and Molly, my sister. I inherited my mom's water aptitude. The end of the first night found us heading out to the Gulf without running lights . . . Dad was lost on the water for the first and last time in his life. The next day we went out for another day of joyful fishing. As we sped across the water—deep, dark green water on one side of the boat and a clear view of hermit crabs on sandbars on the other—Mom was still less than secure. When the inevitable happened—stuck on a sandbar—Mom was uptight. Dad jumped over the side, willingly accepting his role of boat pusher. He disappeared, save for his trademark brown cap floating on the water. Seconds later, light years after Mom declared herself a widow, Dad resurfaced, sputtering some words about how deep the water was. From the water, he calmly handed Mom his wallet, new watch and cap. He asked her to throw him a rope. As she performed her backswing for the throw, Dad yelled "Not that rope." Mom was about to throw him the rope . . . the one with the anchor on it. Ah, poise.

Mom's gravestone describes her as "A Tender Mother and A Faithful Friend." I could probably leave it at that, but I won't.

In 1974, Molly and I gave Mom and Dad this poem on Christmas:

There are two stones
Simple rocks of granite
Which have held me up
And kept me at it.

Rocks so soft
On which to lay
Tablets of wisdom
And words to say.

Shiny and smooth,
But weathered on edges
Nonetheless strong,
Steady and rigid.

Slabs to lean on
When exhausted and old.
Foundation for a home
When winds get cold.

These enduring stones
Are part of my life.
Forever Mom and Dad,
Husband and wife.

What type of woman was this? Many of you are here in honor of Mom; many of you are here for her family—thank you for that, but you really should know her.

Cute, athletic and a great dancer in her youth, she married a man who couldn't/ wouldn't dance. She must have been something. As Dad described their first meeting, Dad was working late at a gas station. A muscular, cocky 20-year-old boxer pulling long hours. From the station he saw someone snooping in the house across the street. Grabbing a pistol from the desk, he walked over and asked the peeper what he was doing. The peeping Tom said he knew the people there and was trying to get their attention. Dad took the man to the door, knocked and asked the woman who answered if she knew him. She said "no" and Dad told him to leave and promised he would shoot the man if he did it again. Dad asked the name of the young woman who answered the door. All attempts to find out were answered with "I'm in the telephone book." Dad went back to work. He told his fellow late-night employee that he just met a gorgeous woman and was sure that she was the woman he would marry. Quite a statement for Dad at that time in his life. The woman, of course, was Mom. After dating three years, they married . . . seven years into the Great Depression, a life-affecting circumstance.

She remained active all but the last few years of her life, but shied away from the spotlight. She often cited her ability to do cartwheels with Molly's friends. Mom was 50 and still playing like that.

Marriage to Dad and his poor Mississippi family, living through the meagerness and tough times of the Depression, and raising four kids—and one foster child—across two generations were managed . . . with poise. Calm, steady, always supportive.

When we talk about Mom we see visual images. Snapshots of memories pass amid our tears and laughter. The things she did, the life she had, her experiences:

Snapshot—Her years as a child: Her Polish-Catholic immigrant mother divorced when Mom was two; her mom died eight years after that. Her mom, intelligent, able to speak five languages, and strong-willed profoundly affected Mom. At 16, Mom moved out on her own . . . met Dad at 17 . . . married him at 20.

Snapshot—A young mother watching as her small, 14-year-old son sat atop phone books to see out of the cockpit prior to his first solo flight. Jim was flying at 14.

Snapshot—That same young mother, making treks with Dad to Mayo Clinic in Minnesota and John Sealy Hospital, holding Ann, their dying daughter, on a pillow as she went through the suffering of leukemia before she died at the age of 5.

Snapshot—Behind the stove, making divinity that filled the house with a wonderful smell and that served as appreciated presents to kid's teachers for decades. And, behind that same stove, filling the house with the noxious odor of greens for her husband. Ugh.

Snapshot—Cool, calm intermediary, liaison and conduit between the kids and Dad. We each had our . . . "issues" during our growing years . . . have they stopped . . . and Mom always promoted "easing us through." She guided with a gentle hand and a faith in our principles to do right.

Snapshot—The mom who helped her daughter pull off Little Broadway in Memorial Bend, a play that offered attendees soda and homemade cookies and boasted of press coverage. A play presented by a bunch of kids. It was quite a community event.

Snapshot—Mom discussing with neighbors our totally destroyed front yard. It was the playground for half the children in Memorial Bend from 1956 to 1970. Having a safe place for kids to play was more important than having a nice yard in the developing subdivision according to Mom and Dad.

Snapshot—A warm welcome smile to all her kids after they came in from their adventures: amateur spelunking in the hills of San Antonio, scuba diving using homemade air tanks, exploring the bayous and creeks in the Memorial area, first dates while a protective father panicked.

Snapshot—Tender and courageous caregiver to everything from kids' colds to Ann's leukemia to Dad's cancer, from her husband's mom's slow demise to the grueling two months of her husband's death in ICU.

That is just a couple of pages from our mental scrapbook on mom, sister, aunt, friend . . . .

She was such a good example for us, though always modest about that role. When she commented on how well Molly took care of her during her illness, she was surprised to hear Molly ask, "Who do you think I learned this from?" She was surprised, but pleased, of course. She was always there—tender and faithful—with a smile, an ear and a backrub. Always giving others rope, whether they built bridges or nooses was up to them. But I don't think Mom would ever pull the noose if someone made it. Infinite in patience, she moved gracefully through life, taking the rhythm of life with the smoothness of the dancer that she was. She was never flustered by what God had in mind for her. I don't recall Mom ever blaming anyone else for any condition in her life, except maybe the doctors who she felt took her beloved husband away. Over the years, I have come to appreciate her ability to never blame others but to have the courage and will to say "This is my life. I will make of it what I will." In this time where people look for others to blame for failures, hurt and imperfections, it is nice to look to Mom as an example of someone who accepted life and moved forward with faith. She had a wrought iron spirit. Don't mistake her for rolling over for life, she had the knack of knowing when to draw a line in the sand and when to let the tides wash it away. The line was only to be drawn when it came to issues of supporting her family.

An extended review of this family's memory collection would show a seamstress, fisherwoman (with an incredible knack of fishing while doing crossword puzzles), housekeeper, and so much more . . . always done with poise.

I believe all of us are here today because of what she taught—always matching her actions to her words—on how to love genuinely and selflessly. How to sacrifice. How to give. Perhaps her greatest legacy is what she taught those around her: how to be a tender parent and a faithful friend. All of us here today appreciate her lessons. There can be no greater legacy.

Wednesday, June 29, at about 3:00 a.m., she left us. Greeting her was Dad, with a fishing pole in one hand and little Ann holding the other. After a soft kiss and a tender pat on the bottom from Dad—a love pat as they called them—Dad, Mom and Ann went fishing. And we're happy for her because we love her. Today, we aren't burying our mother, sister, aunt and friend; we are celebrating a reunion.

"Forever mom and dad

Husband and wife."

It helps to have a great mother and father when growing up to become a parent. I wished that I could have shared my thoughts in a eulogy for Dad, but I guess I had not grown enough in the right areas of my Self to enable that. I am sure that Dad knew how I felt about him, but it would have been great to tell the world, or at least those attending his funeral, why he was such a special father.

Watching parents in action provides great lessons in responsibility. Watching kids in action provides great insight into what they've chosen to learn.

We never spanked the boys, though a pop on the bottom was sometimes called for in order to redirect a little one's attention. A little dab of soap in the mouth served as a technique, but only for the first, I believe. I don't recall us trying that on the other two. Parenting techniques change based on each child's behavior and how the parents have changed/aged. Yet, they also learned early that actions came with responsibility and accountability.

Dion experienced more "college life" than I ever dreamed of. When I realize that I have only heard a smidgen of his adult life—scenes of which could have come from Hemingway scenes—I shake my head. And I nod, in admiration for his ownership of the full range of his experiences.

He worked hard for the monies he needed for college. Despite the aptitude to earn scholarships, he found other activities that he deemed more important, so the working, borrowing and scrimping became ways of life. And there was fun . . . college fun. His apartment used various traffic signs and a large wooden sign from a restaurant as decorations. Someone who came to his door because he had a bone to pick with Dion decided to notify the local police department about the décor. The officers were fine with merely confiscating the street signs, but the restaurant owner wasn't as easily satisfied. Dion negotiated for him and his roommate: pay the several thousand dollars of replacement cost over a few months and no charges would be filed. The business owner got more than he expected, faster than he expected. Dion owned the dilemma in which he found himself.

My mom and dad used an effective method of helping us learn to be responsible, not that we always were perfect in that regard. But Mom would say, "You will get in much more trouble for lying about things you've done than for having done them. Be truthful and we'll be fair." Neither Mom nor Dad ever spanked us, but we feared one thing more than anything: to disappoint their trust. I say "we," speaking for myself and interpreting some of the things that my brother and sister have said over the years.

I tried to carry the same message to the boys, and, for the most part, it worked. When Justin was about 20 or 21, he, Cameron and I went fishing. Most of the time was spent talking together or in pairs. I heard Justin begin to "educate" his younger brother in the ways of high school and the misdoings that sometimes occur.

Justin shared the story of the pick-up incident. A few years prior to this fishing trip, Justin came home after curfew one night because he had gotten stuck or had a flat tire or something similarly innocuous. His telling of the story was fishy, but we didn't grill him. After a few questions, his mother and I let it go. His conscience got the best of him and then we learned about getting really stuck, about the mud-caked clothes now hidden in the pick-up truck and about the Hitchcockian nature of the evening. Justin shared the full story with Cameron while fishing.

Justin and some buddies, and a girl or two, drove around in some back road areas. It was his first "date" with the girl he had with him that night (despite the night's activities, they dated for a couple of years). They ended up on a dirt road that had an embankment on each side. At the end of the road, a house stood in the darkness. Seclusion, solitude and darkness: Perfect ingredients for high schoolers to have some fun.

I don't recall what they were doing, other than it was not dangerous or illegal, except for the trespassing part. They discovered the dirt road was really a private drive when a voice from the darkness yelled out, "Get off my damned property or I'll call the cops!"

The kids jumped into their vehicles and attempted their escapes. Inexperienced and scared, they didn't fare well in the fast getaway department. Justin's rushed efforts landed him and the truck too far off the side of the road to be able to drive out. His cussing and anger was not enough to move the truck. Combined, the group didn't have the money to secure the services of a tow truck. No one wanted to call their parents. As high school boys are wont to do, they opted for brute force.

As the boys dug and pushed and pulled and cussed, only silence came from the house. They wanted out; they didn't want the cops to arrive; they didn't want to call parents; they were determined to make it out on their own devices. And some of their techniques were dangerous. Remember, high school boys.

During a lull in the effort, Justin looked toward the house and noticed a small, orange glow that brightened and dimmed. The resident was invisible but the sight of his cigarette ember as he stood on the porch watching was just visible enough, just present enough, to be a strong reminder that he was watching. And watching.

"I swear, Dad . . . I kept watching that ember thinking if it disappeared I would be watching and listening to make sure that guy didn't sneak through the trees to get to us."

By the time they extracted the truck and got everyone off the road and away from the man's house, the guys were caked with mud, the underside of the truck and hitch had weed-filled mud caked everywhere, and the wheel wells held mud spun on in layers. And they were about to miss curfew.

Quick attempts to clean most of the evidence, and borrowing someone else's clothes comprised the strategy to create the appearance of a more palatable story, Justin figured.

After sharing that story with Cameron, Justin said "The moral of the story is to not be doing what you shouldn't be, and if you do something you shouldn't, tell the truth and deal with it. It would have been so much easier to just call home and get some help."

Cameron nodded knowingly, probably feeling he had just learned about both how to steer clear of trouble *and* the kinds of fun that awaited him in high school.

I smiled, and added, "There is another moral to the story for when you become parents. Don't make the consequences of telling the truth so difficult that your kid would prefer to bear the stress of hiding over the unburdening of coming clean."

They both nodded.

Different milestones remind me how the growing process is going for the boys, and for me. Cameron was 17 and deep into his junior year in high school when he had to take again the Texas Assessment of Knowledge and Skills test, a standardized test in Texas that students take a few times throughout their education. He shared the news of the day's test.

"We had TAKS today. I think I did real well. We also had an essay component."

"I'll bet you rocked on that, buddy."

"I think so. I mean what I wrote was legit. I used big words and everything."

We both laughed. He is a good writer, so it is amusing when he talks about his work in those ways.

"And, you were in one of the essays, Dad. We had to write about independence or feeling independent. So I wrote something that didn't really happen the way I described it, but was from a lot of different times together, sort of. Anyway, the story was about you and me fishing and me realizing then that I could go off to college and continue to grow. To be a man. And, that you'll still be my dad and there for me. And always will be."

I am sure there were times that his confidence was not so strong. Nor was mine. When I made the decision to move from the family, I realized that I took the risk of losing my sons. A risk that made my blood stop flowing. Whatever decisions I made along the way were ultimately determined by what I thought would ultimately help them. It took a while to gain a greater sense of sureness about things . . . for all four of us guys.

About a year after I moved, Cameron shared some of the frustrations of being the 12-year old trying to accommodate his mother's frustration, anger and hurt over the situation. "It's not like it's not hard not having your dad around. But at least you're not gone," he said as his voice cracked. Hearing his honesty reminded me of a poem I had written less than a year before:

I'm sorry I caused you anger
I'm sorry I caused you pain
You are my dear, dear son
You are my rainbow after a rain

It's been raining a lot
On and around your ol' dad
Inside him, too, for that matter
And sometimes it makes me sad

These thunderstorms and lightning
Are scary from time to time
They are drenching and chilling
But hey, do you like my rhyme?

I'm sorry I caused you anger
I'm sorry I caused you pain
You are my beloved son
Hold my hand, we'll play in the rain

June 9, 2003

I hoped that despite the rain, my boys and I could find a way to find happiness. We did.

I could not be more proud of his essay's message. And I'm reminded of the role that fishing has played in the processes of growing. When Dion was about the age of Cameron when he shared the TAKS story with me, I wrote an essay called "Cutting The Monofilament." I found it to be both ironic and affirming how the consistency of our images and similarity of our thought processes make a linkage between us in the growing. The essay follows. Cameron's comments gave me a view from the other end of the "leader."

Yeah, sure, there is a process called "cutting the apron strings." Just as surely, there is one called "cutting the monofilament" or whatever string metaphor there is for what a father and son share. Either way, the process is not for the weak.

I look back to a time a few years ago. In a three-week period, my not-yet 16-year old son, my namesake, had experienced the death of his second, and last, grandmother. He had packed suitcases for a one-week missionary trip to Mexico. He had interviewed for a position among 300 students to spend his junior year in Germany, and he received acknowledgement of his acceptance as part of that group. That interview took place while his last grandmother rested in ICU waiting to be unplugged from the machines that kept her falsely alive. He served as a pallbearer and reader at her funeral. And sure, he had caught a few fish, caught a few young women's eyes, sank a few baskets (a lot of them, he would say), lifted some weights and shaved a few fledgling whiskers. With each occurrence, he moved another step away. Another nick in the monofilament.

I recall it all too well. Time moves fast, and memories linger.

In the next three-month period, he was to add driver's education, testing for his license, and quite possibly his first job. Flashbacks from my mid-teens crept in at the most inopportune times.

Old letters, old songs, and old images short-circuit neurons and the arc lights the memories as I watch him, as I interact with him. Our training drives at the ranch in Texas and in the subdivision (he and I having similar experiences to my dad and me), his good ideas, and the young man's accomplishments as he makes his way, nick the line near the knot that connects us.

In his next year, I expect to see time at a job, time with those interested in stealing his heart, time with those who enjoy his company and humor, and time exploring the world by foot and wheel. I can expect to see less of my son.

I have to wonder if there is such a thing as a parental leader, a leader similar to those used in fishing: An extra-strong piece of line or wire that connects the bait, or lure, and the reel's line. No matter how far the fish runs, there is always a connection. As we move closer to the day that he runs off to college, I wonder if my terminal tackle is ready for the task at hand.

A leader should be tougher, nick resistant, and capable of handling the playing of the fish. It is the best chance of keeping the fish for the duration of time that the fisherman and the fish are joined. The leader must be flexible, not brittle; tough, but not injurious: perhaps our parental leader is a braided line of love, patience, understanding and communication.

Fishermen go to great lengths constructing appropriate leaders: short, long, monofilament, braided steel, supple or stiff. No matter the size of the fish, there is likely a leader for it. And so it is with our children. No matter the age or personality, we construct leaders of various styles. Yet, they all nick.

Interesting materials make for desirable leaders.

Pool cues are excellent. Spontaneous games of nine-ball provide quick connections while late night marathons of eight-ball and rotation provide long, supple leaders that allow for substantial playing time with little resistance on the drag. Despite the rigidity of the stick, this connector flexes well over time.

Six-inch, flat, silver leaders can be deceiving, especially when they are music CDs. Fishing leaders are usually measured in inches; CDs as leaders can span decades. Lounging and listening to tunes uses notes and rhyme to compare stories across the generations. Each generation's balladeers sing of love, hate, fun and injustice; the lingo is different.

Fishing line and fishing time, now there's a natural connector. Time on the water can join the feisty child to Dad for years and years of play, give-and-take, and the struggles of coming of age.

And so I watch that young man of mine and consider that the leader does nick, that the fun is in the playing on both ends of the line, and that, if Dad has done his job well, the sport of fatherhood is about catch and release. The leader keeps us together; mutual respect requires that he be released into his world, and, hopefully, we'll come together often in years to come.

Indeed, the acts of catch and release happen with great frequency. And on each re-connection, I note how they have changed, grown, and developed as men. I've enjoyed watching the various events or actions that reveal another mark on the door jamb or another ring on the tree.

In 2008, a lot of activity hummed for Dion and Justin, and Cameron earned his first job—cleaning boats. He loves boats and yearned to be around them. He loved the work, but, in comparison to his brothers' grand achievements, felt he had nothing exceptional to claim as his own. His situation at home presented its own challenges, and the summer of 2008 would be his first living with a stepmother (he spends June, and sometimes more, with me during the summer, and in 2008 he spent it with us—Kim and me). Out of nowhere, an anonymous observer and fan began sending him a package each week. The first contained a note to say that this was to be the "summer of Cameron." Creative, handmade cards with notes and a small gift accompanied each package. Every mailing addressed something special about Cameron—an interest, trait, hobby or characteristic. Each week he received a reminder that he stood out, and in no one's shadow. He was growing to be his own man and the mailings acknowledged that.

With 11 years separating the first and last son, observing all three is like watching a time line. How is the youngest's behaviors and comments similar or dissimilar to his brother at the same age seven or 11 years ago? That sort of thing. And though I have plenty of gray hair, I still have memories of my own times at their ages. This combination of lenses provides wonderfully rich views to partake of their lives as observer. I also realize that I am not, cannot be, the same dad for each. As they change over time, so do I. I was the caboose of my family, so I have no understanding of the roles that Dion (first born) and Justin (middle son) play, though I try to. I have struggled at times at the differences in the experiences each has had with their dad, and then with how I haven't provided to them some of the good things my dad gave me. In the end of each evaluation, after exhaustive analysis, I allow that I am me, Dad was dad, and I am proud of the type of dad I am to the boys.

How different the scouting experiences with Dion, when I was a young dad. Both of us first excited by our roles. Now, Cam is excited and I am "numb" to the fun of scouting events, lock-ins and songs. I'm "the old" disciplinarian, it seems, but I struggle to show Cameron the same joy that I shared with Dion and Justin. I can't be too concerned about each getting the same experiences. How happy I am that my brother and I had such different experiences with our father. Such is the greatness of changing as you age and being willing to share that with your kids.

June 17, 2002

New bonfire plan ignores ban
A&M student group building smaller, though unauthorized, stack

Associated Press

COLLEGE STATION — The sounds of buzzing chain saws and toppling trees filled a nearby forest Saturday as Texas A&M University students and alumni worked to revive their bonfire tradition, on hold since a deadly collapse in 1999.

Wearing colored hard hats signifying leadership positions and wielding axes and machetes, the volunteers searched the woods east of College Station for dead elm trees to cut down and eventually burn. They plan to light a 10- to 15-foot-high, off-campus bonfire Nov. 24.

"You can still feel the spirit of bonfire out here. You can smell the dirt on your pants, pick up an ax again. It's an amazing feeling," said Luke Cheatham, spokesman for Unity Project, the group behind the effort.

University officials are discouraging the effort to resume the 90-year-old A&M tradition, on hold since a 59-foot-high bonfire collapsed in 1999, killing 12 people and injuring 27 others. The wedding cake-style stack of more than 5,000 logs fell while it was under construction.

"Our concerns primarily are one of safety — safety for our stu-

Texas A&M student Dion McInnis chops a tree for an unauthorized, off-campus bonfire to be held

volunteers who sometimes have been injured in the process. But in February, then-A&M President Ray Bowen announced the bon-

Cheatham said the Unity Project's effort is the only one that adheres as closely as possible to the tradition

during the week of the Aggies' Nov. 29 football game against archrival University of Texas.

The bonfire traditionally has been lighted on the eve of A&M's football game against archrival

In fall 2002, the family had just moved from Albuquerque to join Justin and me in Houston. Dion had found new family at Texas A&M—the students and alumni interested in rejuvenating a new version of their bonfire. I share more about that in other parts of the book. He invited me into his new family that year. Proud of his work, and proud of his father's photographic work, he blended the two by asking me to photograph "the cut" and the bonfire. The cut occurs with the strong wills and backs of a couple hundred college men and women, and some adult participants/overseers, who chop down trees, haul the trunks to trucks and hoist them on the flatbeds for hauling to the site of the bonfire burn. A photograph taken by an Associated Press photographer captured Dion taking a swing with his trusty ax during the time of "the cut." The photo ran around the world. Watching him and his family in action prompted this journal entry:

The bonfire went perfectly. Good crowd, secure, no problems. Dion takes—as he rightfully should—great pride in the work. My gift to him—and perhaps the greatest gift that I can give anyone or everyone—are my words through writing and spoken love, and my images. Images of the fire, of him and his friends . . .

photos sought for and created out of love and respect, not "snapped" for the sake of simple posterity. To capture and to share is, for me, to love. These acts of love are the greatest gifts that I can share. In these ways, I desire to love often, always. At any rate, the project went wonderfully. I called Dion to share with him my pride in his work and his passion. My boys are my heroes.

This was three months before his mom and I separated.

He invited me into his college world a few times, and each gave me a different view of how he developed as a man, a friend to others, and a son. His passion for life and living flowed over and around an inner source that sometimes would erupt like a magma flow. I appreciated the chance to experience his world.

I had never attended a Texas A&M football game, but the chance to witness the traditions and routines of an Aggie game against Notre Dame proved too irresistible to miss. Besides, I would be with my son. As of the date of the game, it set the record for the largest attendance at Kyle Field at A&M. The record has since been broken, but we enjoyed history together.

Students never sit during an Aggie game. And they all sit together, theoretically. Standing, not sitting, in the stands, one can feel the structure move with the pounding of feet, swaying of bodies and general movement of humanity. Kyle Field holds a well-deserved reputation for being among the loudest in the country. After the game, I understood why. Cheering and yelling incessantly fills the air, until the Aggie team needs silence. Students, with arms on each other's shoulders, form long lines of cheering, swaying fans who are creating memories while encouraging their team. I'll never forget my memories made there with Dion.

Universities have cheerleaders, and Texas A&M is no exception. At football games, fans also witness a legendary team of spirit leaders called Yell Leaders. This tradition comes from the institution's roots as a Corps of Cadets school. Until the 1960s or so, only men could enroll in the university, and they had to also be members of the Corps of Cadets. Many of A&M's traditions grow from that history. The Yell Leaders are one of them. Yell Leaders earn their role by vote. The student body votes for their leaders and the campaigns demand energy, spirit and dedication, as well as a few impromptu demonstrations of one's commitment to tradition, knowledge of the cheers and strong vocal chords. Like public elections, candidates may face a runoff situation.

Dion ran for Yell Leader. He loves all the traditions that comprise A&M and wanted to be one of the few who would lead the maniacal crowds in tradition-based cheers. On one of my visits to campus, he proudly walked me around, showing me the campaign posters on campus and in almost every window in his dorm, Walton Hall. "Dion for Jr. Yell." The odds were stacked against him, but that sort of thing has never bothered him. Ever. He did not win, but he has yet to give up his outspoken spirit for the university.

DION MCINNIS
JUNIOR YELL

Howdy! I am Dion McInnis, proud member of the Fightin Texas Aggie Class of 2003 majoring in Sports Management. I was born in Houston, raised in Huntsville and for the past few years have lived in Albuquerque, NM. No distance could have kept me from Aggieland, and I am proud to back home, prouder to be home in Aggieland and prouder still to be your candidate for Junior Yell Leader. I cherish the opportunity to even be running for such an honorable position for you and my school. For years I have had a fire inside, a burning I am sure you all are familiar with. And if you know that fire, I am sure you know how satisfied it feels when you hump it at Kyle Field, or say "Howdy" or even just being an Aggie. And then you know how that fire grows when you feed it. That fire is why I am running for Junior Yell Leader. I have loved Texas A&M for years for myself. I have done my best to show the world how much I love this school, and now that passion has grown so intense I can't contain it. I want to show the world how much YOU love this school. That is the core of the Yell Leader position. Yell Leaders aren't exceptional simply because they love the school, they are exceptional because they love the school for the 12th Man- without regard to recognition or notoriety. And with that in mind, I offer my shoulders to carry the 12th Man's passion, the Ol' Ags' pride, and the future Ags' dreams out to the rest of the world with the honor Texas A&M University deserves. And if you see me around, please be sure to stop and say "Howdy!" I'd love to meet you. Thanks and Gig 'em Ags!

Click Here To Vote Online!!!

This was not the first time he pursued such a role. He first developed the role while at St. Pius X High School in Albuquerque, New Mexico. Dion tends to re-invent himself with each move or relocation. The change from a semi-rural Texas college town to New Mexico's largest city comprising thousands of people with disdain for all things Texan provided Dion the chance to hunker down or flourish. He chose the latter, and it provided him his first foray into yell leader roles.

The school's mascot is the Sartans. Not SPartans, but Sartans. Don't bother checking Wikipedia or the dictionary. According to the high school's web site, "The name is a contraction of Pope Pius X's name, Giuseppe Sarto. It is used because our patron saint embodied the characteristics of charity, good humor, fair play and faithfulness—the same ideals that St. Pius X High School hopes to instill in its students. In Italian, Sarto is translated 'tailor.' Thus a Sartan is one who tailors his life after those ideals and supports his motto: 'To restore all things in Christ.'" The image of the mascot looks remarkably like a court jester with a shield bearing symbols of the Catholic faith.

The new guy at school from a state of disdain chose to make something of himself, by himself, and for others. The odds were stacked against him. Charm and persuasion go a long way.

After a few conversations with appropriate school leaders and staff, Dion recreated the yell leader role for his school. The reputation and campus acceptance of his unique re-manifestation of the role captured the imaginations of student and parents. Not unexpectedly, his efforts also gave rise to competition and envy. But, he did it for others—to rile and rouse both fans and spectators at athletic events. First, he performed his work at football games, and then came basketball. For baseball, he recorded classic rock songs for each Pius athlete as they came to bat and funeral dirges for the opponents as they warmed up.

As high school yell leader, he strived to inspire more than entertain, though both could, and did, occur. Dion painted his face in yellow and white or yellow and black (the school's colors), and wore a Pius team shirt, black and yellow checkered shorts, and waved a large black, yellow and white flag as he yelled, screamed, taunted and cheered with and for everyone in the stands. Flips, tumbles and pom-poms were replaced by passion, zeal and exuberance. He wrote the number nine under each eye, making a "99," his graduation year.

Dion McInnis
The Spirit of St. Pius (Class of '99...saving the best for last)

He came to epitomize spirit there. He held the role of spirit leader. He also deemed himself the protector of Pius pride. He won the school's Spirit Award for his efforts.

He brought his schtick to soccer games, too. At one game, the opposing team's cheer squad kidnapped Pius' inanimate mascot or flag. Dion planned an incursion to the opponent's sideline to protect the honor of his school and recover the absconded item.

He ran to the opposite side of the field and dove to keep from being spotted. Unfortunately, he slipped on the way down and caught his fall by extending his arm. After recovering his position, he dashed into the opposing cheer squad, took back the Pius piece and returned to the Pius side to the cheers of fans. Somewhere out there, a parent holds a video of Dion coming up off the ground, arm dangling uselessly, as he raced into the cheer squad.

I didn't see the incident. I had just landed for a business trip in Dallas when I received a call from a Pius coach. He asked me to get Dion and take him to a doctor. I gave him my wife's phone number. Four hours later, thanks to some medical mishandling, he received a healthy morphine shot so the doctor could re-locate his shoulder. It had been separated to the second rib. Less than 24 hours later, he took the SAT test, scoring only 50 points short of National Merit Scholar level.

As passionate as he was for team spirit, he was equally frustrating to some. Yin or yang, but never middle of the road. His high school career could be described as eventful, adventurous, curious and boundary breaking. Perhaps I should simply leave it at that. Oh, and add growth—his high school years included much growth—personally, at school and at home. The wheels of the family wagon began to get wobbly during those years.

Many times I have recalled Dad's words, "I wouldn't want to be a day younger or older than I am today," and understood the power and inevitability of them. Time passes and there is no better place to be in that continuum than right where you are now.

Like the tic marks on the doorway or the rings of the tree trunk, growth has its markers. These visible or memorable signs remind us of different stages. One of my early steps involved a six pack of Budweiser beer.

Dad and I were going fishing somewhere. I don't recall where. I was probably five or so and the location has nothing to do with the story. Our short stay in a small store serves as my only recollection.

Dad paid for his purchase and said, "Grab my beer, bud." The store clerk said no and cited policy and law that prohibited kids from handling alcoholic beverages. Dad again prompted me to gather the six pack. The clerk again objected. Dad wrapped up the conversation, "He's my son. If he wants to help his dad, he can. I've paid for it and he's carrying it." As an adult, I look at that occurrence differently, but at the time the scene revealed a dad who was willing to break rules to allow his son to help if he wanted to.

I don't use that example of how I would teach my boys a similar lesson. The concept stuck, but not the method. But, I remembered this incident when some 40 years later, Cameron and I took our seats at Denny's for breakfast. The waitress asked if we wanted a child's menu. I looked at her, then at Cameron, and said, "There are no children at this table. You must be thinking of a different table."

When the two older boys were of age to begin a new tradition of us sitting on the deck with a cigar to commemorate an important event or night in need of special conversation, I included Cameron who was too young. He was 15. Old enough for a new tradition.

I never smoked, actually. Not until I separated from the family. I had little money, and an overabundance of thinking and writing to complete. Cheap cigars smoked while I sat on an old blue folding chair on a 30 square foot patio at two in the morning created a new ritual for me. And it was cheaper than food. Once the separation and divorce passed, I quit smoking except for the unusual occasion where a nice cigar made for a pleasant accompaniment to thought or conversation. Into this tradition I brought my boys.

Another mark of growing (older) included marking, of sorts. Dad and I worked on a variety of projects together without the benefit of scouting programs. Fathers and sons did such things. The older I got, the more cuts he received while working. I questioned the reason and he explained that older people had thinner skin and it cut easier. Mom confirmed the reason when I commented to her, or when Dad came in from working on a repair job with a cut or scrape. "Cutting easily equals aging." These past few years, I have begun to cut more easily. Yet, I don't want to be a day younger than I am today.

Visions of my aging dad
Greet me in today's mirror.
Lines to wrinkles to crevices
And a developing pot belly creating a berm between my chest
And pubic hair now sporting a gray hair or two.
Laughter with my sons strikes resemblance to the jokes shared between

My dad
And
Me.

2003

I caused you hurts
And made you laugh
And together we grew, you and me
Struggling together
Struggling apart
Like the life struggling in a seed
Living our lives
Living our dreams
Always believing in what's to be
I've always loved you
As only a father can
You'll always be a treasure to me

August 25, 2003

Many habits and experiences that I saw in Dad continue to influence me today. Some are so sublime as to be feather-strokes of memory that make me smile or sigh. For some reason, I vividly recall some of Dad's eating habits, perhaps because they served as markers as I grew up. If he came home later than the family had dinner, I would watch as he ate from a TV tray, enjoying the meal after a day of work. As I grew older and learned to enjoy some of the same foods, I remembered how he seasoned his meal, or cooked it (if it was fried fish, steak or fried oysters).

I remember my dad eating:

- Grapefruit, peeling them like large oranges, and then sprinkling them with salt after removing the semi-transparent, thick skin off of them;
- A plate completely full of grits, greens and pork chops, all heavily peppered and enhanced with a sprinkle of homemade hot sauce on the greens, and a rum and Coke highball on the little end table next to him;

- Steak—what was once a luxury became as commonplace as he wanted it to be, and he took great pleasure in cooking them in the black iron skillet, fat spitting hotly across the stove and a dish towel wrapped around his waist like an apron to protect his clothes;
- Oysters—another luxury that became as common as he wanted it to be, whenever Mom bought them in the pint jars from the Lewis and Coker at Lantern Lane shopping center . . . raw or cooked, either was fine. He relished cooking oysters in hot oil that bubbled just right in preparation for the meal that had been tumbled in a clear plastic bag (dare I recall when he did it in paper bags because we didn't buy the plastic bags?) one-third full of his concoction of flour, corn meal, salt, pepper and whatever seasoning caught his fancy that day;
- Soft peppermint sticks—a treat that Mom would get when Lewis and Coker had them—and now I wish I had photos of him enjoying them with his kid-like smile because now I would understand how little of such treats he had as a child yet how happy he was to provide them for his children;
- Ice cream cones from Baskin Robbins ice cream shop . . . I believe he liked butter pecan, or was it chocolate mint? . . . though I believe he liked them more because he was able to enjoy his family's company as we ate them together;
- Fried chicken like only Dad could cook it in the bag-full-of-concoction, and the ever-present-while-cooking highball on the kitchen counter nearby.

I know that I follow many of his examples, with my own twists, to those foods.

I believe some of the first memories of Dad's behaviors must have begun when I was about three. Three is a great age. Now that I have seen my boys go through that phase, I can only imagine the life I lived when I noticed how Dad ate, walked and moved.

Each time one of the boys hit age three, I witnessed magic. In fact, I want to be three when I grow up. Or, at least maintain the spirit of three.

You see early in their lives indicators of character. Even at three.

At the age of three, the hill near our house became too much for Cameron to resist. As we began the turn up the short hill, into the cul-de-sac where we lived, he asked, "Can I run?" From that time on he was an avid hill runner. I jotted this in my journal after one of his runs.

Cold or hot; wet or dry; day or night, the side door of the van would open and out he would fly. Or he would be lifted across his dad's lap from the front seat and onto the road. In either case, we would drive slowly behind him as he ran—first with arms straight at his side like a young cheerleader, and progressively like a runner, with arms pumping to get him up the incline—to protect against any other traffic. Blonde hair bouncing with his steps, his head would turn as he looked over his shoulder to make sure he was beating us up the hill. His smile of satisfaction was greater than any he could ever display crossing a finish line.

The boys showed me that at three . . .

. . . you can keep sticks in your pockets as treasure, toys and mementos of adventures from earlier in the day. It is always good to keep such things with you.

. . . A smile can get you out of almost any kind of trouble, particularly when the expression comes from genuine joy or excitement and not for effect.

. . . You are big enough to roam your world and small enough to still be carried by mom, dad, grandparent, aunt, uncle, brother, sister . . . someone who cares for you.

. . . Tears are okay. Feelings get hurt, as do fingers, knees and elbows, and tears are natural. Likewise, tears dry up just like hurts go away, and then we can go about our life's adventure. And every day holds the opportunity for adventure.

. . . Every day of life's adventure brings new discoveries, new perspectives and new experiences. Be open to them.

. . . Simple sandboxes provide great places to play, create, enjoy the company of friends or self, and explore with your imagination. It is good to find simple sandboxes and learn to play well in them.

. . . Everyone likes those who look good in shorts. Shorts make you look young, active and in search of fun. Wear sandals or go barefoot—it makes a difference.

... In your way, you do own the world you're in, but that doesn't give you the right to be arrogant about it. Enjoy your world, explore it, grow in it—but don't let it go to your head. Others are doing the same.

Three also represents a time where innocence and intelligence come together in unintended ways. As a three-year old builds a knowledge base to apply to newfound discoveries, the result sometimes captures greater meaning than they intended.

When Cameron was three, he had a 35mm film container—a gray plastic container with a black cap—in his hands. The boys saw this sort of container throughout their lives and we always had extras to be used for kids' projects, fishing hook or weight storage, and more. When I asked Cameron what he had in the canister that day, he replied, "Magic."

Children's new realities and understandings become part of how they understand life, comparing and contrasting information with the situation at hand.

Cameron always struggled as a student because of apathy, boredom and frustration. Not until his junior year in high school did he take ownership and responsibility for his grades and put in the effort to keep him clear to compete on the swim and water polo teams. Texas has a "no pass, no play" policy that prevents students from participating in competitive sports if failing a class. Cameron's tendency in high school was to "pull it out at the last chance" when the grade review deadline was upon him. It always worked, except when it didn't. The time it happened, he learned a new type of disappointment.

He is clearly a smart kid and always has been. It took a while for his sense of responsibility and accountability to grow to the level of his intelligence.

As a kid, he could not muster much interest in, or dedication to, the things he was supposed to learn in school. "I can't learn it," "It's too much to learn" and all the other explanations parents are accustomed to, served as responses to each grade that missed the mark.

One day Cameron tried to explain to me the games based on the Pokemon character and their trading cards. The cartoon entertained millions of kids each Saturday and the cards provided distraction (and sales) on the other six days of the week. As we played, it became clear that he knew each character's name, as well as its characteristics and traits, weapons, weaknesses, key adversaries and so on. The information for each character affected every other character, depending on which cards were involved in the moment. All combined, Cameron held an incredible amount of information that he had memorized and was fluent with for the changing conditions and contingencies of the game.

"So, let me understand this," I said. "You possess an incredible amount of knowledge and details for Pokemon, but the test at school the other day was 'impossible' because it covered too much information?"

He smiled.

"Well, yeah, Dad. Sure. Pokemon is fun to learn."

Part of a parent's role in their child's growth, I believe, is to find the "fun" that inspires growth. Mandate and edict do not light any fires in a child—they only instill fear of failing.

Years later, his oldest brother, Dion, shared frustrations about a college class. "I love to learn," he said, "but I hate to be taught." So true.

"Dad, is this the music that grandpa grew up learning to hate?"

The question was yelled by our 15-year-old over the sounds of The Turtles. They had followed Gary Lewis and the Playboys, The Crystals and The Grassroots. Still to come: Tommy James and the Shondells. His mother's dad sat on the tarp that eight of us shared while listening to the music on the soggy hill at the Cynthia Woods Mitchell Pavilion.

Indeed. The music that one generation of gray haireds and bell bottoms rocked to, was the very music that another generation of same had come to hate as their children played it "too damned loud." Happily, for the younger of the gray haireds, it still sounded best when played loud.

This Wonder Years concert, a Woodstock for the hypertension set, created a wonderful flashback. At the time, the boys were the ages their mom and dad were at the time the tunes were created—11 and 15—making the circle more enjoyable. And poignant.

The pieces come together in mysterious ways. The boys' mom and I attended church classes and the topic arose of godliness in our lives. "God wants us to aspire to be like him," the instructor guided. "We'll never be as complete, of course, but He calls us to his likeness. He sent His son as a way for us to see the potential."

The words echoed for years, and have now come to a new meaning: ". . . a way for us to see the potential." I look at my sons as they grow, behave, misbehave and develop their personalities. The new teenager swings from a swing set, root beer Popsicle dripping from the desert heat, and he epitomizes the future—full of hope, life and unfilled potential. The high school senior exercises his confidence through honest, albeit sometimes still rough hewn, commentary on the world as he sees it. The kindergartner steps into a new world every day, akin to Lewis and Clark as they traveled west. The ways our young ones live, and live out, serve as examples to us of our potential. Sometimes they remind us of potential lost—things that we could have done, but didn't.

Paying attention to the boys' lives and moments provide me glimpses of how that progress is coming. A few months after Dion began attending Texas A&M, I took a business trip to Houston from Albuquerque and was able to spend some time with him. It gave me a great weekend with my son and a glimpse . . . both in time and back in time.

Saturday morning I drove out to TAMU to hang with Dion a while before we headed to Huntsville. We toured campus, scarfed Shipley's (a southeast Texas donut favorite) and went to lunch with Sara. I'm proud of my boy. He is learning about life and I pray that his curiosity doesn't lead him to danger. We all flirted with different dangers as we boldly went where we thought no other generation had gone before. Fishing on Lake Conroe with Richard was good. I didn't drive the boat but I enjoyed watching Dion: a young man's face, blown by the wind as we dash across the lake at 45 mph. His young, strong, hairy arms extend to the steering wheel and throttle. Did Dad think the same when I drove the old Hollywood (my dad's boat)?

April 2, 2000

Not all his college times were great. They certainly were his own.

I was what is called a "non-traditional" student. I went part-time, hit the campus for class and then departed to run my photography business. I never lived on campus and did little of the "college life." Dion was a traditional student who experienced college in non-traditional ways. And Justin, who thought he would never go to college, had the most traditional experience: five years of classes, a useful degree, and career employment a month before graduation. I graduated only after taking a couple of "special projects" that enabled me to complete six hours in one semester so I could graduate in August 1981. Dad died in June. I took eight years; Dion took ten. Cameron enters college in just over a year from the time of writing this piece. There were rough patches along the way for his dad and brothers, and there have been for Cameron; we'll see how he grows in college. Their paths were not always clear along the way.

Dion has dropped out of college. Justin doesn't want to go. B (the boys' mom) is succeeding in school at 47 but is upset with her B+ grades. Cameron is on the verge of failing 5th grade. What is going on? Dion has a brilliant future and he'll get there if he remains focused. Justin will make the world a better place if he can find his spot to do it from. Cam's brilliance is now beginning to show on several fronts—math not being one of them. I admire the team that Dion has brought around him (a team he showed that he and I both piss people off); I appreciate Justin's need for seclusion and solitude.

April 4, 2004

My Mom used to say "No use worrying over something that likely isn't going to happen." So it is that as a parent, one can't worry each time it appears that a wheel may be coming off the wagon that is your child's life. Patience and perspective are required.

At no time does a parent have the full image of what their child is, or of what they will become. To project greatness or failure on a kid because of a good or bad day is to rob them, and life, of the vastness (and scariness) of potential and fate. When the boys would come to me, concerned that someone projected something bad in their future because of a grade, misconduct or subject-based apathy, I would try to remind them that we can't add up the score of our life until we die. And even then, it isn't ours to score. Opportunity always awaits.

Each stage of life makes for a stage of growth. Where we see our kid may not be how they see themselves.

Cameron was midway through his entry into the teens as we talked about the future and how our topic choices would change over time. I mentioned that about eight years from then he would talk to me like in the Cat Stevens' song "Father and Son," in that he would be facing changes and challenges and would want me to listen as he would say "It is time for me to be a man now, Dad." He smiled, despite the fact that he was quite sick that day, and said, "You're looking at 100% man now!" We both laughed and I reminded him, again, of his comment a few years before: "Ain't I a piece of work?" As I laughed, I thought, "He's still a kid." No matter how old and developed as men they are, they will always be my boys . . . and each a piece of work.

Cameron was quite young when he declared "I'm using my good brain," when asked how he figured out the answer to a problem. How he uses his good brain varies to the circumstance, of course, but invariably he finds a way to be thoughtful, wise and intelligent at the same time.

Trying to decide what to do with the job offer from University of Houston-Clear Lake created the opportunity for me to chat about options with Justin and Cameron. Dion had already moved away to college by that time. Cameron was about eight and realized that I was looking for something more fulfilling. I accepted the job offer, made preparations to move, and the day came for me to move to Houston. Cameron handed me a small plastic bag with a note. The bag contained grass clippings; the note read, "So you can see if the grass is really greener in Texas."

Always insightful beyond his years, he also sensed trouble some two years later. I struggled with my marriage, confusion of what to do for myself and my kids, and the tension was thick at home since the family had reunited in August 2002. Cameron wrote a poem on loose leaf paper and gave it to me. Moved by the message, I asked, "Where did you get this poem, buddy?"

"I wrote it."

"I see that you wrote it, bud, but where did you find the poem? It is really quite beautiful."

"No, Dad. I wrote it. I wrote it."

I read it again and looked at him with love and amazement.

"How did you come up with this? What prompted these words?"

"Well, I knew that something was wrong. And I thought to myself, what words could I use to let you know that things would be okay? So, that's what I wrote."

In a child's scrawl, these words stood before me:

The garden of life is no normal place... no it is the love of life. The love of livig (sic) it. This is magic, easy, good, SO live this miracle... don't wish it.

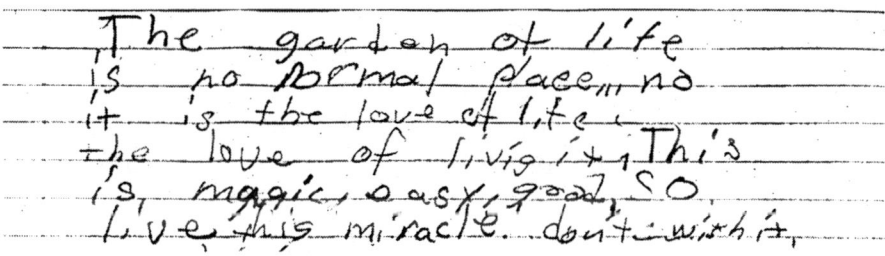

Many occasions reveal the inconsistencies of growth—boys as men, men as boys. I guess wives would say the same thing about their husbands. But that's another book.

In May 2000, Justin graduated from eighth grade. I worked at University of New Mexico at the time, only a few minutes' drive from Justin's school. He waited at my office before we headed to his school for the ceremonies. It was a big day, his last day in kid school and the opening of the door to high school. As I took care of some things at the office, he kept himself busy at my desk. With binder clips. He placed them together in ways to resemble the star fighter craft in Star Wars, of which he was a huge fan. I watched and thought, "He's still a kid."

Later that summer, I received a call from Justin while I was out of town on a business trip. He wanted to let me know how cross country practice went—"Eight miles, Dad. It was crazy."—and inquired about my trip. As we wrapped up the man-to-man conversation of updating each other on our lives, he said, "Oh, Dad . . . on the flight home, don't forget to get me my peanuts." "He's still a kid," I thought to myself.

In 1977, at the age of almost 21—short by a month—I obtained my first DBA to start my photography business. At the age of just past 21—by four months—my oldest son is getting his first DBA. At the age of 16 I got kicked off the track team for not cutting my hair, in the '70s no less. At just past 17, my middle son's thick long-ish hair is inspiring his track peers to grow theirs—he is becoming a leader.

October 12, 2002

About a year after that entry and about nine months after I had moved from the family, I offered to assist Justin with his road trip to College Station, Texas to visit his older brother at Texas A&M. My help came by switching vehicles so he could drive a safer, more cost-effective vehicle than the one he normally drove: my "new" Mitsubishi Lancer instead of his 1987 Ford pickup truck that I used before getting the Lancer. The experience of using his truck provided me more than a view into his world, but also affirmation that the boys and I would make it through the changes that we were in the midst of.

I journeyed into my son's world today, or I journeyed with it. We traded vehicles today so he could more safely get to his brother at TAMU—he in my Mitsubishi with air bags and me in his pickup with his schtuff.

I first untangled the base of the seat belt. Two water bottles rolled out—he's a varsity runner and consumes mass quantities of the clear stuff. At every other stop sign or red light, another bottle rolled out from under the seat. That in itself was amazing considering the amount of stuff he has packed on the back floorboard and back seat. How could anything move?

Amidst the papers and wrappers is the notice of the SAT test he took this morning. It is folded haphazardly forming what looks to be a flattened origami road kill. A simple note on loose leaf paper rests atop of who-knows-what on the floor of the front passenger side. "You did a great job this evening. I'm proud of you. Love always, Elaine." No longer does he have just his mom and dad passing such notes to him. I dare not look at what is under that beautiful note.

Perhaps only in a teen's truck can the back seat hold as much as the truck bed can. The runner has sweats, shorts, a towel, running schedules, and more water bottles. The high school junior has a mannequin head, school books, school notices, school flyers, school stuff. The truck driver has a Club for the steering wheel, jumper cables for an aging battery, a battery terminal cleaner, a wire brush, a hydraulic lift and a mondo tire tool. My son has his world in a truck, like his father did in a Karman Ghia 30 years ago.

November 1, 2003

As each boy passes through their phases, I see the things that they come by honestly, genetically, and those things that come from other forces.

Watching a movie starring Michael Douglas. He was committed, enraged to his purpose. I miss the rage. So much has to be tempered by roles—can't be too angry as a boss; can't be too wild as a dad, etc. But, is that true?

So, I understand completely Dion's rage and his conclusion that he is successful when he allows himself to be mad. The difference is that he seeks revenge and I seek expression. But he is right that we both seek our own worlds to live in, worlds only we create. He is right. I understand completely.

All the boys and I share a fire inside that can be used to warm our souls or start a pyre. We know it is something into which we can tap, as well as something we need to focus.

His passion burns, this young man Dion
The smoke from the incineration—
The visible clues—
Being energy, smile, charisma.
He embraces his life and living
With joy, emotion, conviction
Moving through obstacles as air—
Smoothly, cleanly, completely.
Others marvel at his work

Which he sees as game or play.
He is untamable
His yawps are howls at the moon or passionately persuasive conversation
To beat him back is to beat back the tide.

Ah, this young man Dion, my son
And his father some time ago.

September 25, 2003

Typically, family photo albums serve as the visual markers and evidence of a family's development. There resides posed and candid images of gatherings, parties, fun and comedy. The boys' mom holds the albums which include images we all created. As a photographer by vocation and avocation for my entire life, it comes as no surprise that we possessed myriad images. Some of them were created as part of my profession, too.

Dion's first photographic experience "in the business" came when he was less than one. A beautiful young model with long, gorgeous hair wanted to try a few images of her topless, and covered by naked Dion as she held him. As I created images, he peed on her.

His first "modeling" job for publication served a healthcare client of mine. The image included his hand reaching for an adult's—his mom's. At about two, he posed on a makeshift diving board in my garage photography studio to create a semi-silhouette of a youngster at the edge of the board, prepared to dive. He held the pose—knees slightly bent, hands together and pointed over his head, head tilted downward—just as his teachers had taught him for the "first dive," which appeared more like a controlled tilt and fall into the water. A light from behind gave the feeling of a bright summer day. The hospital magazine's cover story detailed ways to keep children safe during the summer.

Cameron had one brush with photographic experiences as part of his Dad's business. His image occupied the back cover of the magazine that I created for the University of New Mexico School of Engineering.

My job entailed writing and designing the magazine, as well as working with alumni and donors to secure support for the school. We had just begun the early stages of planning for a new building, which provided naming opportunities for donors.

To make the point, I created an image of six-year old Cameron writing his name in blue chalk on a cinder block wall. The shape, size, direction and angles of the letters clearly came from a kid. As he retraced the letters, I created images. The tag line for the photo stated, "There are other ways to put your name on a building." Neither one of us became famous because of that image, but it created another story and provided another visual marker of his growth—and mine.

Image-making followed my various professions. I believe it is the McInnis way to explore jobs more out of curiosity than anything else.

I always placed in my imagination little markers of my dad's growth by the stories of his many jobs. He worked in a garage and delivered ice when he met Mom, and he also boxed in 1933—no money in that! After marriage, he delivered ice, delivered milk, mixed paint, and drove buses for the City of San Antonio. Born to work for himself, he followed the path of some of his in-laws—business owner. Eventually, he became an accountant in 1946. When he, Mom, my sister and I came to Houston in 1956 to rebuild, Dad tried working for one of the Big Eight accounting firms in the Esperson Building in downtown Houston. That did not last very long and then he began working for himself again, like he had done in San Antonio. Hard work and independence go well with McInnis men.

Not unlike many young boys in suburban America in the 1960s, I tried cutting yards as a kid. I completed a few, but did not have the entrepreneurial spirit. I tried selling seeds on "commission," lured by the enticing advertising on the back cover of a comic book that tempted with great items to be had in lieu of commissions for sales. Mom and Dad bought a lot of seeds that year. Mom didn't think that I could pull it off; I was painfully shy then and she was right. At 13, I talked to Ken at Oshman's about working as a stocker. At about five feet tall and less than 90 pounds, my confidence far outstripped my stature. Ken's polite encouragement to try again when I was older only frustrated me, which I shared at dinner. Dad said, "Son, you can't even see over the shelving units. Your time will come."

At about 14, I had been lured by the joy of our times at April Fool Point Marina where Dad and I launched for fishing trips. I watched as straps were placed under the boats while they sat on trailers, and were then lifted off and into the water. On the sides, tanned young men worked with hooked poles to maneuver the boats by their cleats into positions for their owners. I could do that! When I heard that one of my Dad's clients owned a marina in the Tiki Island community on Galveston Bay, I imagined working there, deftly moving boats around the marina. Dad said, "Son, you're not big enough to handle those boats and you're not even driving yet. Your time will come."

I tested for my driver's license when I turned 16. Within two weeks, I garnered my first speeding ticket. This new freedom of movement expanded my employment opportunities. An ad in the now-defunct Houston Post newspaper caught my eye. It sounded too good to be true. The advertiser sought people who loved sports and wanted to work in a sports environment. Commission sales, as I recall. Wise Mom and Dad suggested that the job may not be "as described," but did not prohibit me from trekking the 40 miles from our house to the address listed.

The big day came, so I dressed in nice, brown corduroy pants—casual, but nice; nice, but casual—and a burgundy, ribbed pullover shirt with a zipper at the neck that could be opened to expose my hairless chest. I drove to the specified location—and was a bit surprised to find the location was actually the Astrodome sports arena—and then to the specific entrance. I parked the car, noticed that everyone else had dressed in jeans and t-shirts. I was a minority in the group.

The job involved hawking "popcorn, peeeanuttts, and soddddaaaaa heeerre." After the boss explained the rules and procedures, I managed to get lost in the labyrinth of stairways in the Dome and took in a few innings of the game. The boss found me and told me to not get lost the next time. He and I both knew there would be no next time.

As I applied for other jobs, I also practiced in my imagination how an interview might proceed. Neither Mom nor Dad practiced with me, but both encouraged my success. Still shy, I envisioned each step of the process. I would lay in bed, imagining how I would say hello, present my hand confidently for a handshake, introduce myself, and so on. (I later used this technique of visioning to help young runners imagine the details of how to beat their nemeses.) I still believe in the technique.

None of my job applications yielded calls for interviews. Dad told me that he had heard a radio ad that Handy Andy grocery stores were coming to Houston and looking for all levels of employees. "Your brother's first job in San Antonio was in the produce department at Handy Andy," Dad said.

I applied at their office on Westpark Drive, just a few blocks from where I had received my speeding ticket several weeks before. Early in my junior year in high school, I received a call for an interview. A job as a package clerk soon followed. I worked at a store only three miles from my house in a spot where my family had picked blackberries for weekend fun only 15 years before. That area on Memorial Drive had nothing but open land, horse pastures, fire ant mounds, and a few big homes, particularly "the Kickerillo home," that caused quite a buzz in those days.

I loved the job and it broke me—pushed me—out of my shyness. I loved interacting with the customers and often hummed the chain's theme song as I pushed the carry-out carts back into the store: "Han-dy An-dy . . . a grocery store and so much more . . . Han-dy An-dy."

The stores were great, full of young employees, particularly eye-catching young women as cashiers. Handy Andy provided me my first post-pubescent co-ed experiences since my high school was for boys only. Handy Andy women gave me my first exposures of having my butt pinched (thank you, long-haired Suzanne, as I bagged groceries for you; I had no idea my butt was pinchable!); first plays at first base, second base and third base; one of my early nude models (she was better than most any model I've had since); first wedding photography client (and second and third); early, genuine friendships with girls; believers in who I was (runner, poet, photographer); first responsibility over a lot of money; and, much more. Mindy, Suzanne, Sally, Sue, Kathleen, Laura, Laurie, Nancy, Wendy, Lisa, Robin . . . they all helped define me. I will always be grateful for their, and Handy Andy's, influences. And there was Barbara—who became my wife and mother to my sons. Funny how that first job can work out.

I earned a promotion to office cashier quickly and worked there for five years. I financed my love affair with photography and my first two car purchases with Handy Andy earnings. At one point, there was talk about me joining the management program. "You'll be a manager before our stores have those new scanning things," a beaming manager told me. Stores didn't have UPC scanners in those days. The call to photography was too strong and Dad offered a safety net to help me make the leap into the photography profession full time. I made the jump, and somehow the store survived. I learned a lot about work, colleagues, politics, good bosses, bad bosses, customer service and interpersonal dynamics. Every young person should have similar experiences.

When Barbara and I were engaged, I talked to Dad about the idea of me getting involved in his accounting business. I'd be a married man and needed to consider how best to support my wife, and, hopefully, kids someday. He smiled lovingly and said, "I would love to have one of my kids take over my business. But I don't think the work is you. Here, read this book and then let's talk." He handed me an accounting book. "If it works, we could split the year. We'd each have half the year off. Read the book first."

That semester, I took an accounting course at college, too. At the end of the semester, I returned Dad's book to him. "I love you Dad, but . . . that accounting stuff is . . . ."

"I didn't think it's you. It's okay."

The photography business treated me well and comprises much of who I am at my core. I am blessed to have found something so early in life that means so much to me. I could write a book on my years in the business but won't clutter this story with it. But, for as much as I loved it, I had to leave it in 1987 to better provide for my family, which then included two sons and wife.

My move from beloved photography to the great unknown of higher education came as a matter of necessity. More than 500 letters, calls to automated job lines (there was no internet then), cold calls and more finally brought me to University of Houston from where I had graduated five years before.

The interview went well, with the wrap up being with the dean of the Cullen College of Engineering, Roger Eichhorn. He would be my boss if I got the job. Near the end of our conversation, he asked if there was anything else I wanted to add.

"I don't need the job. I have a job I love. I promise that I wouldn't accept an offer if I were to get one unless I really wanted to do the work you need done."

He nodded. Minutes later, the interview was over and I headed home, kicking myself in the butt the whole time. "What do you mean you don't need the job, stupid?" I said to myself. "You need the job. The insurance. The stable income. What the hell were you thinking?"

Months later, Roger called. "So, when do you want to start?" he asked.

They hired me. When the elevator door closed for my ride up to the office on May 15, 1987, my first day of work there, I wondered aloud to no one around, "What the hell am I doing here?" I knew nothing about working in higher education or about engineering, but I did know writing and photography, and those were what I came to the job to do.

Tapping into lessons learned while running my photography business—chamber of commerce involvement, working with volunteers and community members, communicating messages, and so on—I changed my roles a few times and created a new operation for the Cullen College of Engineering: the Office of Engineering External Relations. I stayed seven years, though I had intended to stay only three before returning to photography. I learned about higher education, politics, good bosses, bad bosses and myriad other things that set me onto a new career path. For Christmas 1987, after seven months of gainful employment with the university, I gave my wife a checking account with money in it and a savings account. I was to earn, and she to manage.

Success continued amidst speed bumps. I left UH in 1994 and spent three years at Sam Houston State University, four years at University of New Mexico School of Engineering, and have been at University of Houston-Clear Lake since 2001. Each experience could inspire a separate book involving politics, alumni relations, fundraising, leadership, management and lessons learned.

In all the experiences, I have realized that my favorite boss is me, but I never figured out how to pay myself as well as the universities do for my line of work, and it takes money to support a family. Or pay for divorce.

I bring all these stories and insights when watching the boys develop their work ethics and means of earning funds for the things they want, as well as developing job responsibility. The boys' willingness to perform honest labor for honest wages has brought them a variety of interesting experiences.

Dion hungered for money early on. I developed a business card for him that included a light bulb, a slogan about him having good ideas, and a list of services he could provide. He was about 13 then, and the tag of "good ideas" could have accompanied all his business cards since. His mom attached the cards to magnet strips so he could hand them out to select neighbors for their refrigerator doors. It helped, but his entrepreneurial spirit had not completely kicked in yet. At 16, he was ready to work and we hauled him to a Target on the opposite side of Albuquerque from where we lived to get him to work. When he began to drive, he picked up a job closer to home at a Texas-styled restaurant. Dion's first job there placed him in the dining area so he could demonstrate genuine Texas Two Step dancing. "Not all Texans two step," he said. His future as a fry cook began.

Dion's jobs always included charming customers and/or persuading bosses to allow things against their better judgment. Dion as a fry cook accomplished both. Soon he concocted special items made on demand for special customers.

Before heading to college, he took a stint at the nearby Discount Tire store where he enjoyed the sweat, exertion and labor of schlepping tires up and down stairs, cleaning floors and other "duties as assigned." While he appreciated our neighbor's assistance in landing the job—the same family that provided Cameron his first money-making gig—he swore off tire store labor after finishing his summer duties.

Financial realities of attending college without much help from Mom and Dad led him to more creative solutions. Early in his stay at Texas A&M, a minor transmission leak went ignored and became a major problem. He may have been the only person over the age of 21 in College Station without a vehicle. But, he made do.

During one summer at college, Dion trained to be a member of a group of people who travelled around state fairs during the summer to educate people about agriculture programs. Frankly, it seemed to be the ideal challenge for Dion. He had to learn a lot about agri-business (he loves to learn), speak to audiences (he never met a crowd or microphone he didn't like), he had to travel to new places around the country (he loves, that, too), and at times he was placed in charge of the team (he really loves that).

The work required a lot of gear, so he travelled with a couple of huge bags filled with materials, clothes and paraphernalia. Lucky for him.

The phone rang. I answered.

"Dad, Dad. I'm in Indiana, you know. And you're not going to believe what happened. I'm down in the baggage claim at the airport and I heard this voice call out 'Harmon. Harmon Killebrew.' Dad, Harmon Killebrew! I heard it a couple more times and headed to the voice. I got to the voice and looked up. It was Bobby Knight. Bobby Knight, Dad! Anyway, I looked at him and said, 'Coach Knight. It is a pleasure to meet you. I'm a big fan of yours. This is great. But, coach, did you say 'Harmon Killebrew?' And then Knight said, 'Yes, I did. You want to meet him?' Of course I said yes, Dad. Then Bobby calls out, 'Harmon, hey Harmon. You have a young fan over here. C'mon.' And up walked Harmon, Dad. Man, he's got wrists the size of my biceps. Huge. I guess that is how he could have such a fast, strong swing. I said, 'Mr. Killebrew. It is an honor to meet you.' And Harmon said, 'I'm surprised you even know who I am. You're pretty young. But thank you. Would you like an autograph?' I said, 'Oh yes sir.' Then I had to scramble to find something. I opened up my carry-on bag and there was the book I got for my birthday ("The Science of Hitting" by Ted Williams). 'Here, can you sign this? You're in it!' 'I know,' Harmon said. Then he signed it, Dad. After we chatted a second, Bobby said, 'You want my autograph, too?' I said yes, of course. 'OK, but I'll leave room in case you ever meet Ted Williams. Have you ever met him?' For a minute, I thought Ted may be in the airport, too. It was crazy. As I walked away, I thought I didn't have the heart to tell Coach Knight that he just signed a book titled The Science of Hitting."

The summer job helped. A few scholarships helped, too, and to meet other obligations and wild ideas, he worked at restaurants and eventually started his own business, Old Army Supply Co., an online purveyor of irreverent t-shirts and other products that honor Texas A&M Aggie traditions and slam its key rival, University of Texas.

To better promote his company, he needed a capable and attractive web site. He couldn't find anyone who would provide the ideas he had in mind at the quality he expected and at a price he could afford. So, he taught himself. Once he became capable, he began bidding online for coding jobs around the country. I remember when he called with the exciting news that finally broke the $25 per hour barrier on a project.

He now works as a business consultant and web page designer. He doesn't design pages; he builds sites with the express purpose of making more money for his clients. "I'm motivated by the chance to make others a ton of money," he told me. Over the years, even when money came hard to him, Dion donated services to help collect funds for the family of a friend who died, to promote a traditional bonfire reincarnation and other needs.

I completely understand his path of being self-taught and self-employed, and if/when he ever has to leave that form of work, I'll both empathize and sympathize. I miss those days for myself, too.

Justin always put his back into his labors, literally and figuratively. When in New Mexico, he sought neighbors who could benefit from the force and energy of an early teen with a great work ethic. He garnered several jobs hauling rocks. In Texas, we order dirt to patch the yard, fill the gardens and such, whereas, in New Mexico people order yards of rock for the xeriscaping. Justin helped neighbors with his near-limitless energy and serious commitment to getting the job done right.

The requirement to keep his grades in passing range postponed his job searches for a while when we returned to Texas from New Mexico. Once able, he joined a skate and surf shop in an area mall. His hard work earned him extra hours and awards, including two for chasing down and tackling shop lifters. The business was poorly managed. When the owners had to close all but two of their stores, Justin sought employment elsewhere though they offered to keep him at the store.

Justin's years at Lowe's reinforced his love of manual labor, knowledge of plants and all things dirt, and provided experiences with good and bad bosses, good and bad customers, and politics.

When the time arrived in 2005 for him and me to move from our little two-bedroom apartment into a "beginner home," I sought his knowledge learned at Lowe's. He commented on the plants at the two houses that made it to our finalist round as factors in the selection because of the maintenance required. He helped in my new start of homeowner supplies and tools by getting us an employee discount on purchases such as lawn mower, weed trimmer and such. Lowe's also introduced to him several fine people and allowed him to transfer to Texas State University in San Marcos, Texas because they allowed him to transfer his job, too. The assurance of income from the first day made Justin's transition easier to manage.

There were plusses and minuses of working for a box store hardware store, but a great advantage included the combination of steady income and working outside. He worked in the garden section and met a few special friends there. He also practiced the plant knowledge he learned in school while working among the plants at the store.

Justin required extra time for studying and he was willing to commit the time for college courses—a far cry from the high school days. (Another reminder to never jump the gun on a child's future based on something he is doing in the present.) The time requirements forced him to quit the job and focus on school, though the increasing student loan burden served as encouragement to get part-time gigs when he could. An older school buddy who had a small construction business hired Justin for various projects. Justin learned a lot, including how bad things can get in an old attic, and the importance of wearing masks when working around clouds of roach and mouse excrement stirred up from old attic insulation.

All the experiences of retail and construction, and working for the Student Conservation Association (SCA) to teach high schoolers about the environment combined to place him in his dream job, even before graduation. His interview preparation, including a mock interview of sorts with me, helped him land the job and provided him practice for the next big interview that awaited him.

About six months before graduation, Justin noticed an ad for a position with the United States Geological Survey. They wanted someone with a degree. In just a few months, he would have a bachelor's degree in geography with a minor in biology, a master diver's certificate and a geographic information systems certificate.

We chatted about the situation and I reminded him of the great preparation he conducted for the SCA job. We agreed that he should apply for the job and convince them that he was the person they wanted, and it would be to their benefit to hire him early. He could work there while wrapping up school and begin full time when he graduated. During the interview, they asked why he wanted to work for USGS. Thoroughly prepared, he cited a quote from one of the early USGS directors who described in passionate terms why he worked in the profession. After citing the quote, Justin said those were the same reasons he wanted to work there. The room fell silent. One of the interviewers commented that he had forgotten why he first entered the work, but was re-energized by the recollection of why. Within a month, they hired Justin.

Justin immediately was a pig in slop (or a fish in water, bat in a cave, etc.). He could not be happier or more proud. We talked about the job and salary and taxes. "You're not a dependent any more, buddy," I said. "You have officially left the nest, and you're doing quite well."

He's a far cry from the kid who swung from tree tops for exhilaration and new perspectives, but he's still exactly that. Recently, he called to share how well one of his data gathering projects was being received by the bosses.

"I may end up having my name on a patent for this," he said. How far and fast they grow.

Due to the family relocations, then separation and divorce, Cameron lived in four homes within 10 miles of each other between the ages of 10 and 17. At 17, he said he wanted to move away for college "to start again, to find a home."

Work will certainly be part of his future, too. That shouldn't be a problem.

Cameron's first work occurred when we lived in Albuquerque. Just as his brother hauled rocks instead of cut grass for money, Cameron too had to adapt to the circumstances. He also had to accept jobs that were negotiated for him by his mother: picking up dog poop and cigarette butts for a neighbor.

He would head to the neighbor who lived a few houses down from us and who were particularly good pals with his mom, and sometimes grumble, but would still put the sandwich bag on his hand for gloves and bring a plastic garbage bag to hold the refuse. He would usually return with a dollar or two. Perhaps those memories are what made it a bit more challenging to pursue his first job as a teen when he needed to begin earning money. Of course, not having transportation also complicated his plans.

Thanks to a conversation in a church men's group, I discovered that Cameron's goal of becoming a boat salesman could possibly begin with boat cleaning. That's the way it worked for one of the men in the group. He is a successful yacht salesman whose career began by cleaning boats. His offer to connect Cameron to the man who cleaned the boats at his dealership led to Cameron's first job that extended for a few summers.

It wasn't until his third summer on the job that he had his own transportation—my hand-me-down Mitsubishi Lancer. Prior to that, either his boss or I gave him rides or he walked to and from work. And he worked hard. Very hard. And loved every minute of it.

His job for summer 2010 provides him new experiences, less physically demanding but no less exhausting. He works at Space Center Houston, a space-themed entertainment area in the shadow of NASA's Johnson Space Center. He learns daily the joys and frustrations of providing patient customer service as he works at various entertainment stops in the complex. Simply by having the job, he learned that there is recovery after "disaster," even when it occurs on an interview.

"Dad, I really blew the first question of the interview, but I think I did well over all. I got better as it went along," he said.

"Cool," I replied, leaving the door open for the rest of the story.

"One of his first questions was 'Do you know who was the first man to land on the moon?' I knew it and blurted out 'Lance Armstrong.' As soon as I said it, I knew I goofed. The guy was cool and all, and laughed and said, 'Well, no.' He asked more questions about NASA's work and I couldn't answer those either. But then he asked, 'If someone comes up to you and they seem unsure of themselves or maybe uncomfortable about asking you a question, maybe because they don't speak English well . . . what would you do?' I told him that I would smile at them. He really liked that. Everyone else said 'Shake their hands' but that's not right. I think I did good, Dad."

He earned the job and within his first month he was recognized twice for his customer-oriented attitude. Each day he grows as he learns about work, pay and people.

It still won't surprise me if some day he lands that job as a boat salesman.

I've talked about Dion's wedding toast when Kim and I married—"Ask Dad for a stapler and you may end up in an hour-long conversation about the meaning of life." He said more, too, that presented a view that I hadn't seen but was happy to have revealed to me. Just like we used to mark their growth with hash marks on door frames, he marked one for me. He said, "Dad's thing, in everything he says and does is about growth. From one second to the next, one moment, one day to the next."

Those sorts of conversations yield great insights—usually about the boys, and always about myself. All three have always been wise beyond their years and tend to be good listeners and conversationalists. These ongoing interactions over the years provide us better mutual understanding, which then opens the door for more gnarly conversation, and pearls of wisdom. I hope this sort of intellectual and emotional relationship with the boys has helped them see that even when they become "as old as dad," it is okay to wonder about one's own growth and potential. And to honor Socrates' words, "An unexamined life is not worth living."

A few months before Dion turned 26, we engaged in one of those examination sort of conversations. He said, "That's why we're not understood—we see the big things in the little things." Comments like that jolt my sense of understanding—I realize then that my boys understand me better than I thought, that they are growing to understand themselves, and that they can frame their observations in the context of themselves and their dad. They show this clarity on points in which we are not similar, too. My mom always appreciated the poster I bought freshman year in high school: The wording was David Thoreau's "Different Drummer"—"If a man does not keep pace with his companions, perhaps it is because he hears a different drummer. Let him step to the music which he hears, however measured or far away." I was proud that she saw that in me and honored the sentiment, and I always hoped to instill the same sense of courage and independence in my sons.

I tried to replicate that feeling for Justin. He took a backpacking trip with a friend to the San Juan Mountains of southern Colorado when he lived with me, and returned to the area for a solo trip shortly after he moved to San Marcos. When he returned from the first trip, a banner awaited him. I taped together several sheets of paper and lettered it by hand: "Welcome home, Justin! Hiker, explorer, fisher, photog, seeker . . . ." For his second trip, I made another banner with similar craftsmanship and sentiment: "Seek and you shall find . . . . Adventure, stories, experiences . . . and yourself! Welcome home, Justin!"

Later that same year, Dion said, "You always encouraged my personal cartography—to map out my own way. Not many dads do that." I could not have felt more proud. The boys map their lives, and I celebrate their courage and adventures. It works well for us.

Watching one's children grow serves as a distinct reminder of one's own growth. Dion is now older than I was when I took a photo that has always described to me the first 27 years of my life.

I took the photograph in the old Westwood Mall in Houston where I had a one-man photography exhibition. It was less than a year after Dad died, and Dion was almost two. The image shows the exhibit, which included about a half dozen free-standing displays that held large prints mounted on boards that were then screwed to "walls." The base of the wall stood a couple of feet off the ground. In the foreground was a large print that I created on a trip to California with a few of my friends. We went for friend time, and I specifically went to see my friend Kathy in Walnut Creek. One of my friends on the trip I had known since third grade; the other two were high school additions. I had known Kathy since seventh grade. The exhibited photo showed the four of them standing on a large rock at Muir Beach not far from San Francisco. The rock is so large that they are dwarfed, though still recognizable by their clothing and shape. On that rock stood the history of friendship and a moment of my "coming of age" trip.

A 30x40 inch print of that scene made the foreground of the image taken at the mall. Behind that image stood Dion. My then two-year old son stood looking at his daddy's photos, but all that is visible in the image is his chubby legs. In that one image was photography, my past, my coming of age and my future: fatherhood. It was all about growin'.

Since June 26, 1981, fatherhood has been an integral part of my life (Dion was born); since December 25, 1962, photography has been an integral part of my life (Santa brought me a Kodak Fiesta camera). The image in the mall brought those two influences together, but there have been other times where our interests grew together.

While attending College of the Mainland, Justin took a few photography classes. At one point, he called to say, "I guess that I'm not a photographer. I can't find inspiration to even complete the one roll of film I'm supposed to do for my assignment."

We chatted about inspiration and I asked him to consider the things that move him. At the time, he loved surfing and skating. I said, "Why don't you try to get some photos related to skating? You've told me about how it feels to be low to the ground and skating under the cable barriers in parking garages. And you told me about how lonely those places are in a great way. Stuff like that. Or anything about skating, or anything else that means a lot to you and is part of who you are."

"Yeah, maybe. I'll give it a try."

A few hours later, he called in an excited voice to say that he shot three rolls of film already and looked forward to the next shoot to come. The fire had been re-lit by him paying attention to himself and growing his vision. Some of the images of that day appeared in a student photo exhibition in the college later in the semester.

A few months later, we decided it would be great to both photograph in a parking garage at night, the time that he and his friends adventured for their adrenalin rushes. We would each come to the situation with our perspectives in creating images. My then-girlfriend (and now wife) arranged for us to get into the parking garage where she worked. For an hour or so, Justin and I worked together and apart to create images of the environment in which we worked. As the images revealed, our visions were different, but we were both visually curious and explorative.

Soon after he began his job at USGS, they asked him to purchase a camera so he can document the work and stories of the organization while in the field. I'm not sure it can get much better.

Each of the boy's life vision, as well as creative one, has been forged and influenced by experiences. The same is true for you and your kids. I have been lucky enough to notice it as it happened.

With each son in different phases of their lives, it is easier to make a composite image of the lives of the McInnis men. The divorce was not yet final when I caught this view of each of the boy's lives in stark contrast to each other and their dad.

Justin is going to buy a surfboard
Dion's trying to purchase a meal
Cameron is saving for a camera
Their dad is trying to heal

June 26, 2004

That day was Dion's 23rd birthday. He and his dad were working on dealing with moments, while his brothers moved to the future. Such is the ebb and flow of life and living, and its beauty. Pausing to reflect on the view of the moment provides us more grounding for memories in the future.

Cameron and I drove to Austin to pick up Justin at the airport after his work with the Student Conservation Association, and then took him home in San Marcos. It was to be a McInnis men weekend, and a chance for the brothers to catch up. It was late by the time we got to his apartment, and exhaustion took the place of adrenalin. Justin slept in his room and Cameron and I each got a couch. Sleep came fast and deep.

The next morning, I awoke to sounds. Shaking slumber away revealed the muffled sounds to be voices. Voices of men talking. My sons. I lay on the couch and just listened for a bit, as two brothers, men-in-the-making, shared stories and ideas. There was much to be shared since they had not seen each other in about three months, and Justin had some harrowing times on his journeys, including working in parks surrounded by urban gunfire. He had time to jot us a note or two, but the visit provided the time for catching up.

Occasional letters have marked growth among the McInnis men, including those written by me in support of a son to a third party. Justin wrote a letter about me to the Olympic Torch Run selection committee and I ended up running for torch for a quarter-mile stretch in Albuquerque in 2001 for the Winter Olympics held in Salt Lake City. Similarly, I have written notes and letters for the boys. A few stand out:

Parents were asked to provide input to the high school counselors at Dion's high school in Albuquerque. The instructions read, in part, "Please provide any information that you feel will be beneficial regarding your student's strengths in the following areas . . ." and it listed a range of activities and accomplishments. I wrote:

Dion's traits and characteristics are the sort that only some colleges and universities would be interested in . . . only schools interested in students with: enthusiasm, natural scholastic and musical ability, leadership skills and the confidence to use them, analytical skills and the ability to communicate what he learns and discovers, and Texan pride and independence.

Dion loves life and he does so with common sense, a strong set of values and a willingness to test the world, his mind and those around him. He has always been involved: church (volunteer and myriad youth ministry projects/services), music (symphonic band, marching band), outdoors (fishing, fishing and fishing), sports (baseball, football, soccer, swimming), school (clubs—including creating a German club, class socials, homecoming and other committees, and a created role as high school painted spirit leader at games), and more. He is a very poised young man; while his grandmother lay in a hospital waiting to be unplugged from life support, Dion completed an interview that earned him a spot for an all-expense paid year of student in Germany. He declined the offer, but he earned it in the most difficult of circumstances.

Dion is strong willed, strong minded and rarely daunted by challenge. Despite his excellent grades and many honors, accomplishments and accolades, he is still a gem in the rough. He understands that to the extent that he believes his future is still in the making and he has six routes in mind: teacher, coach, writer, businessman, traveler and fisherman.

He and I tried to be creative when exploring avenues for additional scholarships. I encouraged him to send a few letters to businesses that likely supported youth and might have unseen scholarship programs, particularly those businesses that tied to his passions. One such company was the Bill Lewis Lure Company that makes Rat-L-Trap lures. He sent them a letter explaining his situation, his love of fishing, and his request for support to go to college. They replied with a form letter thanking him for his interest in being a lure field tester. I was not pleased. So, I wrote to the signer of the letter and copied the CEO of the company:

I'm embarrassed for you, and disappointed.

Today the societal cry includes negative attitudes about our youth's ability to set goals, to work hard and honestly for what they want, to think creatively and to work together for what they want. My son, Dion McInnis, sent to you the attached letter that requested your company's support of his goals that he is working hard to accomplish. He suggested a creative "partnership" between him and Bill Lewis Lures. Granted, the request for consideration of a scholarship may not be terribly clear—he is only 17 and new at this—but he clearly states in the first paragraph that he is searching for scholarship support and he'd like to include the fishing part of his life in that search. He said nothing about being a professional fisherman and was seeking some response, trolling as it were for an indication of whether your company would entertain such an idea. And you replied with the attached letter. No name in the salutation, and no indication whatsoever that his letter was even read. I understand the need for form responses sometime, but this wasn't even close. That's embarrassing.

At a time when the media is featuring stories about kids massacring their classmates, or about dropout rates that are threatening society, a young man presents himself as an articulate, goal-oriented person who hasn't lost his sense of human-ness in his quest for education and success: He includes fishing, kids and shared good times in his dream of the future. And you reply about his desire to be a field staff member? That's disappointing.

Perhaps you'll reconsider. But more importantly, I hope that you and the company pay more attention to youth who are trying to be what your company and our mutually beloved avocation aspire to: intelligent, informed, thoughtful, family-oriented and with a vision for the future.

A few days later, Dion caught the phone call from the recipient of the letter. The caller was full of apologies and thought he was talking to me because he started out the call with, "Is this Dion McInnis?" Dion gladly obliged with "yes." After the caller realized he was talking to Dion the son instead of Dion the father, he adjusted his message, clearly directed to the right party. I appreciated his call, and Dion enjoyed the man's message. He told Dion that "a little something" would be sent to us. Not long thereafter, a box arrived.

A couple dozen lures, two fishing caps, an apology letter and copies of multitudes of examples of how the company supports youth and youth programs awaited us in the shipment. We took a photo of him and me in front of all the items displayed on the kitchen table. I prepared a thank you note, along with the photo, and sent it to the author, and the CEO.

Justin moved from Albuquerque to Friendswood in December 2001 so he could enroll in the high school that he would be in when the family arrived. He would begin in Friendswood High the spring 2002 semester. Because of his dyslexia and ADD, he qualified for Section 504 accommodations (which he never took full advantage of . . . he wanted to deal with school on his own terms) and therefore required a "staffing meeting" so the counselors and staff could meet to discuss how best to accommodate his needs. The first such meeting in his new school was to be held in January 2002. I prepared a note for the counselor to provide his teachers in hopes of giving them insight into the young man they would be working with and his growth.

Since all of Justin's teachers won't be in the staffing meeting, I'd like to jot down a few points that can be shared so everyone gets the same message about him. This is in no way to infer that your team would not communicate clearly to the rest of the team; please don't misunderstand me. There are, however, a few things that I think it important for all his teachers to know.

Thanks for listening.

1. *Justin is hard working.* To get the grades he has, he works incredibly hard. When we put him into a private school in Albuquerque in seventh grade, he went from an hour of homework per night to four hours until he got the flow of the new style. He didn't complain. He didn't curse his reading disorder. He knuckled up and worked at it. He has spent hours and hours on his Spanish as well as gone for tutoring (though his most recent teacher wouldn't show up at the appointed times), and he keeps working at it. For geometry, and other math courses, we've had him in tutoring the past few years. He is a worker in school, at home and in sports, yet he still has teenager spirit, too. He's well on his way to an Eagle rank in Scouts, too.
2. *Justin is motivated.* He has battled with and compensated for his dyslexia and ADHD since we first discovered it, which was very early on. But ask him where he wants to go to college. He'll say Air Force Academy, Naval Academy or Notre Dame. He wants to be a Blue Angels pilot. I'll never bet against my son's tenacity and will to achieve. He relished being in a college prep type high school in Albuquerque so he could work toward his goals. A few examples:
    a. He lettered in cross country his sophomore year. There wasn't much in his freshman year performance that would predict that, except that he is hard working and very coachable. But he was determined to make it this year, and he did. The only sophomore to get a varsity letter in cross-country in his high school.
    b. He has a very difficult time reading, but he reads! He loved one of his summer reading books for this past summer. Loved it. It took him all summer, almost, to read it. And he read it on trips, in quiet times at home. Struggles don't deter him. And three years ago he began writing a history-based war novel.
    c. He writes from the heart, albeit not from the spell check. His essay about me garnered me the opportunity to carry the Olympic torch in Albuquerque on January 12.
4. *Justin has been flexible to change.* My sophomore chemistry teacher at Strake Jesuit told me that "how one handles diversity reveals the making of a man," or something close to that. I remember that when I watch him trying different things to help him: colored flash cards, color filter to diminish the noise in the letters as he reads (and colored glasses for same), tutoring, and other adaptive techniques.
5. *Justin has high standards.* Though he doesn't measure them in grades, he measures them in attitude, spirit, dedication, desire, willingness to work, etc.

6. *Justin has never been a discipline problem.*
7. *Justin is excited about learning. He loves it. He has an insatiable curiosity about writing, photography, war history, the stories of the elderly, and the stories of women . . . life.*

I may be biased, but I've also worked with many wonderful youngsters and young adults (coaching, ministry, volunteering, etc.) and I am sure that Justin has outstanding, not-too-common traits for a young man his age. My wife and I have always endeavored to do what we can to be sure his educational experiences support him and his traits.

Letters and notes provide good milestone markers of how things are going and how things look and feel. E-mail is useful, but a letter requires putting many thoughts into context for a single, purposeful message.

Several years ago, Dion shared an e-mail exchange between him and a columnist for Sports Illustrated. The short version of the story concludes with the columnist telling Dion that maybe Dion should be the columnist, and the writer be the fan. Dion's writing can catch your attention, raise your spirits, inspire grand actions, or cut you off at the knees (or a bit higher). So it came as mixed emotion surprise when he shared with me the note he sent to the columnist about the origins of his writing prowess.

According to his story, as a kid he would bring his writings to me to proudly show off what he created. I, according to the storyteller, would then mark boldly in red ink and bark out, "Now do it again!" Trust me, it didn't happen that way, but we have shared our love of writing throughout the years.

To Dion, writing is just another implement in the expression tool box, as it is for his persuasion and curiosity boxes. He used words to explore, provoke, inspire and express. That started when he began to talk, whether anyone listened or not.

A quick digression. Dion's grandmother had some floor work done when he was a little boy. At one time, Dion rattled incessantly with the worker for a couple of hours. It was a monologue. Only later did we find out the man did not speak English. But Dion had an audience, and that's all that mattered.

His first formal audience possibly occurred in the pre-school, Mothers Day Out programs. There he began to speak out with great confidence and determined that he was smarter than his teachers. He retained that opinion of most of his instructors ever since.

Throughout his life's love of words and expression, he retained his love of knowledge acquisition and sharing. Those functions serve him in communicating his views of the world, but also break ground for him to continue his discoveries. His expressiveness enables him to break boundaries and shells, allowing him access to the marrow of life.

Justin's view of the world has always been influenced by experience more so than words. Dion was the cautious big brother and Justin the risk taker. It is the perspectives of those risks that helped shape Justin's views as he grew and used experiential means to convey his messages.

Justin was nine to twelve years old when we lived in Huntsville, Texas. He rarely spent time indoors, while other kids in the area preferred video games and other air-conditioned options. He spent his thinking time outside, frequently in the tops of trees, some young and supple enough for him to sway them until they were at 45-degree angles to the ground. He has never met a tree that he didn't like to climb.

From this high, adrenalin-filled position and perspective, he has witnessed, observed, thought, contemplated and experienced. It continues to be so.

Part of his rebellion and expression in his late teens included tattoos. His first work included the molecular structure of adrenalin inked onto his inner right bicep. The second tattoo portrays a colorful, breaking wave nearly the length of his upper arm as it washes over the adrenalin. Nothing could be more accurate and insightful. The power and chemistry revealed through art describes his approach to life and growth: natural, persistent, consistent and colorful.

Justin's view of, and connection to, the world has largely involved nature. From the tree tops in Huntsville to the top of the Continental Divide in Colorado, and from undersea to inside the earth, he connects to the world through his actions; they have always been part of his growth process.

Along the way, Justin added a greater use of, and appreciation for, words—both written and read. He tackled his dyslexia head on as a kid, which could have been a great indicator of how his wave and energy would address any other challenges. His persistence beat back impediments until now when his writing and reading abilities have become instrumental parts of his success.

Cameron's growth, like many last-of-the-bunch children, shows a blend of both his brothers' traits. Writer, poet, fisherman, thinker, athlete, charmer, quiet, conversational, and humorous, he presents contradictions similar to his complex brothers.

The activity Cameron loves most defines well his approach to life and living, so far. He is 17 at the time of this writing and an avid fisherman. Not a zealot, not a fanatic—just a fisherman. A knowledgeable, informed, motivated guy who can fish for hours or call it a day in less than an hour. He has not always been so. Such is the growing process.

Until he was about 11, each fishing trip usually came to a halt quickly as he surrendered to boredom or distraction. His brothers were more persistent when they were young, but he reigns supreme over them now in the fishing persistence category. They seek his wisdom and ideas. Something happened to cause the change. No one knows what; we all know when.

His mom and I were separated, and she and he went camping at Huntsville State Park, one of their favorite spots. One of those mornings, he sought the solitude of fishing on the pier and remained there all day. The addiction and the attitude began on that trip.

Since then, he consumes fishing articles as both student and teacher of the game. All throughout his teen years he used spiral notebooks or sheets of paper to develop guides and tip sheets for specific species in specific fishing areas. He never surrenders, though he may cut a trip short. Whether bank, pier or wade fishing, he invariably can catch when no one else around is doing so. He proudly cites those times. Less often one will hear about the times others catch and he doesn't—those are rare. His room at our house displays photographs of him with his fish covering the past eight years.

- Falcon reservoir holds big ones on the rio grande
- they will be on or near holes the bigger the better
- hole big = 100-200 ft long, with not up 2 for them to snag on
- When feeding they move upstream on sand bars against the current when they reach the end of the sand bar they just go back and forth on the same sand bar until not hungry anymore be you want to fish the ~~slow~~ the more slower parts of the water on the sand bar

Setups

Setup 1
- 7 foot rod
- 30-50 pound line
- wire leader
- Shakespeare Tide water reel

Setup 2
- 130 pound line
- 8 foot
- 130 pound leader

Slip rig

- Slip float for bite indicator not to hold bait up keep bait down to around 12 to 14 feet away from t end line Put in 8 foot water

Cameron is a student of fishing, using information that he learns from reading and watching television shows to create his own strategies and tactics. He has been doing so since he was about 10.

Cameron fishes alone, with buddies, with his brothers and with me. He can go either way as long as there's water with fish. That's pretty much his life view—he appreciates solitude but enjoys the company of others; his persistence pays and he's a good sport when things turn out less than he hoped; and, he is philosophical about the process while finding the positive in most any situation. He shares his positive perspectives with smiles, laugher and kind words. Usually.

On one of our wade fishing forays when he was about 17, we weren't able to find the key to getting the fish to unlock their mouths. No bites, no action. He was getting frustrated and I was running out of ideas.

"Hey, bud, what do you think we ought to be using now?" I asked.

"Use whatever the f*!@ you want to," he responded in a heartbeat. Silence followed before I began laughing.

"Now there's the friendly customer service attitude that is sure to build your fishing guide business," I said.

We both laughed and I refer to the situation when he talks about being a guide.

Within the realms that each of the boys has grown, they have done three things, though differently:

1. Define, defend and protect boundaries
2. Balance patience and passions
3. Integrate kindness with firmness; expectations with fairness

I guess that means they are complicated, not unlike the complications of the tree trunks' rings.

Likewise, growth never stops and the variations in appearances don't change the essence of the trunk—the formation from which all else grows. The boys share some similarities in their core.

They don't suffer fools gladly, and they expect no quarter. They are generous, compassionate and competitive. Part of my job will be to keep reminding them as they continue to grow.

When I was an early teen, my mom said, "Your enthusiasm will take you far." She repeated this often as I grew and I recall it at times when I feel like I've lost my North Star. As a tree grows, it builds around what was once a tender sapling. And it pursues the light. The beginning becomes the basis. The boys continue to grow, adding rings of experience around a strong, stable center which keeps their eyes on their guiding light.

Growin' changes parent and child, but, like the acorn that becomes the sapling and then the tree, it is in growing that others can see the trunk—the substance and strength and essence of that which is growing.

There are times when we get a special view of our children's development to adulthood.

Dion commented how he, Candice and Hutch (his roommate) had all seen their future this summer or had experienced it—Dion and Candice, marriage; Dion, his business; Hutch, his cooking future; Candice, Peace Corps. He then talked about the need to discuss it—what are the implications and the new paths? Very wise. Add to that, me and Kim—married life because she moved in and Justin—his SCA internship experiences. I believe that Cameron had age-appropriate ones this summer, too. Ah, life.

September 7, 2007

We part at the door
Leaving him behind with his coach
"Have a good race, son"
"Will do Dad"
A hug
Before I head to the airport
And he to his track meet
"Love ya, Dad"
"Love ya, too"
Teen years can be great.

April 15, 2000

Freshman status on a varsity team
Muscling up against the "big boys"
Cameron holds his place, his cool, his humor
As his team is decimated.
He and his peers
The future of the team.

September 2007

Some years ago I commented to a photography group that I had loved watching them grow in their craft. I had given presentations and reviewed their portfolios for about three years and had witnessed wonderful changes in their vision and work. One of the members said afterwards, "and we have enjoyed watching you grow, too."

I can't really expect
My boys to understand me
This action has been taken
As a self discovery.
Their dad has it together
Probably less than they thought
But I'm also more complicated
And with perplexes I am fraught.
My inner view was very clear
To me, but to them transparent
What they saw was my loving dad
Supportive, bread-winning parent.
Glimmers and glances of my fire within
Surely have they seen
But not until this action I've taken
Do they realize what I've been.

May 18, 2003

Essentially, none of us are static. I hope not, anyway. We're all growing if we allow ourselves that room. I've noticed those changes in several ways. And I have changed, too.

A poet at fifty
Is pretty much the same
As the poet of youth, but
With time's seasoning of the rage.

Many of the questions remain
Of life and loss and love
But time makes one wonder
Beyond the simple and the cause

I wonder and I rage inside
I seek through words to understand
I'm still curious and desire love
Still the poet, just an older man

I do not know anyone here
No one from my neighborhood or church
These are the parents of my son's friends
They are strangers in my world.

We sit in the bleachers under the "visitors" sign
I look for the section titled "intruder"
They cheer for kids whose names I don't know
I listen while they root for him or her

I watch my son as he dives and strokes
I cheer with a nod and a grin
It's not their world but his I enter
It is his that I'm welcome within

September 25, 2006

I write now at 47
Like I did when I was a young man
Watching the darkness yield to light
While my words and ink flow.

2003

Many times, what provoked those words were my sons.

This is going to hurt me more than you
Was what parents used to say
Before a spanking or punishment.
As I watch you grow
To now—moving upward and moving on
To life's adventure fraught
With joy, pain, laughter, sorrow and
Beautiful discovery
I consider these old words differently.
Onward and upward to your new life
I couldn't be more proud.
As you move on I know
This is going to hurt me
More than it will hurt you.
I love my child.

August 2, 2002

Who of these young ladies—
With strong, lean legs,
Firm breasts,
Sparkling eyes,
Soft, sweet hair,
Wetness and hardness
Laughter and tears—
Will capture my youngest son's
Eyes
Then attention
Then heart?
Will any of these in team swimsuits
Provide the inspiration for his words
About touch, taste and scent
Of Woman?

September 6, 2007

Little boy blue overalls with snaps
To get to diapers
Are replaced by Carhartts
With buttons places to allow a quick piss in the woods.
Cute little sandals holding soft little feet
For treks or trails or beaches
Are gone for the sake
Of steel-toed boots
For working or schlogging in fields.
Little cuts would bring him kisses
Making boo-boos easier to heal
He now carries many proudly on his muscled arms
As marks of labor and tests.
That little boy now looks eye to eye
Though we don't always see that way
A god, a hero, a wonder to behold
He is first . . . my son.

November 2, 2003

I don't need to understand you
To love you with all my heart;
I don't need to agree with you
To respect what you're thinking;
I don't need to live in your world
To accept it without judgment;
I don't need to share in your dreams
To wish you all successes.

August 2, 2003

LEAVIN'

I'll always, always be your dad
Even if your mom is not my wife
I treasure all you are to me
And I'll love you all my life

2003

Never in my wildest imagination did I believe in my 20s or 30s that "leaving" family could mean anything other than leaving my family of origin as a young man, and my own children doing the same someday. Life changes perspectives.

When the time came for me to leave my home at the age of 22 to marry Barbara, I left a home of security, comfort, love and support. I dreamed of creating the same conditions for my own family. The songs referenced in the Havin' chapter signified leaving home as a change in the parent-child relationship, not a separation from it. Mom and Dad raised me to make my own decisions and be my own man. I don't think I've always done as well as I should or could in those regards, but those are noble aspirations for a parent to provide their children. I wanted to provide the same for my children; I believe that I have, but under very different conditions.

That, perhaps, is the greatest reality of parenthood: conditions change.

I don't recall any great fears in leaving home to become a husband. I had lived essentially in the same house for all my life. I had been loved and was in love. Life was expanding for me. I was growing while I was going on with life.

Even then, I realized that there were different types and levels of leaving. One can physically leave, moving bodily from one location to another; one can leave emotionally, detaching in healthy or unhealthy ways; and, there are stages of leaving. A quarter—century later, I heard similar information from a marriage counselor as Barbara and I began work to save our marriage. The style of leaving is also influenced by one's role. I have now left, or witnessed leaving, as a young man, son, husband and father. There are similarities. There are tremendous differences.

Amidst the changes of life and living come the changes of death and dying. For me, that sort of "leaving" provided the greatest challenges and uncertainties.

I grew up on Faust Lane in Houston, Texas. Twenty-two years there inspired an ongoing collection of stories under the title "Faust Lane: Quarter Mile of Wonder," as a reference to the time and feeling of the Wonder Years television show. They were fun, secure, wonderful times.

I did not leave home for college. After graduation from Strake Jesuit College Preparatory, I attended University of Houston (UH), immediately starting a photography business. Mom and Dad supported my entrepreneurial efforts—my bathroom also served as a darkroom when necessary and I could improvise studio space in the living room. I had no reason to leave home. I had a girlfriend that captured my attention at the time and UH provided a convenient way to pursue an education on terms that served my dreams. At home, I had the company and respect of two friends and mentors—my parents. When the time arrived, I left home as son to enter a new home as a husband.

Barbara and I moved to an apartment, which included an improvised darkroom in the second bathroom. Although I had to work on my knees to work on the tray stand I built for use over the tub, I still effectively produced quality prints. My office comprised a narrow walk-in closet where I wrote articles and stories on an old IBM Selectric typewriter that Dad gave me from his office. It would be a few years before I moved up to a correcting typewriter. The second bedroom made for a 100 square foot studio space. I created a lot of images on location!

Six months later, we found a house in the Mission Bend development in the Alief area west of Houston. My father in-law and I converted the garage to a studio and darkroom facility and one of the three bedrooms served as my office. The office moved to the studio area when Justin was born—both he and his brother had their own rooms. We remained in that home for 15 years. Not quite three years after we moved into the home that Dad helped us secure, he died.

Because of the senses of love and respect that I grew up with at home, I was strong enough to leave. Because of the same things, we were able to deal with Dad leaving.

Dad's stay in the hospital made for a nasty roller coaster ride. False calls persisted for both good and bad news. The final bad news call was not a false alarm.

My mom, sister and I sat with Dad's doctor in the reception area. He described Dad's further deterioration and suggested that we hang on a bit longer. He left out information that one of the nurses shared with us, detailing what was happening to, and in, Dad's body and what was to happen next as organs continued to decline.

I asked the doctor if the nurse's information was accurate. I don't recall him saying yes or no; he expressed uncertainty and how it was impossible to predict what might happen next. His face said more than his words. I believe he liked Dad. Most people succumbed to Dad's style, charm and sincerity blended with a healthy dose of confidence. This patient, I believe, was in the doctor's blood.

"If that is true, would you subject your dad to that?" I asked.

He didn't answer.

"We have more respect for Dad than that," I said, communicating what our family had already talked about. "It is time to remove him from the machinery."

"Okay," the doctor replied quietly, "but he may linger for a while."

The doctor left us. Shortly after his departure, the horizon began its sunrise glow and birds began to greet the light with song. A few minutes later, before the sun fully created the new day, the doctor returned.

"He only exhaled."

Dad left us.

I wrote this essay that appeared in the local newspaper a few days after.

My dad died.

That may be of little or no concern to you, and I understand that. That is OK. He should not have died—that is not OK and should bother you tremendously because someday a loved one of yours will be in a hospital and subject to modern medicine.

Now I'm not beating a malpractice bush or starting a witch hunt; I won't even name the hospital because it is not in our area. But if the care and attention afforded my father in his 54-day stay in intensive care is any example of modern medicine . . . it scares me. Hopefully doctors, nurses, hospitals and maybe even the AMA will respond to this because frankly, the things my family saw in those eight weeks scared us spitless.

Modern medicine. Saver of lives. Extender of life expectancy. These points cannot be argued but the price families must pay in order to provide these benefits is frequently too high. Almost eight weeks spent at a hospital's ICU waiting room (neatly disguised to look and smell like a bus depot) provided many horror stories and few pleasant ones. For example, a man's doctors said "we cannot save but cannot let die" did indeed die only to be revived 25 minutes later producing a comatose symbol of the vitality once housed in that human frame. The result? Doctors happily reporting "we saved him" to a wife and family that had to spend another eight days for death to once again conquer what was once solidly in its grasp. Lives are altered forever . . . all to save a man that "could not be saved" but could not be allowed to die.

Unfortunately, this was not the only case of lifesaving of hopeless cases that resulted in comatose patients being prompted along merely by medicine's miracle machinery. Even worse, all died.

Fortunately, my father had signed a "Living Will" years ago, that precluded the use of "heroic attempts" to save/prolong his life—exhaustive effort is to be expected but some measured taken to prolong life are absurd. It was needed as he, clinically dead, was kept breathing by respirator and heart pumping by the surgically implanted pacemaker. Per request the machine was turned off; not another breath was taken. It was quiet, peaceful. The horror to come, as described by the doctors, was inhumane.

Something else that is absurd is in whom patients must place their lives. It's not the doctors. Easily, 90 percent of medical care is provided by nurses. Nurses that work 16-hour days per hospital policy. Nurses that are guardians of the thin thread of life yet are spaced over four CRITICALLY ill patients over the 16-hour period. Nurses, who in some cases, were found to be inserting IVs incorrectly or refused to check on a man who was going into shock due to internal hemorrhage.

That man was my father. My mom won't forget that sight any time soon. But we also won't forget the compassion and empathy of these overworked ladies. They cried with us. They fought with us against the doctors to allow my father the right and dignity to die as he desired: peacefully and without pain.

What was to be a "simple" triple bypass (that surgery went well, his heart performed perfectly until the end) ended in a rain of complications, misdiagnoses, infections and problems. A total of 12 doctors handled my father's case. At one point they were all changing one another's orders treating their "specialty." As a result, the unit, the body that housed all these "problem areas" suffered. Chemical levels were nowhere near nature's intentions. Dehydration resulted from the fight against fluid buildup. Questions concerning my Dad's progress often waited for hours while trying to locate doctors—one of who was invariably "at the bank."

It was this doctor who had to turn off the respirator and sign the death certificate.

Doctors, please, treat the patient as a whole unit that is tied to an even larger unit—the family. We ask questions because we are afraid and would like to know. We have feelings so be careful, but please tell us. Of the doctors working on my father, four spent time with the family, answered questions and told us the situation (sans "medicalese") as they saw it.

One heart specialist had the audacity to giggle when asked "do you pray?" Maybe he believed there was no power above that of modern medicine.

That power greater than medicine is now taking care of my father; God bless him.

Thirteen years later, Mom quietly left us in her sleep, with my sister next to her.

Mom's passing did not come as a surprise; Dad's was. Mom died when I was 39; Dad when I was 26. Mom met all three of the boys; Dad only saw Dion's first year of life. Dealing with the losses, therefore, was quite different. I delivered Mom's eulogy. It helped others understand why we would miss her, and helped in my own healing and coming to grips with the loss. Her gravestone reads "A tender mother and a faithful friend." No truer words could be spoken about her. Dad's stone reads "He left for us a most noble pattern." True, indeed.

After I returned to the Houston area in 2001, I found a way to take actions that expressed my appreciation for Dad amidst the loss. That was two decades after his death.

At the time, I struggled with several issues including concerns about my marriage, and family. The seeds of concern had been planted previously and grown over time. My mind seemed like a jungle of overgrowth. Time alone could help sort things out, I believed, so I set out to fish at Brazos Bend State Park and visit my mother in-law's grave in hopes that both activities would provide me a clearer view and understanding of what was happening in my life. After spending the night in my car at the park, I then drove the highways and byways of my youth. The urge to return to the marina where Dad and I launched the boat in San Leon grabbed my heart and imagination. En route to the spot—I didn't remember how to get there but figured I could look for signs along the way . . . which was pretty much what the weekend was about anyway—I conceived an idea of how to address Dad's death.

I remembered that many years ago, when Molly and I were quite young, Dad dropped a bottle with a message into the ocean at Galveston. We forgot about his act of curiosity until the phone rang one evening after dinner. The caller had found the bottle.

I vaguely remember that the call came from Mexico, but I'm not sure. It wasn't from "here," I am sure. The caller had been fishing with his daughter when they found the bottle and its message that had our contact information. Looking back at it, it was serendipity that a father and child would find Dad's bottle that was an adventure of father for child. To be fair, I was too young and it has been too long ago to remember whether the idea to create the message was Mom's or Dad's. They both had young spirits. And I remember Dad taking the call.

My idea to honor Dad involved another message to be thrown into the sea. This time, however, I decided to send the message by casting an orange and white fishing popping cork like the ones we used when fishing Galveston Bay and beyond. I could toss the cork from the marina from which we launched our boat in the old days. We fished out of April Fool Point marina which resides on one corner of a rectangular-shaped peninsula. I purchased the cork at a large sports and outdoors store that didn't exist in our fishing days and no longer exists there at the time of this writing. I muddled my way from the store to my destination by following signs, recalling landmarks and salvaging a few wrong turns. Sounds like life.

I made it to the marina. Things had changed.

What once served recreational boaters now hosted a mosquito fleet of shrimp boats. I parked in an area that would have been filled with cars and trucks and their trailers after having had their boats lifted off the trailers and into the water in the "old days." Here I learned old fishing stories and expressions like "Old fisherman never die, they just smell that way," or "This bait'll catch ya fish or die tryin'." But on this day of healing, the shrimpers remained in port because of the winds. The primary language spoken there was Vietnamese.

While the marina was different, the bay was recognizable. Standing at the point where the wood seawall caught the forces of the waves, I could see the opening to Moses Lake, the buoys where Dad and I would turn to head to some of our favorite fishing spots, and more. Memories flooded as the wind blew, the waves beat, and the cork awaited its mission.

The cork bore words written in red permanent marker, paying tribute to Dad as father, friend and fisherman.

I sent a few thoughts to Dad and hurled the cork into the bay. The wind caught it sooner than I had expected, forcing the bobber into the bobbing waves. Between the wind and the waves, the bobber soon headed back in my direction, and I thought "How like Dad. Coming back to his son."

The bobber never made it back. The waves bounced off the wall and returned to the bay, creating a force that stalemated the cork's return. It began to travel parallel to the shore, about 30 feet away. And I realized, "THAT is Dad. He is dead. He cannot return, but I can 'see' him in my memories like I can vaguely see the writing on the cork. He cannot return, of course."

I felt a sense of calm at that moment that I had not experienced since Dad died. I had made my peace.

Dion was one when Dad died; he was 21 when I found my own deep-rooted peace that comes with goodbye. In that time frame, I faced another "leaving" experience—Dion moved to college.

We used available minutes to shoot hoops in an ongoing game of basketball that lasted for months. Sometimes we would only have a few minutes and sometimes an hour, but we would use the time to play together and talk. On the final score, Dion beat me. Badly. But it was a thrashing worth taking.

He lived with us after graduating from St. Pius X High School in Albuquerque. He first attended University of New Mexico. While he broke into college life at home, Texas A&M suffered the bonfire tragedy in which several students died when the bonfire structure collapsed during construction.

Dion fell in love with Texas A&M at 16 when he attended a summer camp there. He felt the tragedy of the bonfire loss, which strengthened his desire to return home to Texas and to the university of his choosing. The university doesn't allow mid-year transfers unless students come in as members of the Corps of Cadets. Dion decided to meet those requirements.

The family drove from Albuquerque to College Station, Texas to set him up in the next phase of his journey. He was excited; we were nervous.

We stopped at the Walmart in College Station to pick up the limited personal items allowed a cadet: storage trunk, black shoe polish, white socks, white underwear and white t-shirts. I believe the toothbrush and toothpaste could be any color.

The family trekked up and down the store aisles to pick up the required and allowed items. The shopping spree was short lived and we then transported him to campus. To his new home. To his new family. Little did we know how true that to be. The goodbyes included brief hugs and "I love you" before he disappeared into the designated area. It seems to have lasted less time than when watching him at the bus stop on his first day to catch the bus to school. The time between those two incidents moved equally fast.

Dion left while the family was a unit. Justin's turn to leave for college arrived in very different conditions. He graduated in 2004, 30 years after I did and 15 months after his mother and I separated. His and my circumstances at that stage of life could not have been more different; his and his brother's were significantly dissimilar.

Dion scored 50 points short of National Merit Scholar status on his SAT test while under the influence of morphine because he separated his shoulder less than 24 hours before; Justin struggled with school grades and standardized tests, and was convinced that he was "too stupid" to go to college. Dion chose Texas A&M because of his love for the institution and the state; Justin chose the college he could afford and get into because of applying at the last minute. Dion graduated from A&M after ten years; Justin went from College of the Mainland to Texas State University to complete his degree program in a total of five years. It took me eight to graduate from University of Houston.

Justin's first "leaving" for college came as a product of procrastination and circumstances. His weak academic record in high school and poor testing results (thanks to dyslexia, ADD and the changing family circumstances, none of which he would accept as excuses) made acceptance into college a challenge.

He did not enjoy the experience of being taught while in high school. He enrolled in a biology class at College of the Mainland, a local community college, with a renowned biology professor—renowned in these parts, anyway. He did not become a convert to post-secondary education, but he learned that teachers can be knowledgeable, challenging and demanding, none of which he seemed to have gleaned from his high school experiences in Friendswood. He took her summer course, balancing classes with surfing and a job.

His girlfriend at the time headed to Texas State University. He didn't like the idea of her going away, her being in college and him being out. He considered joining the military as perhaps his only opportunity to gain education and employment.

With only a few weeks remaining in the summer, he decided to attend college. I suggested that he move in with me; my lease for the one-bedroom apartment that was home for me would soon expire. A two-bedroom apartment could be had and managed, and we could use that time to get him on his feet academically. With good community college grades, he could then transfer to Texas State, if that was his choice. He accepted the offer and the challenge. As with most of his challenges, he nailed it.

Justin's first "leaving" for college ended up being his returning to me. He found a new direction and a purpose. Within a few years, he was ready to leave again. He had prepared well for school and was prepared to grow again. He was also concerned about how his dad would manage alone. The call was strong.

He knew in his heart that he had to go and I knew it was time. When he expressed concern and angst over his decision, I reminded him that all such thoughts were normal for a young man heading to independent adulthood.

I burned a CD of key songs for him (see the Havin' chapter) and asked him to listen to it. The songs carried messages about growing up and growing on. I guess that is a fairly unique approach since Better Homes and Gardens Magazine mentioned it in their August 2008 article about seeing kids off to college.

He made his decision and the time came for the move. We had moved from the two-bedroom apartment to a three-bedroom house, still close to my work, my girlfriend and his classes.

"Don't pick this house for me," he said. "I likely won't be here more than a few months."

"I picked this house for me. You are always welcome in it, to live temporarily or to visit later."

After about a year in the home in the Meadow Bend subdivision of League City, Texas, Cameron asked how I liked it. I expressed my comfort with the home and where things were going in life.

"Of course, Dad. You loved where you grew up—Memorial Bend; you enjoyed where we started—Mission Bend; and, now another M Bend."

Somehow, I found comfort in that observation.

Seven months later, the time arrived for Justin to relocate to San Marcos, Texas for college.

His departure had an inauspicious start.

Everything was pretty much ready to head to San Marcos the night before we left. Justin, Cameron and I only had to wake up early, and put finishing touches on the packing and car. It would be a long day, so our only goal was a long night's sleep.

"Cameron and I are going to explore those open fields," Justin said, referring to an area where open fields and new construction came together a stone's throw from our house.

"Okay, guys. Just remember that we need to get to sleep early."

Justin had purchased a used Saturn VUE not long before, and enjoyed its back road abilities. Soon he would be wondering how to get back on the road.

"Dad," the voice said on the cell phone. "We're stuck. Can you help?"

The boys had only been gone a few minutes and it seemed impossible that they would already be stuck.

"You're kidding, right?"

"No, Dad. Serious. And we're stuck good."

Justin gave me instructions to find them. Little daylight remained when I saw the VUE only 100 yards away from a concrete street and stuck in the mud.

The Houston area in July owns a reputation: 90-plus degrees, 90-plus percent humidity, and 90-plus buzzard-sized mosquitoes per square inch of skin. There we stood in a field muddied by rains, near dusk in July. Mosquitoes love night feeding.

The vehicle bore the marks of failed efforts to get out—throw patterns of mud on the side evidenced many tire-spinning attempts. The boys were already muddy, having tromped around in muck and mire in hopes of getting out before having to call for help.

The less light we had to work with the more hungry mosquitoes we had for company. The more mosquitoes we had biting us, the more irritating the lack of progress became. I believe anemia due to blood loss likely began to set in, but I'm not sure.

We each ended up with roles to play. Justin had been the one behind the steering wheel in their previous attempts to get out. Cameron did not have a driver's license, much less know how to handle a standard transmission. When I arrived, Justin and Cameon chose brute strength roles. I had the ways of wisdom—techniques for digging out when a jack disappears into the mud and methods of providing traction to tires despite conditions of mud, water or weeds—borne of experience.

Each using their strengths—literally and figuratively—we tried solution after solution until we got the magic combination that released us from the muck. The vehicle looked like a motorized mud clod; the boys looked a bit like the mud men of New Guinea in jeans; and, the inside of the car became a repository for pounds of mud and millions of mosquitoes. Thanks to materials from nearby home construction sites, patience and laughter, we had extracted the car, lived out new stories, and lost any chance of a long sleep before leaving for college.

All things for the 200-mile journey went well enough. Everyone contributed to the efforts of moving boxes and furniture up the stairs and into Justin's new apartment. I lingered a bit after Cameron and his mom left.

From my journal afterwards:

I haven't shared the story of moving Justin here (in the journal) yet—perhaps because I knew that I wanted to digest it first. Now, nine days later, that I am moving into his old room to make it my office, I can share the story.

It went well—some things ran late, all of it was exhausting, but we got him moved in, set up and supplied from Walmart. I drove the U-Haul with my car on a trailer behind. Cam and J drove in his Saturn. Barb went separately—I passed on the "offer" for us to go up together. Dion and Hutch met us there which was great since the muscle was useful in moving the big stuff upstairs! On Monday, J and I with Cam had moved the stuff from grandpa's, and then the three of us moved the stuff from the house to the van. By 10:30 p.m. when I got the car rigged on the trailer, I was whipped. 5:30 a.m. was going to come much too soon. We left at 6:30 in the morning and I left San Marcos at 6:45 that evening. Youthful muscles were very good assets on Tuesday.

I told Cam that I may have to hire movers by the time he is old enough to move, that I would still do what I could, but I doubted I'd be up for hauling big stuff again. ☺

Today, as I take a break from setting up my office, I realize age—my ankles hurt, my little hernia is irritated. Growl. I don't know if I'll accept aging gracefully, but early indicators are that I'll be fretting the loss of capabilities—physical, visual, etc. Harumph.

August 4, 2006

Justin and I talked about changes, growing up, and my pride in his developments. After a few hugs and "I love you's, I headed to my car. "You're a great roomie, bud," I said. "You, too, Dad."

As I drove home, he and I texted a few messages of mutual appreciation, love, support and "best roomies." There were many leavings to his leaving, but such is parenthood. Being a parent requires a catch-and-release mindset.

One of my greatest fears when I chose to leave the family was that my decision would separate me from my sons. I knew in my heart that our bonds were strong enough, but that did not alleviate all the fears. The change had a rocky start and a year or so later, Cameron said, "I'm not sure if moving out was the right thing to do, but I do know that you were right to not come back."

Breaking the news to the boys that I wasn't going to return home presented an emotional, intellectual and spiritual challenge. I had been out of the house for about 18 months and had been through personal searching and financial indebtedness. All the thoughts, prayers and counseling yielded the same response—it was time to heal and move forward in life.

I wanted the boys to know before I told their mom. On the day that she expected me to return—"When you come home, there will be a price to be paid, but come home"—I instead communicated that I wouldn't. By this time, the boys and I had had much time of communicating, giving each other strength and coping with life's challenges. I called Dion first.

He said, "I believe you subconsciously waited until you believed we could really understand why."

All the boys expressed sadness, understanding and support—for each other, for their mom and for me.

I advised Justin of the news and he offered to take Cameron "for a ride" as a ruse to bring him to my apartment so I could tell Cameron man-to-man with big brother there for support.

After I explained the situation, the gears in Cameron's head began processing. "You're not coming back home?" he asked. "No." He put his head down and cried softly. I won't even pretend to guess what sort of thoughts ran through his mind. I assured, and Justin affirmed, that Cameron would not lose his dad. His mom was losing her husband. We talked for a while longer and I answered their questions. Having built up a hunger, we drove to the nearest sandwich shop for lunch and more conversation. As if someone had flipped a switch in the middle of our conversation, Cameron paused and looked at me. We sat next to each other in the booth with Justin across from us.

"Dad, are you going to be okay? What can we do for you now?"

I did not know.

I told him that I'd be fine and we'd all be fine if we stayed strong, supported each other and remembered to live the best lives we could.

As I seek the stories and images of others
I miss—
Watching my sons and their friends—
Boys and girls;
Spending time with their questions
And wisdom of their years;
Seeing their clutter
And smiles and freckles—
I have not taken the easy path.

May 17, 2003

My Dear Treasures:

This must be a confusing time for you—chronologically challenging at the ages of nearly 22, 18 and 11, and emotionally, as your dad has left. I hope to somehow explain that in re-finding me, I am not losing you. Well, I hope that I am not. Some of that is your decision; I understand that it is not mine alone to say we haven't lost each other. I pray that we haven't.

I'm not sure how best to explain all this except that if I had stayed, you would have had a father's body, but lost his soul. You wouldn't have lost it, actually. You would have had all that I truly possessed, which was becoming less and less. Less and less approaching zero.

I did not gamble. Years of stressful thinking, wondering and discerning how much of me to lose possession of was adequate. Perhaps I should leave that part where it is—I have travelled now the road less journeyed. It is scary, but I could not die not knowing what was there. Specifically, am I there?

I love you more than you can ever know. I'm not gone. I never will be gone. Even when I am under the tombstone that reads "people knew he loved them," I won't be gone from you. Soon I will be more fully available to you as I reclaim parts of me I had forgotten were truly mine.

I'm learning to live, with appropriate encouragement—divine and other, by the words I believe and preach: "To empower others you must find the power in you."

Your daddy once had great power—internal, shared and gained. I'm reconnecting to it now. I'm feeding it.

So far, this maybe sounds quite selfish. My celebration of my Self will be for my lifetime. This distance between us won't last much longer. The connection will be different, but more full.

You are the three most magnificent young men I know. So bright, charming, witty and honest about your struggles. Never let the world take any of that from you, for it cannot take it if you have not somehow allowed yourself to give it away. The world can't take it, but it can influence you, persuade you, reduce you or guilt you into giving away your laughter, your tears, your hopes and your power. Never, sons, let that happen to you. Never give that away.

God has plans for you, and He doesn't. He plans for you to be his children, and all the potential, hope, love and power that brings. After that Original Gift (much more powerful than Original Sin), He allows you your journeys, faults, foibles and always honors your greatest potential—to love yourself and others.

May 27, 2003

I miss my boys, my play times
I miss the feeling of family
I miss the sounds and touches
But no longer do I miss me.

I don't miss me 'cause I've returned
From two decades of hide and seek
Next step is to share with my sons
My love, my soul, my chi.

What they'll get after this
Is better than what they had
They'll get back the poet man who loves them
They'll get back their only dad.

June 3, 2003

Christmas 2003

Christmas is bizarre this year
My dear God, take me from here

The pain I'm in, the pain I've caused
To think that I once was Santa Claus.

This year perhaps it's the Grinch I be
But I love them all, don't they see?

Is it true that I can love my Self?
Or is that unreal, like Santa's elf?

Forever my boys will remember this season
Though they know not the why, nor the reason.

How could they know that I almost died
Like the poet I feared would die inside?

How could they realize the flowing tears
Stopped . . . so I could address my fears?

I fear their lives are forever marred
I fear their happiness has been abruptly jarred

I fear more that they almost lost their dad
To fear and pain that he once had.

I'm breathing some, though through a straw
This Christmas season, there comes a thaw

I pray for a gift—just a simple little thing
Please God let me make it until spring

And let me bloom, come alive once again
My boys'll then say "Now, I recognize him."

All I can manage is one day at a time
To come out whole, to more than survive

Christmas is bizarre this year
My dear God, catch my tear

There is no end to the catch and release of leaving, I guess. Just as the boys and I held fears of losing each other because of separation and divorce, there is also a fear of leaving borne in marriage.

A few days before I remarried to Kim in November 2007, the boys and I had a chat. They were happy for my happiness but were also willing to admit that they didn't want to lose their dad and their best friend.

Two years later, Dion married Candice and his brothers and I feared losing him. The fear of loss through leaving is natural, and primarily of importance to those who care deeply for each other.

I miss family sounds—
Children's laughter
Parental conversations in the background of play
TV babble and water boiling bubbles in the kitchen
Thumpa-thumpa of a driveway basketball game
Giggles and whispers in bedrooms long after bed time
Yelling and screaming between siblings that show spark and independence
Blessing at meals
Incessant questions already answered to simply make conversation
Tears of pain or fear that only parents cause to cease
Lawn mowers running—or stopping in deep grass—on weekend mornings
Splashes of water in blue wading pools or huge swim meets
Quiet talk while lying on the floor, just being.
I miss family sounds.

July 15, 2006

My Dear Sons:

If your mind is confused but your heart says your daddy loves you, listen to your heart. A heart is a pretty good compass, though it makes a lousy gyroscope, almost impossible to keep steady in tumultuous times.

There are a lot of things that your heart is trying, has been trying and will forever try to convey to you. In your heart is you, is truth and is the secret to inner peace.

I knew this when I was younger, that is at the ages that you are now. Over time, I began to doubt those confident McInnis feelings. That is not uncommon, according to what I have read, and the people I talk to in workshops, etc. But we're not common, are we? I think not. Nor should you ever accept being so. More than being McInnises, you are Dion Christopher, Justin Anthony and Cameron Matthew—you are you. Just as God intended.

Cameron, you said not too long ago that you knew to listen to your stomach because it gave you answers. Remember? Remember our talk of "gut instinct" and "gut reaction?" Your brothers know those feelings well—it is gut reaction that drives Dion to his decisions for his business and Justin in his races and friendships. Y'all don't want to lose that either.

When our stomach talks it is tapping you into instinct. Your stomach is instinct and your heart is truth. They'll guide you well.

In case you've wondered—I miss you terribly. But I cannot die in your presence. So, I can be some distance away and struggling to find life or I can remain close where I will die inside. I can't do that to me or you. I saw what a de-spirited parent looked like and it took six years after my mom died for me to fall in love with her again because my recollections were tied to the 13 years after Dad died . . . she wasn't herself.

I hope that you find a partner, a purpose and keep a clear head. Life is always about compromising while tacking your sails on the journey, but never, for any person, any job, any expectation, any role, any fear—never bring your sails down young man.

So you set out in life in a journey in which you're constantly adjusting your course and your sails. Your heart brings you truth and your gut brings voice to the instincts you need. See how it all fits together?

You are special men with special gifts. Use them. Let no one or any force take them away from you.

September 9, 2003

Cameron was not quite 11 when I made the decision that the separation would become permanent. As always, we talked about things. I noted one such conversation in my journal. It always reminds me of the travails of growth and decision making, as well as the uncertainty of them.

Tears well in his eyes—"Dad, why did you have to leave? It's a good family." I try to explain what, for me, is still not fully explainable. How do I describe what Marcia (counselor) explained thusly: "Those who don't have the need for a creative environment don't understand and those who do need it can't explain it." How true. So what do I say to this beautiful young man who does not understand but who thinks he might want to? I can only be honest and explain that it is hard to explain. He proceeds with comments about needing to try harder in life, about other people maybe not having the answers. He is processing with his level of wisdom and understanding, as I am trying to process with mine.

March 15, 2003

Life is so uncertain and rarely are there burning bushes to tell us the absolute right thing to do. Leavin'—and havin', learnin', listenin', lovin', playin', fishin', growin'—can only be done with the best intentions and judgment to do best with life and for our kids. For me, it has always been about . . . daddin'.

LIVIN'

Dion once said that when Cameron hits 21 years of age, the three McInnis brothers will go to a bar, and toast to each other, saying "We've done well." And they have. Of course, by then—which is only three years from the time this book is going to press—things will be different. There will be more changes, because life goes on. To my boys, I say, "It is really about living . . . living with arms and eyes open to opportunity, to change, to discovery, to love. Love your life and those in it; love your spouse and your children; and don't forget to love yourself. You're amazing men, and the magic is in living."

Change is afoot as I type. Dion and Candice are expecting their first child the third week of September 2010. Unless the doctors and sonogram specialists are consistently wrong, Lillian Ann McInnis will join the family. She will have a dad and uncles who will love her and empower her, even as they learn how to be around little girls. Her arrival will be the exclamation point to the declaration "Life goes on!"

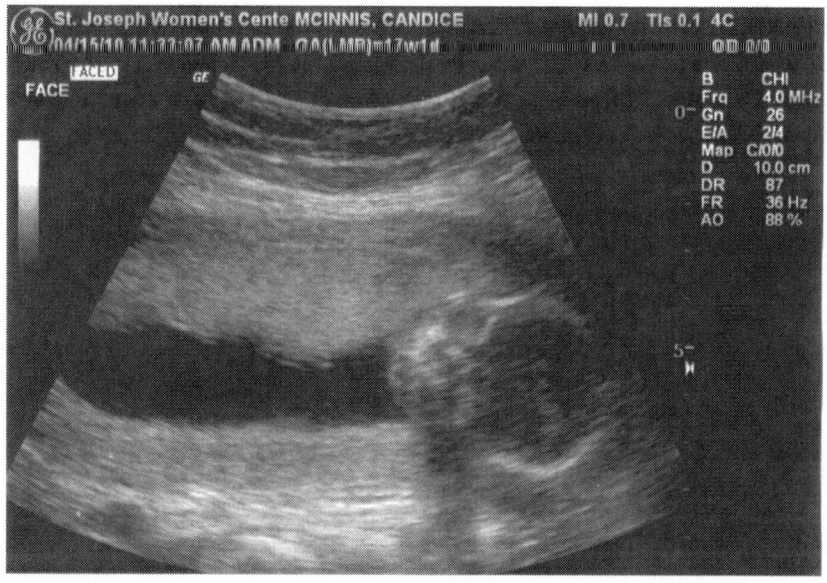

Dear Lillian:

This book was completed shortly before your arrival and before any of your cousins were born to one of your dad's brothers. There are a few things I wanted to share with you here.

Your dad and your uncles are fine men, loving men, living men who believe strongly in what they believe, and love completely the people and things they love. And they will love you. They will laugh with you, play with you, protect you, guide you . . . because that is the way they are. This is nothing new, because the men you will come to know as your dad and your uncles have always been that way. You will see that in the stories in this book.

In a clan of men, you will be new to them as the first little girl. For all the jokes they share about making sure you grow up to be a girl who fishes and can stand up for herself like a boy, rest assured they will encourage and inspire you to be the woman you choose to be. Many years ago, a woman said to me, "One of the great things about your sons is that women will have three fewer men to fear." You are born to a great man, and have great men as uncles. They will expect and encourage you to be a great woman, which I am sure you will be.

First, enjoy being a wonderful little girl. No need to grow up too fast. There will be your own times for learnin', listenin', lovin', playin', fishin', growin' and then leavin'. All the while, live. Live to be all you can be. The men around you will be there to love you. And since you're the first, be sure to guide your cousins and remind them as you grow, okay?

You're not even here yet, and I love you already. See you soon.

Love,

Granddad

Additional Writings

ADDITIONAL WRITINGS

Essays
    Father and Son, Revisited
    Father and Son (Listen to Life, November 29, 2009)
    Important Truck
    Young Love

Father's Day Writings
    1999
    2003
    2004
    2005
    2006
    2007
    2008
    2009
    2010

Kid Art
    Various pieces of art from the boys over the years

Poetry
    Family
    Son's Room
    Voices

Song Lyrics
    Cat's in the Cradle
    Child's Song
    Father and Son
    The Living Years
    With Arms Wide Open
    Younger Generation

Stories
    College Calls
    Daddy, Draw My Hand
    Family Vacation
    Fork in the Path
    Justin, the Shark Slayer
    Moms and Dads
    Napkin Art
    Please Come Back: A Love Story
    Raccoon Feet

ESSAYS

Father and Son, revisited 2002

Cat Stevens sings to me about a conversation between Father and Son, a song that captured me when I was a kid and speaks to me today as a father. I listen as I recall this day's conversations with my son of 16 as we attended church, sought a job for him, and enjoyed a movie together; I listen as I recall the dream of a few days ago in which I spent the entire night in the company of my father. Dad passed away 20 years ago.

As I am father to my son, and son to my father, in this mid-identity midlife, I consider the many topics that I want to share with my son, and ask of my dad. Many are in Stevens' song: girls, happiness, discovery, crying and keeping things inside. Given the "permission" to remain in a discovery mode, we continue to battle the issues of finding ourselves and dealing with "I know, I have to go." As my three sons grow and go, I have to wonder if the time for me to grow and go is at hand.

Life is about growing and going from one realm to another, from one phase to another, from one self-awareness to another. If we remember that, we can better understand our worlds and those of our children. For the moment, I'm trying to understand my own, and seeking the responses of my three boys, great advisers of 20, 16 and 9. By summer's end, they'll be 21, 17 and 10. No more single digits in the family.

How can I have ignored my instincts, my tears and my passions in the name of making a living? How lucky I have been to find a job that allows me access to those things, but not the full immersion that drove me for so long, and now draws me back. Words and images as tools of discovery and understanding of all people—they have been my drive for so long. I feel it at church perhaps because I have the time to watch. No deadlines to move on there.

I'm disappointed in my boys' responses about my writing and speaking engagements when their first comments are "do they pay," but I find consolation when they follow that up with "That is cool Dad. I know you're having fun." Indeed, the fun of being "called out" to create.

Having benefited from a recent trip to Mississippi for a McInnis family reunion, I have many more questions for my father. Questions about why he returned to his origins so few times when so much of his heart resided with the "simple" people of his roots. Questions about why so many of his clients were in the hinterlands of the Houston area, small communities that surely reminded him of his Southern heritage—honest, straight-shooting, and partaking of a good sip now and then. Clients in towns like Winnie, Rosharon, Alvin and Angleton in Texas must have given him a slim connecting root to Vimville, Meridian and Yazoo City in Mississippi. At least, I think so. We never had the chance to talk about that as Father and Son.

But the current conversations of Father and Son cover many of the things I simply want to share with them, and many of the insights and topics that I wished that I had covered with Dad. And sometimes I tell the boys why I'm discussing the topic du jour: "I don't know these answers for my dad, but I want you to know them about me."

Harry Chapin follows shortly after Stevens in this writing-music night. The master storyteller in lyrics and human linkages. I admire both the songwriters' abilities to convey stories, be they of taxi drivers or hard-headed women, in song. I aspire to that in stories, poetry, and images. I achieve that. And then I share them with whoever will listen, including my sons. Father and Sons.

The storytelling is part of the discovery process, which should be an exciting journey instead of a disappointment that I've yet to reach my destination. There are others who believe that I should have "arrived" while I believe I'm still searching. And praying continuously, "God, you're going to have to steer because I don't know where I'm going, but I'll push as hard as I can. Count on that." Too often I'm not pushing as hard as I can, and I'm not trusting that God is steering. And so I seek the map in the writings, images and faces around me.

Cat Stevens' father in the song sang "Look at me/I am old/But I'm happy." I'm happy, discouraged by others and demanding of myself to be without flaw or failure. I wish that I could talk to my dad.

November 29, 2009 Listen to Life newsletter

Father and Son

Forty years ago, a lyrical conversation caught my heart and imagination. I heard it again this past Saturday evening like I had never heard it before.

The song is Father and Son by Cat Stevens, and it recants a conversation between a father and son as the son struggles with the need to make decisions to move on. It is one of the songs that I have brought to the attention of my sons during their different phases of growth for several reasons: youth rarely believes that age really understands, youth always wants to express and feels incapable of doing so, and age hopes to encourage youth to slow down their decision making in order to be happy.

The important thing to me about this song is that the father and son are talking through life changes that all have experienced. When I first heard the lyrics decades ago, I knew I loved the reality of the emotions, the struggles and the coming together of father and son to deal with life's changes. I'm proud to say that the song's description of father and son not listening to each other well was not part of our story, but the sharing of thoughts and wisdom has been a mutual mainstay. I'm also not so naive as to think that there likely weren't times when my sons felt like I wasn't listening as much as they wanted. Welcome to the human race.

My oldest son, my namesake, married on Saturday. It was a beautiful wedding with representatives from all phases of his life, a grand tribute to his influence on many.

Also on Saturday, I heard the song like never before. Deep into the wedding reception, Dion took the microphone and called out, "Dad. Dad, where are you? Come on up here." I joined him at the front of the room and he paid tribute to the importance and pleasure of father-son times together. He called out to fathers, sons, grandparents and fathers-to-be to take the time to join in conversations. "And sometimes, it's just great to have a beer with your dad. Dad, join me at the bar for a beer, huh?" We walked to the bar at the reception and for the duration of the song, we hugged, laughed, cried and shared. We condensed 28 years into about three minutes. It seems like those 28 years have lasted only about three minutes.

Almost three decades ago, I began learning how to be a father, and over the years I've been blessed to be dad to three outstanding young men, my sons. I learned and learn from them along the way. Now, I will begin to learn about daughters. I'm sure I will learn along the way.

I love you Dion and Candice. Have a very happy life together. I wish for you your dreams.

Young Love

Almost three decades ago, I lay on my bed, in tears over the pain of teen love. I was in my room—my favorite place—and alone—my favorite company. The bed creaked as someone sat next to me. I assumed that my mom had come to comfort her poet-son.

A stubbly beard scratched my face, telling me now that Dad was my comforter this day on a matter I didn't expect him to weigh in on. His actions were simple—a kiss on my cheek and a gentle pat on my back—but they were effective. He then left me to my coping with adolescent love. I wish that I could do the same for my two older sons as they struggle with love issues.

The middle son—heir apparent to the McInnis poet title—is dealing atypically flipy with the issues of true love du jour while the oldest—heir apparent to his grandfather's tradition of "so many women, so little time"—is truly, genuinely, lovingly smitten with a woman in a deep, meaningful, vulnerable way that I figured was still a long time coming. Distance and circumstances have not given me the opportunity to do for them what my dad did for me that day—acknowledge that men also realize that love can hurt.

Love, for a young man—and I assume also for a young girl but I've never been a girl, nor have any of my children, all sons—is inconceivably complicated, particularly when trying to move into virgin territory of feelings and expressing them.

Perhaps that is the secret of love, both the good and the bad: it will take you places you didn't expect where you will see and feel things that are unexplainable and bring you life, death and resurrection a multitude of times. My boys are just learning. I wish that I could help them. I'd tell them . . .

Love is being, not feeling. Love could not have access to those protected spots of our soul that bring about extreme joy and pain were it not a part of being (verb). And a part of our being (noun). To just feel love is to admit that love has not been allowed to be the root of our action or the nurturing, stabilizing tap root of who we are. If we are flush with feelings, but how we view and live do not change, we are the litmus paper dipped into the hormonal chemistry of infatuation—changing color to indicate a presence but not becoming or behaving somehow "other." If there is alchemy, it is when the chemistry of love changes us to a richness of loving actively.

Love is about living, not life. No love is worth dashing our selves or our beings onto the rocks, literally or metaphorically. Our life does not end with the conclusion of a lover nor does it begin with the entry of a love. Love affects how we live and share and fulfill our souls, but whether we are "in love" or not cannot be allowed to define us. Our loving ways are living ways, and not tied only to another individual.

Love is sharing, not taking. Sharing with someone, sharing with the world, and most importantly sharing with one's self.

FATHER'S DAY WRITINGS

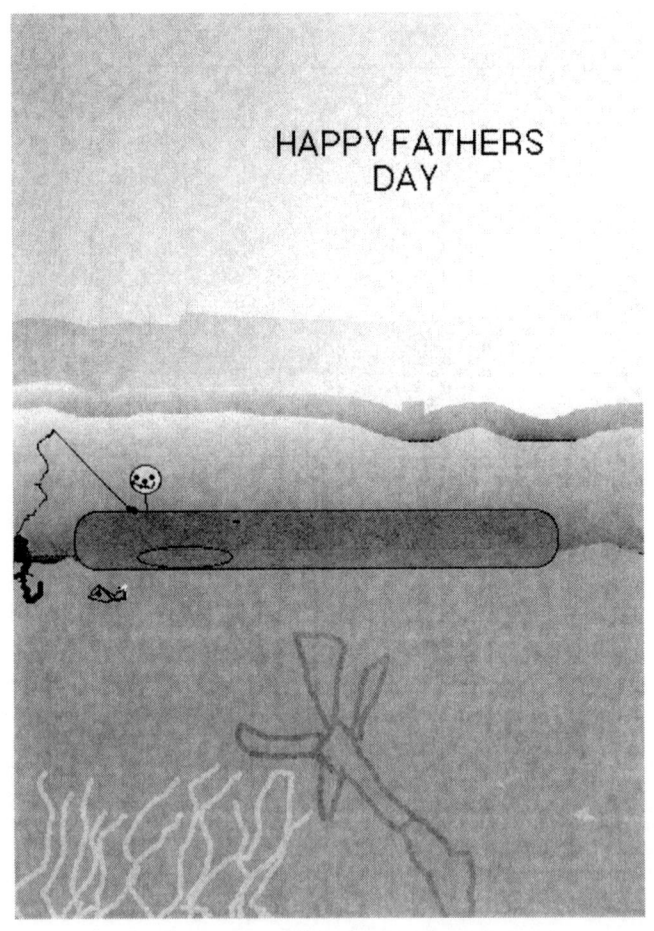

Messages for Father's Day cards changed after my separation and as the boys' style of messages changed with age.

Father's Day 1999

The small voice from the back of the van pierced the chill created by the emotions, the air conditioning and the rain soaked clothing: "Dad, I'm sorry that your daddy died." I couldn't respond, but I couldn't *not* respond either. A long minute later I was able to choke out a quiet "Thanks buddy."

It was Father's Day, the last of the 1900s. On our way to the family vacation in Corpus Christi, at the ¾-way mark of a 10-hour drive from Albuquerque, we drove through San Antonio. San Antonio: the site of McInnis Drive (named for my granddad); where my dad boxed professionally; the town of Mom and Dad's courtship, marriage; the birthplace of their four kids; and where Mom, Dad and my first sister are buried.

Summer torrents were filling all the streets of San Antonio. There seemed to be a respite as we neared the expansive Catholic cemetery on the west side of town. "General McMullen" rang in my ears as I tried to recall at least a street name. I still don't recall the name of the cemetery. Across the entrance to the cemetery was a shopping center, the entire street side covered with vendors selling flowers and other Father's Day memorabilia to be placed at the gravesites. I, my wife of 20 years and my three sons stood by the three plots when the clouds opened up. The rain chilled my bones as shy tears strayed across rain splattered cheeks. Quietly my family returned to the car while I shared my Father's Day solitude with Dad.

There was much that I had wanted to discuss during this surprise visit: the job opportunity in Oregon, the reality of our first-born (my only child that he ever saw) going to college, career developments, fishing stories . . . and so much more. We've chatted this past 17 years, but only in fits and spurts. Hard rain became a heavy-dropped downpour that felt to be of Biblical proportions. The cold shivers began to overwhelm the emotional shivers of crying and missing a dad worthy of the epitaph "He has left us a most noble pattern." The rains and the reality of another three hours of driving shortened my visit. The chatting would have to come later. But there was sufficient time to say "Love you, Dad; miss you so much."

In Corpus, hours later, my middle son joined his dad for a quick visit on the porch, overlooking the beach from our home for the coming week.

Standing at a rail, watching the waves, dodging the wind-propelled rain drops, he asked, "Did you pray to your dad that we all catch fish on the trip?"

"Nope. I said to him, 'Dad, here's my three boys.'"

"Cool."

I'll forever remember the last Father's Day of the 1900s: the surprise of being able to go by the cemetery, the cold of the rain, the mental image of me sharing an umbrella with my wife as three boys—ages 17, 13 and 6—stand strongly by their dad as he weeps for his father they never knew. I very much felt the fortunate father and the lucky son. And the pain will always be overwhelmed by the quiet, caring voice that lovingly said "Dad, I'm sorry that your daddy died."

Happy Father's Day 2002

Son has become father, now telling his sons: Happy Father's Day. I am a happy father on this holiday created by the gift industry to provide another opportunity to sell cards and Sunday brunches. Although the premise is for children to thank their fathers, today I thank my dad by thanking you.

Fatherhood is not without its frustrations, ebbs and flows, peaks and valleys, and confusion. Likewise, it is filled with joys, exhilaration, new discoveries and complete certainty. My dad taught me by osmosis and observation, and I hope that I can teach you through actions and conversations that being a dad will be the hardest job you've ever had, and the most rewarding. "Reward" at your current respective ages means such different things, and all of them are right.

Cameron, a reward is something you get for a job well done, like a candy bar for getting your room extra special clean. Being a dad is that kind of reward. Justin, a reward might be something you get for doing something honorable or just. Being a dad brings that kind of reward, too. And Dion, to you a reward may be something more along the lines of a fulfillment. Being a dad is certainly that, too.

Father's Day 2003

It takes a choice to be a father. And a recent choice made for the most unlikely Father's Day.

I chose to move away from my family a week before my anniversary, two months before my and my wife's birthdays, two months before Mother's Day, three months before Father's Day, and so on. There were 12 months of calendar reasons to not move. But I did. I had to. And that decision, not unlike the decision to become a father, is forever changing my life.

I did not move to flee my family. I had to re-find me. This was no midlife, spontaneous, irresponsible decision to leave my wife and sons high and dry. They have the house, 100% of my salary, 80% of the bills before I left . . . I'm no saint in this, but I'm not a bastard either. I just couldn't go on.

Father's Day. Quite the test for me, the family, the process and the . . . decision.

I saw only one of my sons today. Dion is out of town and called in the evening to wish me well and to discuss our joint business venture. And to thank me for the recent cash. Justin called early this morning to wish me well but couldn't pass his girlfriend heartaches to join Barbara, Cameron and me for a movie. (We are separated, not divorced.) Cam and I then had fried chicken dinner along with some fishing and a movie.

By those measurements, perhaps today is an indicator of bad decisions, hurtful decisions. But it is much too early to tally up the score. If pain and confusion comprise loss, then we all have lost—early and often.

There is much more evidence that this Father's Day indicates that I am their father, and always will be; that I don't, nor have I ever measured or evaluated their love by presents or presence; and, that we're early in a process that is confusing and hurtful to all of us, not just me, not just the rest of the family.

Those who don't "know" are likely shocked by the bold, "irresponsible" actions of such an active, loving father who spoke out often on the value and importance of family, and on the divinely enjoyable job of being a dad. Those few who care to take the risk of knowing me realize that I am indeed still that person. My passionate pleadings and writings were exactly that—passionate. And filled in belief of all of us. Passion is powerful in all manifestations of my thoughts on those matters. That has not changed. I just finally accepted that the lesson also applies to me.

So this year, I bought $13 worth of fishing stuff in preparation for my trip with Cameron. That was my Father's Day present to me. My way of saying, hurts notwithstanding, I still love my boys. And perhaps they see that there is space in a man's life to love himself, too, in a life-preserving sort of way. Cam gave me a 5-pound bag of Hot Tamales candy and his brothers gave me calls. I'm still their father and a good one for how I love them.

Today, I was a good father and a good son. I was true to my Self without relinquishing my Self for the boys. I decided to father. Life changes. Loving sons is constant.

June 20, 2004 Listen to Life newsletter

Father's Way

Father's Day 2004. A day of fishing with two of my sons and we caught nothing but good times, laughter and a ton of conversation. I have a stringer full of good times.

Two men who saw us today wished me happy Father's Day—a pleasant surprise. A guy who cut my hair last month asked "when did you know you were a father?" There is a bond among dads, but rarely do we get to converse about it.

The barber offered his brother's answer to the question; it had something to do with bills. I told him that there are many times throughout the lives of our children, as they grow and develop, when reminders surface that say, whisper or scream "you're a dad." My reply to him was when a little one was on my shoulders. No matter how old they were, when one of my sons rested on my shoulders I felt very dad like. They are all too big now to sit atop without crushing me, but I realize that they still feel comfortable there—letting dad shoulder them, their thoughts, their concerns, their issues, their dilemmas and their successes. It's a father's way.

We don't hear much about a father's feelings. Today is a good day to ask. Some answers may surprise you with their familiarity, and some may surprise you with how different they are than our expectations. Take a chance. Ask. He may answer.

June 19, 2005 Listen to Life newsletter

A Dad's Day

Among my presentations about the things we hear when we listen to life is one that I call "Daddin'." Some of you have heard my explanation. Today is a good day to recall what daddin' is and what it means and what you might discover by looking for it.

In our society, the verb "mother" inspires wonderful images of loving, nurturing, tending and so on. If you say, "I saw a woman mothering a child at the park," your listener likely imagines the interactions between the mother and her child. In our society, the verb "father" connotes procreation. If you say, "I saw a man fathering a child at the park," your listener likely envisions a man having sex. So, for the sake of clarity, I use the verb "daddin'." Being a dad is certainly a verb, as well as a noun, and the role holds whether the man is married or divorced, because being a father is in the heart and soul, not on the finger or license. Consider the times your father was more a verb than a noun.

The tradition (and burden) that fathers are to be the invincible, almighty, money-creating, stoic leader of the tribe robs mothers, children and fathers of the reality of the dad experience. The quest for that ideal destroys women, children and the men who believe they can be those things. I'm blessed to have had the father I did, and equally blessed that there was not a pretense of perfection. His tombstone reads "He left for us a most noble pattern." Not perfection. Not godliness. Not the perfect role model. But he did leave . . . a . . . **noble** . . . pattern, despite his demons and the loss of a daughter to leukemia at the age of five in the 1940s. Your father has had losses, too.

My neighbor told me about the loss of a daughter who was killed at the age of eight. She told me that her husband held their youngster as she died, and that his spirit to grow and live his life fully was almost snuffed out by the loss. It is unlikely that the father you know or see on the street would ever share the pains of loss (death, divorce, career), nor would he share the joys of growth (children, spirit, love). So be it, I guess, but rest assured that the man with a kid on his shoulders and another tugging at his back pocket, or the one fishing alongside a young man version of him, is living the verb of dad and not just the noun of father. Listen to his actions, even if there are no words, particularly if that man is your dad.

Happy Father's Day to all, and particularly to the late J. Russell McInnis.

June 18, 2006 Listen to Life newsletter

Father's (play) Day

Today was a contemplative Father's Day, beginning with a phone call from my oldest son, a day of fishing and goofing around with my youngest, and then a team-cooked dinner with my middle and youngest joining in, each with a responsibility in the steak, mashed potatoes, yams and salad dinner. The mortar that held the day's activities together was my thoughts. Thoughts borne from the conversations and interactions with my boys, from the two movies of the day ("Around the Bend" and "Cinderella Man"), and from the meaning of the day. To be father, and to be son, always provokes thoughts and wonderments.

I provided myself instant replays on the various interactions and conversations with my sons, looking for perspectives into our relationships, and what they will mean to them decades from now when I am a grandfather and later when I am gone. I replayed vignettes of my role as son, and considered the great times that I had with my dad. And I heard something in my head, over and over again: "C'mon Dad, let's play . . ." That phrase would be followed by "catch," or "baseball," or "basketball," or "pool" or some other activity.

"Let's play . . ." serves as a wonderful invitation that dads can't ignore. I consider the things that I learned, and hopefully now teach, in the moments of playing games or playing on the swing set or playing in the driveway . . . and I realize that one's life as father or child gains richness and depth in the play times. Do we teach our kids how to grow up to be fair, honest, balanced, good-humored adults capable of upholding responsibilities and respectful relationships through our lectures? Or in the classroom of play and interaction? Play is not always simply fun, but there are always important lessons.

Kids learn about their parents, adulthood, growing up, competition and honest joy; parents learn about their kids, and re-learn about honest joy and youthful enthusiasm; both are rewarded with relationships that are carried through the generations.

Each time that I hear one of my son's say, "let's play," or I recall the times that my dad would forsake infrequent relaxation time to accept my call to

"Let's play," or in the future when a young child calls out to me, "Grandpa, let's play," I will remember that I have been INVITED into a sacred place. And I will play.

Happy Father's Day.

June 17, 2007 Listen to Life newsletter

Father's Day 2007

"Just think about when I take my kids there, Dad. I expect you to be there, too," my youngest son said. I figured I will be there, just as my dad was with him and me this weekend.

"There" is April Fool Point, a marina on one corner of the peninsula where the town of San Leon sits. From 1968 to 1972, my dad and I used that marina as a point of departure for days of fishing in the bays. Those were wonderful times, providing scores of stories that I have shared with my sons over the years. Five years ago, I returned to the marina to say goodbye to Dad in a different way and was a bit disappointed to find then that the old place was pretty much just a base for a shrimp fleet. But yesterday, my son and I, standing where my dad and I used to stand, watched boats being launched from a ramp and fishermen cleaning their catch. Three decades ago, boats were launched with a hoist that cradled them on canvas straps and then lifted them off trailers for gentle placement in the water. The process was different, but the results were the same: fun and fish.

As the two of us walked alongside the water, I pointed out old fishing spots, told more stories and took him to exactly where I was when I threw my bobber-with-a-message into the water for my dad. I told him how great I thought it was to be able to share this place with him. I felt my dad watching us, smiling as the tradition of McInnis fishing continues through the generations, as well as the tradition of fathers loving their children and sharing time and stories with them. It will likely be a quarter century before he is old enough to have kids his age now, but the stories will still be alive and new stories will be created. And I'll be there, one way or another, just as my dad is for me.

June 15, 2008 Listen to Life newsletter

Father's Day 2008

This summer will mark the midpoint. Father's Day 26 years ago was my 26th with my dad. This year is my 26th without him. My oldest son is now one year older than I was when Dad passed away. There is much to consider on Father's Day 2008. Today I ponder legacy, connection and projection.

Legacy
Dad's legacy comprised various components, many of which seemed to conflict. The same can be said for all of us, particularly if we own each of our elements for our entire lives instead of relinquishing them to one of the many forces that try to shape us to our lowest common denominator. Dad was gentle; he was also an accomplished boxer. He held a multitude of jobs of differing respect levels; he was a successful accountant the last four decades of his life. He was disciplined; alcohol was his demon. He was also loving, caring, common sensical, supportive. All these, and more, make much of his legacy because legacies only begin when those who are influenced share their stories, knowledge and beliefs. What many people know as Dad's legacy is actually what they see as evidence in his friends, colleagues and children that he touched us. Fathers' legacies will surface as the shiny face among the many facets worn and cut through a life of work, success, failure, joy and sorrow.

Connection
The connections that we make with our children, friends and colleagues are what manifest our work as parents. Lousy connections make for lousy manifestations of our beliefs and values in others; in other words, without good relations, communications, honesty and humility, we cannot truly be teacher, guide, mentor or friend to touch lives. I consider the relationship that I had with my dad and how those connections also influence the lessons that my sons pick up from me. Likewise, my relationship with my three incredible sons allows them to grow from my influence and me to grow from theirs. The legacies that each of us creates hinge greatly on our ability to connect to others.

Projection
Legacy tends to be based on a current standing built from historical events and actions; connections are about the here and now of relationships; and projection reflects how our lives and work appear years and decades hence as elements of our morals, values and beliefs imbedded in hundreds of people through legacy stories and connections. If we are truly called to make the world a better place in whatever ways we can, and I believe we are, our influence matters in the here and now, but it comes to fruition for harvest in the future because of the courageous actions, wise decisions and humble attitudes that we possess today.

Dad would be proud and pleased that his efforts, and Mom's of course, have made such a difference because of how his honest beliefs amidst human failings gain immortality thanks to how he influenced others. Your dad would be, too. Tell him.

June 20, 2010 Listen to Life newsletter

Father's Day Memories 2010

"I have a terrible headache and I didn't catch any fish," my eldest son Dion said. "I already feel like a dad," he added. He'll be a father in about three months.

I had to laugh at his comment, not to mention the story behind it. On Friday evening, his wife and he went fishing for their (soon to be) Father's Day fun, and he ended up getting a fishing lure caught in his head that she and another person managed to work out of his skin with much pushing, pulling and pain.

It's no surprise that while he and his two brothers were in town to spend some time hanging out and fishing as a Father's Day weekend treat for me, that we spent some time talking about fatherhood and the stories shared with fathers and kids. We talked about things that brought us to laughter, and things that brought us to quiet thought.

As we fished, Dion said, "I know this sounds cliché, but it seems like 'only yesterday' that we found out we were pregnant and now we're almost there."

"Yes," I replied, "and it seems like only yesterday each of you boys were riding on my shoulders with arms draped around my head, legs wrapped around my neck, and slobbering on my bald spot. It all goes fast. My mom told me so, but there's no way of knowing how true it is until you are in it."

"So, how do you slow it down, Dad?"

"I think by sharing thoughts and stories. We share, which reminds us or triggers our own memories. And writing the stories, taking the photos, and thinking about what's happening."

So, we'll all remember Father's Day 2010 as we share memories and stories of this first as a dad in the making, my last before becoming a grandfather, the flounder we caught, the crazy man who walked across our fishing lines, the crazy people at San Luis Pass Saturday night, the flounder we caught, the throw net I forgot for our gar fishing expedition, and much more . . . including the flounder we caught! We'll forget a lot of details, I'm sure, but we'll remember that again we spent Father's Day together, and again we enjoyed the time together.

As a dad, time passes quickly, the headaches arise and there are some days of not catching any fish, either literally or figuratively. But, we remember and we **work** to remember with fondness, laughter, joy and sorrow the many moments of growing and growing up that make all the days that lead to the singular day of Father's Day so special.

Happy Father's Day to the dads . . . whether we have them with us or only their memories.

KID ART

I guess I had expressed that work was frustrating and Dion used the opportunity to create a visual story of spacing out at work because of the demands.

Another of Dion's characters.

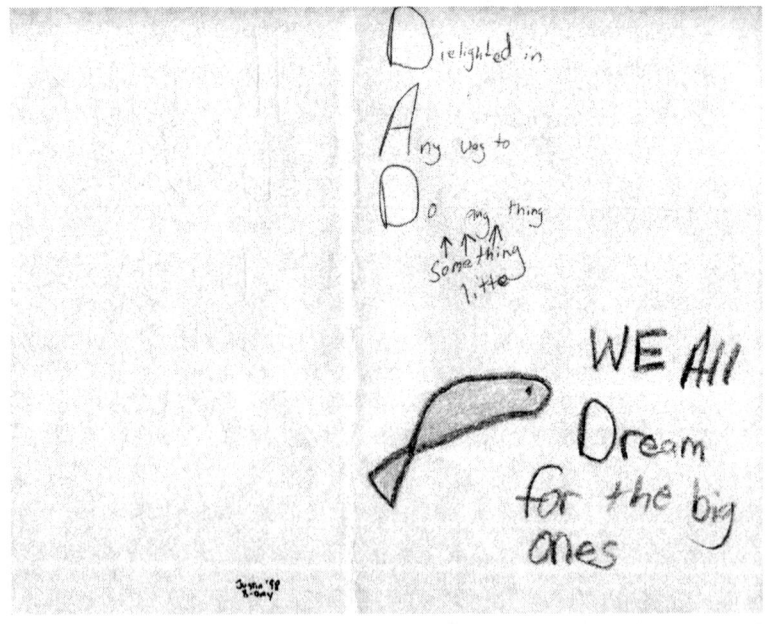

Justin's fun while creating a birthday card for me.

More of Dion's characters, carrying message with a smile.

Justin's life of adventure and discovery made for an appropriate message for his graduation. He supplied the images and I designed the card to convey his message and his essence.

POETRY

Family

The hustle, bustle and potential glory of
Cause
Holds nothing compared to the purpose of
Family.
All the heroics in the world
Provide me less
Than the smile on my freckle-nosed seven-year old,
The introspective chats with my young teen,
Or the charming smile and confidence of my young man.

November 21, 1999

Son's Room

Socks and shoes and toys
Were strewn all over your floor
I looked across the field
While standing at your door
I charged forward
Moving courageously ahead
Until I made it—at last
The destination was your bed
And there we laughed
And we prayed together

Read a few books
Or discussed the weather
The journey from door to bed
Was always an adventurous one
But the trip was always great
'cause it ended with you, my son

August 25, 2003

Voices

In the voices and eyes of my young men
I see inside them, and me reflected
Like a magical looking glass that looks into the future
And the past, at the same time.
The burning of their souls' passions
Were mine;
The curiosity and confidence of discovery
Were mine;
The confidence and knowledge that love will follow them the rest of their days
Were mine.
And in my eyes I hope they see smiles for a lifetime
Will be theirs;
Determination and courage, sometimes repressed, never vanquished
Will be theirs;
The belief in what can be and the confidence to ask for help
Will be theirs;
The humility of vulnerability and humanity
Will be theirs.
I can only hope that we're both seeing when we look
Father to son.

–2003

STORIES

College Calls

The phone rings, stirring me from a not-yet-complete trek to sleep. "Hello" I say while trying to find the fit of the receiver to my head in the dark. There's music blaring on the other end and I smile. It's my college son.

"Hi, Dad, how's it going," Dion calls out. "Hang on, let me turn this down."

"Hi, bud. What's cooking?"

For the next half-hour or so we talk about life for this college junior and of midlife for his father. He's following up on a long e-mail I sent him about his Thanksgiving and Christmas trek home including updates on his old man's life and my pride in who he is. He's quite the young man now, though hearing of the rites of maturation sprouted a few gray hairs while I lay in the dark listening to him, trying hard to listen more than I talked.

I calmly listen to issues of ex-girlfriends and fisticuffs with dorm pals; the topics are connected. I hear of punches thrown and return volleys. Of the mature bonding between him and his friends as they sort through issues. Of working hard to be a responsible young man with a job but without wheels. I cringe that I can't give him a replacement vehicle or even some help for same, nor have I done much for his college education save for financing two years of private high school to prepare him. I could have done worse, but I would love to do more.

He reminds me of those I have met in the dorm previously, and how they fit into the current tales. "Oh yeah," I interject, "I remember him. The guy right across the hall from you, right?" I know this because I spent the night in his dorm a month or so ago so we could attend a big football game together. As it turned out, I was with him and about 100 of his dorm friends to complete our responsibility in forming the largest crowd to ever attend a football game in Texas history. There were more than 87,000 of us watching Texas A&M kick Notre Dame at Kyle Field. As far as I was concerned, there were only two of us there that day.

I'm reminded that there actually are others in the world besides my boy and me when he asks for a break in the conversation so he can answer another call that is clicking in. Bondus interruptus. He returns now that I am fully awake and engaged in our sharing of stories to say the other call is a friend, one of the good guys, who is part of the woman-based fracas of the other night. I sigh quietly. Women. Fracases. Friends. Interruptions. Such is life between friends, even those who are 25 years apart and share both first and last names.

"OK, bud. Take care of yourself. I hope that you get all this worked out." Little does he know how much I wish this harm and powder keg to leave him completely.

"Not a problem Dad. My friends love me, they're helping take care of me."

We both laugh, but I know this to be true. He has that effect on others, as is often attributed to his dad: his passion and clarity bring him the admiration or the disdain of others. Rarely is there an in between.

"Good. Take care. Talk to you soon."

"Love you bud" and "Love you Dad" overlap as it always does when we conclude phone calls.

The phone is returned to its cradle. I lay back, staring at the ceiling, recalling a safer, more innocent time. They each have their magic. They've all been shared in love. And I try to return to sleep.

Daddy, Draw My Hand

"Daddy, draw my hand," my three-year old, blue-eyed smile named Cameron says. It's a fairly routine request. In the routine of fatherhood comes the beauty and the connection.

The exercise comes from the short-legged work tables at his Mother's Day Out program. A varied population of small-toothed, stubby-fingered little artists get to play and learn for a half-day while, as the theory goes, mom gets to take a break and "go out." The concept for the students seems to work; the moms tend not to get their end of the bargain. But, it is in this environment of escape-and-learn that the children begin to discover, in some structured sense, about the omnipotence of glue, potential of construction paper scraps, gems that are uncooked macaroni, and simple sensuality of finger painting. Drawing their hands makes for a simple task that creates unique artwork that can be modified into Thanksgiving Day turkeys, strung together as paper chains or used as Christmas presents for mommy and daddy.

And, after putting away my briefcase, sharing kisses with the young one's two older brothers and my wife, artist and assistant approach the art table. He slides in easily; I fold my legs under the short, light wood table and we proceed. What happens then moves in slow motion through all of my senses. I feel like I am watching a movie that I can rewind and play at any time. And I do.

His smallish hand rests on the artist's canvas, which is actually the backside of old letterhead from my days in the photography business. Minute finger twitches give away his anxiousness to create. His head turns back to me, a smile flashes, leaving me seeing emotional black dots as if a strobe popped in my eyes. I'm temporarily blinded by the smile, the excitement in his eyes and my own pure joy in the simplicity of the moment. Maybe there is something else that hampers my vision.

The flat-nosed orange Crayola is handed to me, not unlike the nurse handing the surgeon a special instrument. Aromas hit me: the wonderful smell of the crayon in my hand and the sweetness of the little boy's hair just beneath my chin. Let the drawing begin.

I trace. The simplicity of the art is its beauty. As for all art, be it headed for a national museum or the kitchen refrigerator, interpretation holds the hook to each of us. This orange-lined hand is much more. It is me.

I am my son's hand. In it is my past. As it grows, becomes heavier and eventually sports a gold band, it becomes what I am now. We're tracing more than the outline of what is to be a holiday turkey, we trace father and son.

The tracing moves along much slower than the perceptions. That is good. It gives me time to sniff the baby shampoo smell, a bit offset by the sweetness of little boy sweat earned in the playground. It gives me time to notice the small, dry, red Play-doh traces on his thumb's nail. It gives me time to feel the soft, still-baby skin as I help keep his excited hand in place for the sketching to be done. It gives me time to see the inventory of scratches, nicks, and little bruises that mark his leaving infancy and moving to the social, interactive world of childhood. It gives me the time to see remains of finger paints in little folds of skin between his fingers. It gives me time with my son.

I can't help but notice my own hands as his are being outlined. The simple gold band on my left hand that has been a fixture there for 16 years. The old band on my right hand has resided there for 13 years; it once was a part of my father, a symbol of more than four decades of marriage before he died. Scars, chewed fingernails and a couple of gray hairs separate a young boy's hands from his dad's. I can almost remember mine looking like his. Will he? I can remember working with my dad on projects and being fascinated by his hands. He had short little fingers that I considered fat, and now his ring fits perfectly on my skinny fingers. He had nails as hard as . . . nails . . . and mine are chewed, made easier by the paper-thin quality of them that I inherited from my mom.

Dad had a small blue dot on the heel of his hand, the consequence of having a pencil jabbed in it. I don't know the story behind the marking, but I remember that dot well. I'm taking in the artist's hands, too. Whose nails did he inherit? Is that finger shape from his mom? Or is it from my mom? A mole is beginning to develop near his knuckles, surely the start of a bumper crop of them, assuming genetics maintains its tradition in our family. Does he notice the big hand helping his draw?

The excitement in his motions and frequent smiles and pride-in-accomplishment-chest-puffing and innocent happiness camouflage the simple wonder of the moment.

His satisfied smile warms me. Quickly he moves. Excitedly he grabs the art and runs to his mom, "Look, Mom, I drew me." No son, you drew us.

Family Vacations

The packing for the family vacation could easily have sounded something like this: socks, underwear, fishing equipment, camera, food, drinks, games, maps, swimming suit and humor. While many family vacations are to see the world with wide-open eyes, this trip has seen our home of Texas through eyes squinted in laughter.

Timing, as they say, is everything. It is not the words that are necessarily the seeds of laughter, but the time and place. Perhaps the greatest thing about the trip is recalling laughing so much. Not that I recall all the circumstances, but recalling laughing at every location, every site and every activity.

It's a big day for the older McInnis boys, me and my two oldest sons. We're booking an offshore trip on one of those charters where half the people are going to get drunk and the other half are hoping to be part of vacationer carnage to the fish population. Us? We're just trying to have an inexperienced experience. We've completed booking our excursion for two days hence and are set to proceed out the door. Son number two lags a bit behind to ask questions regarding what types of fish we can expect to catch. "Kingfish, mackerel and ling," the polite coastal woman replies. The mumble off my shoulder responds, "Yep, we're gonna catch little Chinese guys." My oldest is in fine form.

The cascade of thoughts and collaborative humor begins: the boat freezer plate full of short men in white coats, the fisherman dockside on one knee with his arms outstretched over a little guy as they pose for a Polaroid, the technique of "tlolling" to make the catch, and more.

Things continue to degenerate amid laughs, snorts and dry jabs at any and everything. Words stand alone as triggers to the funny bone, as do actions. Crabbing on the jetties by one of many marinas in the tourism town of Port Aransas has yielded precious little in the way of crabs. Dion decides to fish for seagulls, "casting" the crab line onto jetty rocks, waiting for a hungry seagull to hop along to the soaked meat and then "battling" the prey as it flies off with bait in beak. There is nothing to hook the birds, and the patience of traditional bobber-and-bait fishing applied to seagulls defies description. There's the waiting, the holding of the line and the muttering to the prey in hopes of coaxing them to a "bite." Then I hear a "bait voice" squeaking a tantalizing "Don't eat me, I'm just a dead chicken."

Others don't understand us, for some reason. I can hardly imagine why. Perhaps it is the style of humor, or simply the candor of everyone's comments. As we all pile out of the van, we line up for sodas from the cooler in the back. I dispense Dr. Peppers to the clan, then hug B to the sound of fitzing can openings. A hug and a kiss are interrupted by "Hey, don't put your hand on her booty." The six-year old then giggles to the sound of his own warning.

Maybe everyone laughed at his comments because of the activities beforehand. The bait fishing for seagulls. The appointment to catch ling, or was it Ling? The trolling for kids.

We left the crabbing site and proceeded back to the beach in hopes of a few more rays and waves before heading back to our vacation home-away-from-home. As we're driving down the beach front, in the appointed car lane of packed sand, we hear a tapping sound out the back window of the van. Trailing the van in the wind are a kite, its string and the fluorescent pink plastic string holder. Just as a teaser works in offshore fishing, using a hookless surface plug to attract gamefish, the kite and string have no chance of snagging anything, but behind us lurks two kids as they race down the beach trying to catch the van that caught their kite.

Did I mention that this vacation of family laughter began on Father's Day? It doesn't get better than that.

The Fork in the Path

Well, son, this is the fork in the road. You are on your own path in so many ways now, beginning with these base paths.

For most of my eldest's 15 years, he experienced things very similar to those of his old man. Little league was fun, but McInnises are not genetically bred athletes. So many things were similar; we even share a love for music from the early 1970s—classic rock. In music he began to hear a different drummer, him being capable of playing and understanding music.

I watch now as he is wrapping up his final day of baseball tryouts for the high school team. It has been almost three years since he last played organized baseball. But damn the fastballs, and full slide ahead. He is energized by the coach's requirement to "get naked for the ball." He faces the challenges of other players with a self-confidence and nothing-ventured-nothing-gained spirit that took me some 30 years to claim as mine.

With some envy and reminiscence, I watch these young men running, dancing their feet around at shortstop, and shagging arching hits to outfield. I remember being too cowardly and unsure to face my once beloved baseball once I got into high school. The banter and BS of these hormone machines transports me to ragged fields remembered for the smell of cut grass, the stains of red dirt and the spit-paths alongside the trail of cleat marks leading from the locker room to the field. Suddenly, high school is not so far away: only half a lifetime.

Neither swift of foot nor grace of moves, he tries hard. I smile, but try to remain camouflaged in the row of parents parked in cars under the sunset-lit field lights. The young man shags the first fly coursing its way, rainbow-like, into his glove. He reaches into that pot of gold and executes a throw to a cut-off net, standing in for an infielder in the greening grass of left-center field.

A pot-bellied man turns his head, his jaw moves and words must jump across the line of young athletes as one who just missed two flies is quickly "giving ten." I wonder if this man is the leader who my heir has attached his emotions and convictions to. Who will have the carrot and the stick to challenge him and to bring out the soul of this yet-unchallenged young man? Another fly shagged and I know it will be a pride-swollen drive home.

Gone are the sounds of the cracking ash wood bats, the distinctive clunk of a fungo bat testing the abilities of outfielder wannabes. Gone is the aroma of Atomic Balm, that napalm-in-a-tub used and overused by athletes as muscle relaxer and as the cologne of young jocks a couple of decades ago. What remains on this practice field of developing dreams are the hopes and memories of young men, the recurring youth of dads, the camaraderie bound together by white leather and red threads, and the joy of dirty clothes—a genetic mandate to follow in Pete Rose's footsteps. What remains is the peculiar type of support that occurs between teen jocks as the studs encourage the never-happen hopefuls after muffed plays. The passport across the bridge of innate ability is hustle; if you try you can be part of all the skill echelons. Only the true stars are sometimes forgiven for not giving a darn, and proving it play after play.

Many things separate my world and my son's world, but there is much that unites them at many junctures along the way. Humanity links us.

Justin the Shark Slayer

Something about fishing memories, father and son times, that last and last and last. I recall the first speckled trout that I *possibly* had with my dad (fishing from the shore in Galveston, Texas . . . the line broke, the five-year old asked "What was that?" and my dad somewhat impatiently said "Coulda been a speckled trout."), the first time we used artificial lures (yellow Shyster spinners with black dots used in a stock tank in Navasota, Texas when I was 12), and so on. The memories linger and last a lifetime.

They are no less permanent when the son becomes the father to son. And so it is that I recall the time when my middle son Justin, at 17, caught his first shark. A 15-pound sand shark while we waded in the surf on Bolivar Peninsula in search of bull reds. What a day it was.

We decided to catch our own bait the night before the big trip, which was arranged because of an early, 2:30 a.m. decision of his a week before, that he wanted to do some big-fish hunting. He had had enough chasing small catfish with his brother; Justin wanted a chance to hook a bull red. So, we scheduled an early morning trip preceded by a throw net excursion the evening before in search of mullet, shrimp, piggies, croaker and whatever else seemed logical for sow trout or bull reds. Bait in bucket with aerator in place, we dropped off to sleep in preparation for a 5:30 a.m. wakeup alarm.

The alarm was rude, but effective, as I recall. I got up only to discover that he hadn't made it to sleep at all. So he said. Such are teen recollections of a night's sleep. Anyway, we packed quickly and made the freeway for our hour-long journey from south of Houston to Bolivar Pensinsula. We watched the sky gain light as we crossed the bay bridge heading into Galveston. The man-talk was moving slow, but there is nothing like the simple pleasure of father-son talk; it is memorable as a young man, momentous as a father.

The ferry awaited us; we were one of the first to be on the craft for that particular run. I recall standing on the rail, chatting with him about things of life and sea, while noticing his lean, young physique, scruffy beard, shaggy hair and a smile that could lure a siren off her rock perch. Seagulls make my favorite bird sound and the sky was full of them as they glided alongside the ferry, traveling with us long enough to get closer to the shrimpers that were dredging up the bread of the sea while the sun rose; the son also rose, moving to the front of the ferry to observe more sights, inhale more rich, salty air, and continue the conversation and questions with his old man.

Remember your first anything with your dad? Whether it is using a lure, catching a trophy, riding a ferry or heading offshore, the memories of the "firsts" that occur with dad always seem particularly rich, full of detail, and un-erasable from our memories. Experiences become random-access treasures, capable of being pulled up whenever we want.

We both trolled for truth while on the ferry ride: "How much do those guys on the cargo ship make?"; "Think we'll see any dolphins in the strait today?" and "I wonder when we can do this again?"

The light remained wonderful, but had lost its photogenic magic in the 15-minute ride. We exited and headed to our pre-selected location, complete with new fishing gear, a bucket of bait, a box of donuts and a week's anticipation. I remember distinctly the clarity with which I saw him as a young man, while holding in my memory the mental images of me riding in the passenger seat with my dad driving (me with shaggy hair, no beard or scruff and of no interest to sirens, one way or another).

We stopped at Rollover Pass, a fishably wide pass through the peninsula that is about a half-mile wide at that point. Strong winds had the gulf side coughing up seaweed like wet hairballs. Between us learning how to cast with nine-foot rods and four ounces of weight and meat, tossing into strong winds, and reeling up produce-section quantities of vegetation at a time, we had a rocky start. We lost our bait primarily in the jumble of bile-colored weed. A toss of the throw net brought us four nice mullet: cut bait heaven. Our day was now ready to be changed.

Tossing our bait into gulf waters that looked more like melted frappucino—brown and frothy—discouraged us enough to send us in search of piers or anything that could take us past the brown and weed, and to clearer water. Twenty minutes of driving up and down the peninsula brought us no chances to catch fish, but unending opportunity to snag laughter, man-talk, silence and chatter. We returned to where we started, opting for the bay side.

Fishermen with rods ranging from Snoopy specials for kids to medium action baitcasting or spinning rigs lined the pass in search of barely-keeper trout, panfish and some sun rays. Justin, looking like a bare-chested Forrest Gump with scruffy hair and baseball cap, caught the attention of many who thought him to be a homeless bum, but he caught little more than boredom before returning to the car for a snooze. The long awaited father-son excursion was not living up to the week's hopes.

I recall seeing my 17-year-old boy stretched out inside the car. Within the image of him catching some rest was the recollection of him in a car seat instead of sleeping in a car's seat.

Boredom was contagious; once infected I decided to move along, back to the gulf side, but along the beach. Justin mumbled his acquiescence. The water was inviting so we cut up some mullet, waded into the surf and quickly noticed the near-absence of the dreaded weeds. Having almost perfected our casting, we tossed and waited. Not for long.

Within a few fleeting hours, we had hung and caught several nice sized gafftop that fought like "the train that could," never giving up. We both had massive fish on a few times, me losing mine with poor hooksets, and Justin with the same and a broken line incident. None of that mattered.

What mattered is what I saw: my teen boy some 30 yards from me, (flat) tummy high in the water, brown back standing like a channel marker, rod bent and quivering, him turning his head to me at times throughout the young man and the sea struggle to smile and nod a "I got this one covered" confidence, and either celebrate the fish brought in or throw a fist to the sky for the one that got away. I saw a man in progress.

Rain storm, nap and back to business.

While the desired bull red or sow trout failed to ever make it to the ice box, we continued to try. One particularly rod-bowing experience had Justin so excited that I could hear his heart from 30 yards, and over the sound of the waves. "It's on," he said in a combination of fishingese and youthful rebelliousness that describes a fight. And so it was.

He'd lean back for leverage, and crank furiously on the way back down. The fish took back most of what Justin had gained. The fun was afoot and he kept looking at me, flashing his marvelous smile and nodding his head strongly enough to cause his hair to bounce. Each smile put another image in my mental scrapbook.

A rolling swell about ten feet from his waist drew a new reaction. "Oh hell Dad, it's a shark!" Though we were in pursuit of reds or specks, he had always said that someday he'd like to catch a shark. The long anticipated trip and the excitement of finally catching nice sized fish were now paying off with a bonus: a three-foot sand shark.

I scurried through the waves to get to the car before him in order to get photos of the great shark slayer.

Moms and Dads

One of the best things that a dad can do is listen to mom—his own and that of his children.

Now, I've heard male friends talk about all their work in the delivery room, making it seem to the listeners of their fine, heroic stories that were it not for their efforts, their wives would still be walking around with a baby inside. Granted, the baby would be ready for high school by now, and the mother greatly disproportional with a linebacker in her womb, but thank goodness for dad in the delivery room. C'mon, it might have been a bit better, maybe even easier, to have dad in the labor room, but he certainly wasn't necessary. Nature takes care of necessity.

Nature takes care of parenting, too, in a way. You procreate, you take care of (oh were it that some humans took as good care of their children as animals do) and you send them off. But it is better done as a team. A man can't really take all the glory of daddin' without rightfully giving credit to a mom or two along the way.

Single parents may look more to their mothers, or mother figures, or to a friend-mother, but somewhere there is a motherly influence that positively affects the act of daddin'.

My mom was a patient soul, maybe because I was the caboose child of the family, bringing up the rear of four and 18 years after the first was born. She likely had much wisdom, patience and understanding built up over those years. I was the luckier for it. Goodness knows that she needed all those tools when I came around.

Painfully shy for most of my youth, armed with a sharp tongue, and timid to the world and its opportunities, I was not the easiest child to make independent. She noticed early on that I wouldn't learn something until I was ready, and when I was ready I wouldn't stop until I had learned it. Nope, no history of mother-son lessons in bike riding with the culmination coming one bright, sunny day with little Dion riding, wobbling down the street only to turn around, flash a big proud smile and wave to his mommy-teacher. I went out on my own, failed a few times, deemed myself not ready and then, years later, I declared myself ready, went outside and didn't return until I was a rider. Jumping rope? When the time was right, I came inside with my rough hewn, young-cowboy-lasso-rope and jumped in the living room until I was a real rope jumper.

Those tactics were not lost in my memory which is my best resource book for parenting—other than the obvious, my spouse—because Dad died when my oldest was one and Mom when my youngest was two. In between there were not a lot of parent consultations, just wonderful memories of having been raised by them. So, the memories serve me, guide me, teach me.

As it will be with our children. They will all carry forward particular memories of parental acts that make for a larger memory: youth and growing up. Daddin' is not a solitary activity, but one that is pursued both directly and vicariously.

It was a cold winter day, or as cold as one can expect in Houston in November. Barbara and Dion, our first-born who was maybe six at the time, went for a walk along the trail of the drainage bayou carved through our "master planned" community; both the master and the plan had long since disappeared in the bankruptcies of the dying Houston economy of the 1980s, but it was still a nice place for kids and their parents to grow up. (That all changed, but that's another story, like "watching neighborhood rug rats growing up to be gangsters.") Anyway, along they went down the semi-soggy trail alongside the bayou. Youthful eyes spied something half-buried in the gray clay soil that could suck a shoe right off your foot. It was a bell, a round bell about the size of a baseball. Immediately, Dion recognized it for what it must be, especially with the images of Christmas and words of Christmas stories bouncing around in his brain: It was a reindeer's bell. And so it had to be; it looked exactly like a bell that would be found on the halter of Santa's sleigh engines. Barbara grinned, "It is Rudolph's bell, I bet."

Excitement about that bell ran for days and weeks leading to Christmas. Christmas Eve was the day of reckoning; Dion decided to return the bell to Rudolph, with a short note next to it, which sat by the fireplace with milk and cookies for Santa, and water for Rudolph. We all knew Rudolph would come. He always did. To drink some water. We knew because every year the water was tainted red on Christmas morn. It only made sense that

Rudolph would see the note and the bell when he came to drink his water. Dion's emotions about returning/losing the bell were mixed. He took pride in the decision he made.

Christmas morning was all that story books say it should be, except there was no snow, it wasn't very cold, it was wet, and there was no fire in the fireplace (this was Houston, remember). Dion rushed out to find . . . the bell. And a note, written in magical, sparkly gold ink. "Read it, read it. Rudolph didn't take his bell." His mom read the note of thanks and appreciation: "Thanks for offering to return my bell, I appreciate it, but because of your actions, I want you to keep it."

What is a dad's role in a mom's magical moment? Observer. Photographer. Student.

Napkin Art

The art gallery now takes over most of the lunch box. The art can't go; perhaps we'll need to get Justin a construction worker lunch carrier, one of those indestructible silver jobs that looks like a Jetstream trailer with a handle on top and a thermos of 10w-40 coffee nestled inside.

The medium of choice, napkins, generally has more color to it than the art; this artist motivates, encourages, tells stories and says "I love you" in only two colors: red and blue, the colors of the pens in my pocket.

His mom began the process, occasionally dropping a mommy-drawn note into his lunch box. I would sometimes do likewise. Of late, the art creation has become more of a habit and they don't get thrown away. A collection builds on the bottom of the box: white, square leaves on the floor of his lunch experience.

When his mom had arranged for his bestfriendintheworld to join our friends on the trek from Huntsville, Texas to Albuquerque as a surprise, I crafted a napkin with a man fishing on a mountain lake with a banner that smiled "It's going to be a great day." Later he found out just how great. We're all excited about the upcoming purchase of a new-to-us pickup truck, bright red no less. Today's paper billboard shows snow-capped mountains, sun rising behind them, and a road leading from the corner of the napkin to the heart of the peaks. Of course, a red pickup with blue tires heads deep into the beauty. Granted, the imagination of that image far exceeds the artistic talent detailing it. But to a middle-aged dad and a middle school son, it is love, stories and smiles.

I selfishly hope that he keeps those images, a complementary file to our stash of art, notes, teeth, report cards and class photos that place him in his parents' file cabinet treasure chest. He may. Stories and memories run deep in this household as does the tendency to place great value on the tokens of the past. Baseball cards (for memories, not money), old leather baseball gloves of my dad's, fishing lures rightfully known as classics, photographs of generations spent, gizmos and gadgets from my childhood . . . these surround our children as connections to the scores of calendar pages gone by. Perhaps these primitive drawings on super-soakable, paper media will join that collection.

But one never knows what will stick and be treasured, or what will be discarded as embarrassments. Not unlike the great artists who toiled for the love of creation, only to become "valuable" in decades or generations hence, daddy-artists struggle with their craft for love of their creations, in hopes of being deemed valuable some day.

It's a buyer's market, this napkin enterprise. The recipient names the price, the collectability and the future of each piece.

"Please Come Back: A Love Story"

The neighborhood had pretty much gone to hell in a hand basket since the time the two had been best buds there. "Two decades of gradual decline look like a major upheaval when you only look at it then and now," the young man thought as he made the right turn into his first neighborhood.

When he left the area 20 years ago, his family moving northward into the piney woods of East Texas, he swore he would never heal from the excision of his best friend from his life. He got over it. She tried to correspond; he attempted at times to write as men tend to do—he got out paper and pencil at least three times a year. Letters and e-mails were few and far between from his hand. But she was pleasantly persistent.

Deep inside, from where those little voices live that serves as reminders of the childlike wonder around every day, came the reminder to him of the chalk inscription she left on the driveway. Whether it was her words, preserved in tiny voices and large memories, or whether it was the ingrained urge to go back to the lands of childhood, it didn't matter to him: He had decided to take a drive, alone, while in the big Texas city, to his home of "the early years."

What was once high green grass now stood stiff and dry from the July Texas heat. The yards looked more like fields of dry pine needles that pinwheel from mighty trees and land single point down, leaving clumps of threes and fours standing like mini-pongee sticks. Gone were the manicured green lawns. He realized from his parents' stories that this beginner subdivision of cookie cutter homes was never an Architectural Digest showcase of Southern lawns. But the dryness and lifelessness of the old area seemed to match his feelings: dying from lack of care and overabundance of heat.

No one from the old days lived there, he figured. "Who would?" he considered as he moved at school zone speeds through the streets devoid of kids. Broken basketball backboards stood at about every third house. He could see from the corner that the mighty steel pole his dad erected for him and his brothers had not kept its position at the edge of the driveway. It must have been missing for years. Many years. Where the pole once stood was now an evergreen bush that looked to be at least ten years old. Hard to tell considering it likely was given minimal care.

"Why am I on this street?" he asked himself. The radio station played tunes from his decade, the time of his youth and his first girl friendship. The songs triggered a few memories, but they also triggered many feelings. He shook them off, taking some manly pleasure in his current journey through pain, frustration and self-pity. A relationship of a few years had crashed and burned last month, his job brought him to Colorado (a beautiful state that he recalls visiting as a kid, but far from his mom and dad in Texas whom he still enjoyed seeing), and no one—NO ONE—seemed to understand him.

He parked at the curb, oblivious to everything except the obviously vacant house that was once his world. The towering ash tree's wilted leaves spoke of a dry summer and a family-less house. The rental car's engine ran, blowing a chilly air-conditioned breeze on his profile as he gazed out the driver's window to the yard, the trees, the bushes, the peeling paint and the driveway. He choked on the memories and the lump they caused in his throat. He struggled for good news in the visitation, but found only sorrow.

Scuffed cowboy boots sticking out from frayed-hem jeans gently pushed the car door open. He left the engine running as he perused the place. He thought little of the chance that the car may be stolen while he walked around, despite his feelings that the once beloved neighborhood was now a pit. Nothing remained of the cedar fence on which he learned to hammer; at least three generations of rough, knotty successors had stood their guard, keeping burglars out, and dogs and kids in. He moseyed into the backyard and looked around. The trees he helped plant were missing. Underground, he felt sure, remained the two dogs that he helped to bury. He remembered images of standing on his daddy's shoes in the Houston summer rain as he looked into the eternal hole in which *his* dog had been buried; the memory grabbed his heart. He recalled having placed the dog's favorite ball and rag in the hole. It was a scary time because the dog had been run over and located a few days later. As a kid's love would have it, his memory had lost the clarity of the image of the flies and maggots that accompanied his dog into the hole. He could almost still feel his dad's legs at his back as he stood on the tennis shoes that had powered the shovel to create the grave.

He spontaneously fell, cross-legged, down onto the ground. All noises—the birds in the trees, the idle of the engine—were muted by memories. His chest heaved a sigh and he fell back into the unwatered, uncut lawn. The dry blades poked and jabbed, yet he felt great comfort there.

The voice quietly spoke the driveway words again, "I miss you. Please come back." Those were the words she had chalked onto the driveway, the words that beckoned and called across the years. They sounded soft and gentle like the baby blue chalk that had written them.

He shot upright. Had he really heard it, or was that a voice in the limbo between sleep and wake, between reality and hope? He squinted his eyes. Someone, a silhouette against the Texas sun, stood there. "Hey, you. Get off your back," the voice said. His pupils struggled to open up enough to add detail to the silhouette. He nodded agreement to the visitor; the nod also acknowledged how lost he was, so lost as to confuse the voice in the backyard with the tiny voice of memory.

"Yeah, sure. Not a problem. This was home . . . but . . . I'll be leaving. I hope I didn't scare you lying back here."

"Hey you," the voice said again, "I missed you. I'm glad you're back." A soft laugh followed.

It had been an adolescence and the beginning of adulthood since he had heard that voice. Behind that voice was more than a young woman, it was a friend. A forever-hold-a-spot-in-your-heart friend. "Jess?"

"None other."

Time and distance created some uncertainty. They paused the young conversation as they looked at each other, searching for some indications of where the old friendship stood. He recalled his father's famous mistake of catching up with a friend after 20 years and feeling too comfortable too fast. He analyzed, wondered, and evaluated what to do. As he was caught in the process of evaluation, she plopped next to him even before he could get his sleeping legs to stand him up.

"What the hell are you doing here, Jess? Thank heavens you are. But what the hell."

"Mom and Dad still live across the street. Can you believe it? Dad told Mom that the house would be the last one he ever bought her. He wasn't joking. Dad never much joked about those things," she said, her smile dropping off her face like the leaves off the struggling ash tree. "I try to come by occasionally. I'm not sure why I came by today, actually. But I saw the car at the curb, door open, engine idling. I looked through that big hole in the fence—over there where we used to play hide-and-seek—and couldn't believe that was you lying in the middle of this snake infested, overgrown, weed-ridden thingofa yard." She laughed again. It was music to his ears.

"Uh, yeah. That's what I was lying in? Gee Jess, I thought I was lying in hopes."

"Is that good or bad, JJ?" Actually, together they were JJ, she the Jess and he the Justin, but somehow over the years his nickname became JJ, too. Well, for her anyway, and that was fine by him.

He thought scores of answers in the seconds before he responded. Good hopes or bad hopes? Hopeful or depressed? Hoping for a friendship as an adult like he had as a kid? Hoping for a little more carefree time. For less adult problems. For time with his mom and dad. For a fresh start. He didn't know what. Maybe he meant hopefulness instead of hope, one being a state of mind and the other being something he could define or articulate.

"Pretty much good," he summarized. He cheated her and himself with his answer and he knew it. She knew it.

"JJ. Whassup," she asked without a smile. Her eyes held him in position as surely and as comfortably as a hug.

"Hell, I don't know. I'm 29. Life begins at 30, they say. Or is it 40? I don't want to be 10 again, but there's a lot from that time that I wish I could have again." He conjured images of playing, security and fun. And her friendship.

She nodded. "I miss our friendship," she thought.

"I understand what you're saying and feeling," she said.

He stood up, smiling at what felt like the first plunk of the pebble in the water. The ripples of epiphany were beginning to move out.

"Think my rental's been stolen yet? Considering the neighborhood and all." They laughed in unison as he reached down to help her up. He grabbed her hand and lifted her gently. Another ripple. The light, unbinding conversation continued as they walked through the yard, through the gap in the fence and around the side to the front. The car idled there, cold air rushing out the open door.

"Good tunes. Wanna sit and listen?"

She grinned and shook her head. "Mom and Dad know I was coming over here to check on things. I'm tough, but they still may be worried." She giggled as she punched him in the arm to reinforce her reputation of toughness.

After feigning great injury, he started with "Can I . . ." while she asked, "Will you come over for a bit?" In synch again. Still.

He reached into the rental, switched off the ignition, tossed the keys in the air, caught them behind his back and slipped them into his faded jeans. He was already five years younger.

There were probably less than 50 adult steps between his old driveway and her parents'. As kids, it was probably 75, but they covered it in a heartbeat. He enjoyed the walk from the curb to her front door.

She was smiling and joking as she walked with her old pal: He could see it all from the corner of his eye. Her curly hair, playful eyes, and dynamic walking style: He recorded them all from the side. But up front, ahead, he took in the years behind. A tremendous boxwood bush surrounded the neighbor's mailbox pole. When the plant was small it posed little deterrent to getting to the mailbox what was base for a variety of tag games. A corner of the sidewalk had a large crack in it with crabgrass growing out of it. A couple of decades ago the sidewalk was unbroken until he and she tried to carry a tremendous rock from the bayou back to his backyard—they made it as far as the sidewalk before they lost their grips. His head spun to the sound of a squeaking storm door, not surprisingly Mr. Sullivan didn't come through the door as before, but the door sounded the same. Instead, a knee-high youngster stood at the half-opened door, with a friendly smile covered partially by his hand and thumb that he sucked with innocent pleasure. He felt her hand cup under his elbow. "JJ, whatcha remembering? That little guy reminds me of your little brother when you moved." "Exactly," he said, simplifying the time travel he experienced when looking at the chubby-legged, diapered, smiling thumb sucker.

"Mom and Dad aren't gonna believe this," she whispered. "Stay out here in the driveway." He had no idea what to expect, but clearly her playfulness had not been dissolved by adulthood.

He heard the storm door latch clack open followed by some mumbling from within the house. Her slightly elevated voice set the stage. "There was some bum over at the house," she reported. "I guess it was his car we saw with the door open. He's still over there, but he seems friendly enough."

He muffled a laugh. He knew that this was going to either turn out to be a great practical joke or a disaster. Her dad was once recognized as the gun-toting protector of the neighborhood during some of its less appealing history.

The familiar, gruff sound of her dad's voice spouting expletives about "bums in the neighborhood" preceded him out the door. First, the voices, then the dad, then the mom: They always traveled together. Then, they all stopped: Jess, her mom, her dad, and his voice.

A smile barely revealed itself under her dad's graying beard that looked like it belonged on a commune resident of the 1960s. "Dammitall, Jess. The sonofabitch followed you." The tension of the uncertainty lasted all of about five seconds. Her dad reached out with an iron-grip handshake and her mom's excited laugh-sigh was quickly followed by a hug that said "You're always welcome back. Come on in."

Walking through the darkened hallway was like a trip through the birth canal, except painless for all involved and there was no crying on the other side. Just a rush of life.

The next two hours were spent in remembered rooms reminiscing over treasured times.

"It has been great," he understated as he stood and told her mom and dad goodbye. Handshakes and hugs sealed his words with validity. As the two old friends passed through the garage, she reached into an old coffee can. Her action went unnoticed.

"I'd like to stay in touch with you. Let's get together whenever I'm in town. Here's my number and e-mail address." He continued to gush forth wants, information and hopes. Specific hopes.

"I'd like that," she agreed, her eyes hugging and her face smiling. She reached out to his hand, led him to a seated position on his old driveway. She reached into her jeans pocket—they still dressed similarly to each other—pulled out a small piece of chalk, smiled, squeezed his hand and began scratching a message on the concrete.

"I missed you. Please come back." Years ago the message was hopeful. Today, it was a shared hope.

(Justin and Jess fell out of touch a few years after we moved in 1994.)

Raccoon Feet

Cameron and his daddy were returning from the grocery store and they were talking about mommy and Justin. Mommy and Justin had gone on a week-long Scout canoe trip and were due home at any minute.

"Do you think they're home?" Cameron asked excitedly as they turned into their neighborhood. Justin was twice Cameron's age and very much a big boy to his younger brother.

As they turned on their street, Cameron could see the green van in the driveway and it had red dirt all over the sides. "Mommy and Justin are home!"

After several minutes of catching up on canoeing stories and hugs, mommy said "Cameron, did you see what I brought you?" His bright green eyes lit up in excitement. "It's at the front door."

Cameron dashed to the door and threw it open looking for something but he didn't know what. He looked down at the chunk of red dirt, the same color as was on the van. It had two footprints preserved in it.

"Raccoon," the wise Scout Justin said proudly and knowingly.

Cameron grinned, not sure what to make of these footprints in clay. His mom said, "We'll make plaster casts of them because they'll crumble soon." Cameron wasn't sure about what plaster was, but trusted that mommy's ideas were good ones.

That night Cameron thought of the little raccoon whose footprints sat in a box on his desk. He thought of how raccoons eat, their little feet used like hands. He thought of when he and his family watched a family of raccoons as they ate at the edge of a lake. He fell asleep, only to dream about meeting the little raccoon some day.

Days and weeks passed. The brilliant white plaster cast of critter feet still held a special place on his desk crowded with toys, sticks, books, drawings and other little boy stuff. At dinner one evening, in the quiet after the family dinner prayer, Mom asked, "Would you guys like to go to our canoe spot next week?" Everyone at the table was excited, but especially Cameron. He planned on meeting HIS raccoon.

Over the next seven days, the entire family was involved in trip preparations. They borrowed two canoes, a red one and a green one. They assembled all the necessary equipment: tents, sleeping bags, food, cameras, water jugs and all the other things that get carried, clipped or packed. The growing stacks of equipment held a special, carefully wrapped package: raccoon foot prints.

Early Saturday morning, leaving the house before the sunrise arrived, Cameron and his family hit the road. Mom's green van was FULL and the two canoes on top made the van look like a space ship or something found in the type of science fiction movies that dad loved to watch.

The long drive rumbled everyone to sleep, except for daddy who was driving. Cameron dreamt of sitting quietly by a tree, the gentle breeze off the lake giving him goose bumps. Quietly he waits. Quietly, too, comes a family of raccoons—a mommy, a daddy and three little ones. They walk carefully along the water's edge, pausing to look for danger. They stop right in front of Cameron: they are all eating, drinking and looking around except for the littlest one. The littlest one looks over to Cameron . . . and winks a raccoon wink!

Cameron laughs and wakes himself up. He looks out the window as the van bumps and thumps down the road into a campsite surrounded by trees. The lake stretches out behind the camp. And there was the tree that he dreamed about hiding by.

It was dusk before everything got set up. Mom and Dad did most of the work while Cameron's two older brothers pitched their own tents. All the kids got to run and play and chase and climb while Mom and Dad cooked supper. Over dinner, Dad said, "You all were so loud out there playing, there may be no animals left around here." For a brief moment, Cameron feared the thought and then realized that Dad was teasing.

Four days of vacation passed; there was swimming, fishing, canoeing, napping, hiking, playing games and campfires. But, there were no raccoons. And they were leaving the next morning!

Dusk approached and the campsite was quiet. Everything had been packed up for an early start.

While Mom, Dad and his two older brothers prepared supper, Cameron walked to the water and sat by his dreamed about tree. The orange sun was setting, disappearing behind the line where water and sky play. An orange path led across the water, straight from the sun to Cameron. A few bird songs provided a lullaby to all the critters and creatures. The water lapped gently on the bright red shore, the same dirt that was on mom's van. The same dirt that created the bright white feet that he felt for in his windbreaker pocket. He placed them on the ground in front of him and stared at them.

A soft rustling of leaves caught Cameron's attention. He had to rub his eyes as he saw a family of five raccoons preparing for their dinner at the water's edge. The littlest raccoon looked back to Cameron. Cameron was sure that the little mask-faced critter smiled and winked. He couldn't believe what happened next.

The littlest raccoon started walking to the astonished boy at the foot of the tree. The mommy raccoon did not try to stop her little one. He came closer, and stopped. Closer still he came, and stopped. Cameron's heart beat so loudly that he feared chasing the raccoon away. He sat perfectly still.

The four-footed visitor walked right next to Cameron, raised his paw and placed it right next to the little white feet Cameron had saved. It WAS him! Cameron could scarcely breathe. The raccoon put his paw on Cameron's knee for a second and then darted back to his mom. Cameron began to breathe again and ran to the campsite to tell everyone. "They'll never believe this," he thought, and he changed his mind.

"We were about to come get you for supper," Mom said. "See anything interesting," she asked. "No," Cameron said with a wink. He and Mom laughed.

The family finished eating and the next morning they left at sunrise for home.

Cameron held the memory of his meeting closely. He could almost still feel the gentle weight of the raccoon's paw on his knee.

One day, as daddy walked up the sidewalk from work, Cameron ran to him, jumped into his arms like he always did, and asked his everyday question, "Did you bring anything home for meeeeeeeee?" He always asked like that. Dad grinned a tired grin, and said nothing except for the little "mmmph" he muttered when he hugged the little boy in his arms.

It was during the quiet after prayer at dinner that Dad asked about the big trip. "Anyone want to see my photos?"

Dad passed around a lot of pictures from their trip. Cameron enjoyed the photos, but the greatest image was in his memory. Dad left the table, came back with a big brown envelope in his hand, and said, "This is my favorite photo."

Daddy slid a big picture out. Cameron stopped breathing. There was the purple sunset sky and the orange sun. There was the light path on the water that could lead Cameron straight to the sun. There were the trees and HIS tree. At the bottom of the tree was a young boy with the littlest raccoon touching his knee, and the raccoon family watching and smiling as the two friends finally meet.

CPSIA information can be obtained at www.ICGtesting.com
Printed in the USA
LVOW06s1542080514

384967LV00003B/617/P

[10]